See Jane Run

See Jane Run

*How Women Politicians
Matter for Young People*

DAVID E. CAMPBELL AND
CHRISTINA WOLBRECHT

The University of Chicago Press   Chicago and London

The University of Chicago Press, Chicago 60637
The University of Chicago Press, Ltd., London
© 2025 by The University of Chicago
All rights reserved. No part of this book may be used or reproduced in any manner whatsoever without written permission, except in the case of brief quotations in critical articles and reviews. For more information, contact the University of Chicago Press, 1427 E. 60th St., Chicago, IL 60637.
Published 2025
Printed in the United States of America

34 33 32 31 30 29 28 27 26 25   1 2 3 4 5

ISBN-13: 978-0-226-83949-3 (cloth)
ISBN-13: 978-0-226-83951-6 (paper)
ISBN-13: 978-0-226-83950-9 (e-book)
DOI: https://doi.org/10.7208/chicago/9780226839509.001.0001

Library of Congress Cataloging-in-Publication Data

Names: Campbell, David E., 1971– author. | Wolbrecht, Christina, author.
Title: See Jane run : how women politicians matter for young people / David E. Campbell and Christina Wolbrecht.
Description: Chicago : The University of Chicago Press, 2025. | Includes bibliographical references and index.
Identifiers: LCCN 2024037629 | ISBN 9780226839493 (cloth) | ISBN 9780226839516 (paper) | ISBN 9780226839509 (e-book)
Subjects: LCSH: Women politicians—United States—Influence. | Youth—United States—Attitudes.
Classification: LCC HQ1391.U5 C36 2025 | DDC 320.082/0973—dc23/eng/20240904
LC record available at https://lccn.loc.gov/2024037629

♾ This paper meets the requirements of ANSI/NISO Z39.48-1992 (Permanence of Paper).

To Kirsten,
My role model, always and forever.
—D C

To Ella,
Because Jane got the title.
—C W

CONTENTS

List of Illustrations ix
Preface xiii

PART I. A THEORY OF POLITICAL ROLE MODELS

1 You Can't Be What You Can't See 3

2 A Theory of Political Role Models 15

PART II. TESTING THE THEORY

3 Faith in Women 57

4 Faith in Democracy 85

5 Doing Politics 105

PART III. EXTENDING THE THEORY

6 Intersectional Role Models 131
 with Ricardo Ramirez

7 A World with More Republican Candidates 151

8 Impressionable Years and Enduring Effects 171

9 A Democracy for Everyone 189

Acknowledgments 201
Notes 205
References 215
Index 239

ILLUSTRATIONS

Figures

1.1 Tweets illustrating how women candidates portray themselves as role models 4
3.1 Elizabeth Warren tweet highlighting her "pinky promises" to encourage girls to run for office 58
3.2 These days, virtually all Americans say they will vote for a woman president 59
3.3 Republican boys are the least likely to see women as leaders, hold nonsexist attitudes 64
3.4 The distribution of women candidates for House, Senate, and governor, 2020 69
3.5 When women run, Republican girls and boys are more likely to think America would be better off with more women in office 78
3.6 When women run, Republican boys and girls are more likely to associate women with feminine traits 78
3.7 When women run, Republican girls are more likely to associate women with masculine traits 79
3.8 When women run, Republican girls are also more likely to hold nonsexist attitudes about women in general 79
4.1 After 2016, Democrats became disillusioned with democracy. Democratic girls rebounded, but Democratic boys did not. 91
4.2 In both the House and Senate, a big increase in women candidates in 2018 93
4.3 A prominent example of how the media covered the wave of Democratic women candidates in 2018 95
4.4 In 2018 both Democratic girls and Republican girls saw democracy as more responsive when Democratic women ran 97
4.5 In 2018 Republican girls responded positively to Republican women candidates too; Democratic girls reacted negatively 98
4.6 In 2020 both Democratic and Republican girls became more positive toward democracy when women ran 101

[x] LIST OF ILLUSTRATIONS

5.1 An example of how the news media portrayed Geraldine Ferraro's vice-presidential nomination as historic 107
5.2 Adolescents' political engagement, by gender 109
5.3 Spikes in girls' political engagement correspond to television news stories about women in politics 111
5.4 Spikes in girls' political engagement also correspond to *New York Times* stories about women in politics 111
5.5 Adolescent girls' political engagement, by party identification 113
5.6 When Democratic girls and Republican boys perceive that women run, they become more likely to expect to vote . . . 121
5.7 And they become more likely to envision themselves running for office one day 121
5.8 When women run, only Democratic girls become more politically efficacious 124
6.1 Black girls+ are more likely to be engaged when women of color run 142
6.2 Black girls+ are more likely to say they will run for office when women of color run 143
6.3 Black and Hispanic boys are less likely to say they will run for office when women, especially women of color, run 145
7.1 Republican women candidates lead boys to see women as political leaders 159
7.2 Republican women candidates lead boys and girls to see the political system as responsive 161
7.3 Republican girls become more politically engaged when they see Republican women run 164
7.4 Boys become less politically engaged and efficacious when women run 166
7.5 Greater political ambition for both Republican and Democratic girls when they see women run 167
8.1 When adolescent girls experience a viable, novel woman candidate, they are more likely to vote six years later 185
9.1 A historic woman fosters stronger faith in democracy for young women+ 194
9.2 A historic woman candidate spurs interest in running for office 195

Tables

2.1 The impact of American women politicians on mass attitudes and behaviors 21
2.2 Expectations of women as political role models 53
3.1 Family Matters 2 study 74
3.2 The takeaway: Women role models and attitudes about women's capacities 81
4.1 Family Matters 1 study 90

4.2 The takeaway: Women role models and attitudes toward democracy 102
5.1 The takeaway: Perceived women role models and political engagement, ambition, and efficacy 124
6.1 White men rule: Total number of members of Congress and presidents by race and sex, 1789–2024 134
6.2 2020 Collaborative Multiracial Post-Election Survey (CMPS) 140
6.3 The takeaway: Women candidates of color and political engagement 147
7.1 Time Sharing Experiments in the Social Sciences 154
7.2 The takeaway: The impact of a wave of Republican women candidates 169
8.1 2020 Cooperative Election Study (Notre Dame module) 175
8.2 The takeaway: Comparing adults and adolescents 179
8.3 Educational Longitudinal Study 182
8.4 The takeaway: Enduring effects hypothesis 186
9.1 The meta-takeaway: Summary of evidence for women as political role models 191

PREFACE

Ms. Harris is a role model for my daughter in a way I never can be. It is not, I think, that Ms. Harris's candidacy broadens her sense of possibility, but rather that it broadens her sense of plausibility. Not that the United States could have a female president, but that it might.

New York Times *editorial board member Binyamin Applebaum*[1]

As we finished this manuscript in the spring of 2024, Kamala Harris was not yet the Democratic nominee for president. Thus, while her name appears in various places—especially chapter 6, where we cover her 2020 vice-presidential candidacy—we do not include a sustained discussion of her historic 2024 campaign as the first woman of color to run as a major party presidential candidate. We can, however, draw on what we have learned from our research into role models to provide some informed speculation on the consequences of Kamala Harris's campaign—and her loss to Donald Trump.

In the wake of Harris's ascension to the top of the Democratic ticket, there was a lot of excitement about her pathbreaking candidacy. Her status as a role model for young people was illustrated in an iconic photo taken by Todd Heisler of the *New York Times* during the Democratic National Convention that instantly went viral. In the photo, we see two young girls in braids—Harris's great-nieces—from behind, looking up as Harris delivers her speech accepting the presidential nomination. Harris later shared the photo on her own Instagram account, writing, "I want every little girl across the country to know this: You can do anything—even if it has never

---

1. Binyamin Applebaum, "Why I'm Voting," *New York Times*, October 28, 2024, https://www.nytimes.com/2024/10/28/opinion/voter-turnout-election.html (accessed November 8, 2024).

PREFACE

been done before."[2] Both the photo and Harris's words perfectly represent what we mean by the role model effect, the subject of this book.

Given our research, we also expected Kamala Harris to be a role model for young people. At a minimum, we suspected that she would inspire young women—especially girls of color—to be more politically engaged. In 2020, we found that even as a vice-presidential running mate to Joe Biden, Harris caught the attention and stirred the imagination of Black teenage girls in particular (see chapter 6). As a presidential candidate, we would expect that she was even more salient for young girls who saw themselves in her.

What about boys? As we write in November of 2024, there is a lot of chatter about the "masculine" appeal of Donald Trump and, by extension, the Republican Party—especially for young men. Whatever the merits of that argument, there can be no doubt that sexism was on display during the 2024 campaign. Trump questioned Harris's intelligence—calling her "dumb," "mentally unfit," "slow," "stupid," and "an extremely low IQ person."[3] He also accused her of sleeping her way to the top.[4] Sadly, these are standard tropes for disparaging accomplished women. Given these attacks on Harris, we might expect that some teenage boys would be hostile to her. This expectation stems from our finding in chapter 5 that women candidates trigger backlash from Republican boys. They become politically engaged, but because they are threatened, not because they are inspired.

As a presidential candidate, Kamala Harris likely had this effect too, perhaps even more than the women we study, who were running for comparatively lower-profile offices. Yet while boys demonstrate backlash to women in the short term, we also find that women candidates of either party lead to significant change in young Republicans'—including Republican boys'—attitudes about women. They become less sexist, including accepting that women can be effective leaders. There are no guarantees, of course, but if past is prologue it suggests that one consequence of Harris's 2024 presidential run is that the rising generation of Republicans,

2. KamalaHarris, "I want every little girl across the country to know this: You can do anything—even if it has never been done before," August 26, 2024, https://www.instagram.com/p/C_Ie_ZONL0s/?igsh=ZzgyaHo1NTZpN2pl.
3. Ashley Parker, "Trump keeps calling Harris 'stupid,' offending many voters," *Washington Post*, October 21, 2024, https://www.washingtonpost.com/politics/2024/10/21/trump-harris-dumb-stupid-low-iq/ (accessed November 8, 2024).
4. Michael Gold, "Trump Reposts Crude Sexual Remark About Harris on Truth Social," *New York Times*, August 28, 2024, https://www.nytimes.com/2024/08/28/us/politics/trump-truth-social-posts.html (accessed November 9, 2024).

girls and boys, may become more receptive to women in positions of leadership—even, perhaps, a woman president.

But Kamala Harris lost. The positive vibes after Harris became the nominee turned into bitter disappointment after Election Day. Does that mean that she turned out not to be a role model after all? Not so fast. As we explain in the pages to follow, we have been studying women politicians as role models for twenty years, and have never found any evidence that women candidates have to prevail at the polls in order to change either the behavior or attitudes of young people. They have to be visible, viable, and in some cases novel—all of which describe Harris—but they do not have to win.

Maybe, though, running for president is different. Perhaps because of the presidency's power and prestige, it is a singular office, making an election loss especially crushing. The closest analog we have to Kamala Harris in 2024 is Hillary Clinton in 2016. In a paper we published after the 2016 election (Campbell and Wolbrecht 2019), we found that right after Clinton's loss to Donald Trump, Democratic teens became disillusioned with democracy—and Democratic girls most of all. Their disillusionment did not drive them out of politics, however. When those same teens were interviewed again in 2017, they had become more politically engaged. And those Democratic girls who were *most* likely to question the responsiveness of the American political system in 2016 were also the ones who became the *most* engaged in 2017. Given what we show in the pages to follow about the enduring effects of the impressionable years, these Democratic girls are likely to grow up into Democratic women who are also highly politically active.

Will the same happen with Democratic girls—especially girls of color—following Harris's loss to Trump? The answer depends on whether they see other women engaged in politics. After 2016, Democratic girls had as role models the Resistance, the woman-led movement opposing Trump. As we write in November of 2024, it is yet to be seen whether the Resistance will rise again as it did post-2016. However, even if there is no Resistance 2.0, young people will likely still have role models to lead the way. Growing numbers of women, and women of color specifically, serve in elected office, not to mention the many politically engaged women (again, many of whom are women of color) young people may see in their own communities. Even if the immediate reaction to the outcome of the 2024 election is frustration, or even anger, we suspect that the energy and enthusiasm unleashed by Kamala Harris will result in a highly engaged generation of women—and women of color especially. If so, those women will be Kamala Harris's legacy.

PART I

A Theory of Political Role Models

1 * You Can't Be What You Can't See

On the night in 2016 that Hillary Clinton secured the Democratic Party's presidential nomination, she tweeted an evocative photograph of herself with a young girl. The caption read: "To every little girl who dreams big: Yes, you can be anything you want—even president. Tonight is for you."[1] More recently, the press covered Nikki Haley's special efforts to reach out to young girls on the campaign trail for the 2024 Republican presidential nomination: "'When these girls see me, . . . they just want to see what they can be,' Haley said in an interview this week aboard her campaign bus before a stop in Clemson, S.C., noting she never saw women or 'any brown people' in leadership positions as a child. 'They just want to see someone that looks like them'" (Wells 2024). As Marian Wright Edelman, founder and president of the Children's Defense Fund, often says, "You can't be what you can't see."

From Hillary Clinton's cracks in the glass ceiling to Elizabeth Warren's pinkie promises with little girls on the campaign trail, the idea that women politicians are role models is ubiquitous. Politicians, the press, and the public all speak of how women in public life inspire other women, and especially young girls, to engage with politics. A Nikki Haley supporter explained, "I want [young girls] to know that a woman can be president one day," emphasizing that Haley would be "a great role model for our girls" (Wells 2024). Even Barbie agrees! On the website for multibillion-dollar toy manufacturer Mattel, we are told that "Barbie Celebrates Role Models," as she is "committed to shining a light on empowering role models in an effort to inspire more girls."[2] To this end, the iconic Barbie has been running for president since at least 2000, and a benevolent Barbie president ruled over Barbie Land in her recent blockbuster movie.

The belief that women can be role models is widespread, but that does not make it true. Even Barbie can be wrong. To date, studies that have looked at how the presence of female candidates influences public attitudes and political engagement have been inconclusive, sometimes even contradictory. Scholars uncover role model effects in some studies, under

[4] CHAPTER 1

Figure 1.1. Tweets illustrating how women candidates portray themselves as role models

some conditions, some of the time. They also report many instances—outcomes, times, and contexts—in which role model effects fail to materialize (Broockman 2014; Dolan 2006; Foos and Gilardi 2020; Hoyt and Simon 2011; Wolak 2015, 2019). When one looks closely, evidence that exposure to women political role models changes beliefs or behavior can be elusive.

We are not quite ready to give up on role models. In this book, we offer an expansive examination of political role models. We ask how female candidates affect not only girls but also boys, and we investigate a range

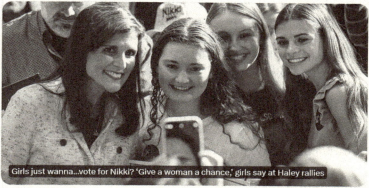

Figure 1.1. Continued

of different mechanisms and outcomes, including perceptions of women's capabilities, faith in democracy, and interest in engaging directly in politics. Building from extensive earlier work in democratic theory, political science, and social psychology to identify key causal paths and gender dynamics, we develop a novel theory of political role models that specifies who is most likely to be a role model and under what conditions, to which people, and to what effect. Our theory of political role models helps us make sense of apparently inconsistent findings from previous research on the impact of women politicians as well as provides a framework that guides the original analyses reported in this book. Given a growing partisan divergence in the gender of elected officials and attitudes about gender-related issues, we attend closely to partisanship. We consider how effects on adults may differ from effects on young people, and how women role models of color might generate unique responses.

Role models go to the heart of what makes for an inclusive democratic system. Without the engagement of women, at every level, American democracy is less than complete. Challenging stereotypes about women's incompatibility with politics, enhancing confidence in democratic institutions, and encouraging the equitable participation of women in political life all serve to bolster and strengthen our democracy.

This book asks: Do women politicians lead young people to have more egalitarian attitudes about gender? When more women run for office, do they increase the public's confidence in democracy as a system of government? Do young people—girls especially—become more likely to participate in politics when they see that the system is not dominated by men? Do girls want to follow in the role models' footsteps by running for office themselves? These are questions that should interest anyone who cares about the state of American democracy.

In the pages to follow, we subject the role model effect to a thorough empirical interrogation, with what we hope is the rigor necessary to satisfy other scholars. However, we also believe that the answers should not be limited to a scholarly audience. We have thus taken up the challenge of writing for people less interested in our methods than our conclusions. For them, we have strived to describe our conclusions straightforwardly and present our findings intuitively.

Defining Role Models

What exactly do we mean by a "role model"? We hear this term in conjunction with everyone from moms and athletes to even Barbie herself. We are not the first to be interested in this question: Role models have been the subject of extensive scholarly investigation by economists, sociologists, psychologists, and even political scientists. Since the term first appeared in social science research in the 1950s, more than 400,000 scholarly articles using the term "role model" have appeared in scientific journals (Morgenroth, Ryan, and Peters 2015). Research in this field explores the psychological underpinnings of role models, the characteristics of successful role models, and the consequences of role models for politics, business, and science—to name just a few. Role models have been found to influence outcomes as varied as choosing a college major, updating beliefs about sex stereotypes, and performing well on a math test.

While there are not quite 400,000 distinct definitions of role models, different scholars have conceptualized role models in different ways. We want to be clear from the start, then, about how *we* define political role models for the purposes of this research. In this book, political role models are women politicians who, as women, are exemplars of the capacity of women for leadership, evidence of the diversity (and thus representativeness) of political elites, and models of women's capacity to engage in politics. In our conceptualization, women politicians are political role models because they are women in positions traditionally held by men.

Importantly, our approach to role models in this book does not require anyone to consciously identify a woman as a role model for women politicians to impact their attitudes or actions. As we will show in chapter 2, our conception of role models is consistent with much of the popular rhetoric about political role models, as well as most of the political science research in this area. The central goal of this book is to evaluate the claim—made by democratic theorists, advocates for women's representation, and even women politicians themselves—that exposure to women politicians can lead some people to change both their political attitudes and their political actions. What we want to know is this: Does it matter if women run for office?

Previous research across the disciplines can and does inform our attempts to answer this question. For example, we are specifically interested in role models who challenge inequality and underrepresentation. A great deal of research has focused on just this sort of role model, and in particular on the potential impact of women role models in fields where men are dramatically overrepresented, such as science, technology, engineering, and mathematics (STEM) (Diekman, Steinberg, and Clark 2017; Hoyt, Burnette, and Innella 2012; Plaks et al. 2001). Similar to those in politics, dominant STEM stereotypes focus on white men to the exclusion of women and racial minorities (Steele 1997). Exposure to role models has been shown to decrease gender-stereotypic beliefs about leadership, improve performance, and increase interest in STEM majors and careers (Dasgupta and Asgari 2004; Herrmann et al. 2016; Lockwood 2006). Importantly, this research demonstrates that exposure to role models can have an impact on individuals, even if those individuals do not consciously recognize or choose the person as a role model.

That said, changing someone's attitudes or performance by simply exposing them to a role model—such as an accomplished woman scientist or a successful woman athlete—is not guaranteed (Betz and Sekaquaptewa 2012; Cheryan, Drury, and Vichayapai 2013; Hoyt and Simon 2011; Lockwood and Kunda 1997; Marx and Roman 2002; McIntyre, Paulson, and Lord 2003; Rios, Stewart, and Winter 2010). In particular, effective role models tend to offer a sense of shared identity, similarity, or belonging (Drury, Siy, and Cheryan 2011; Stout et al. 2011). Same-gender role models are particularly effective (Midgley et al. 2021). The more exposure there is to the role model, and the better the quality of that exposure, the greater the likelihood is of role model effects (Asgari, Dasgupta, and Gilbert Cote 2010). Work in STEM indicates that role models who demonstrate the communal, rather than agentic, aspects of a STEM careers increase women's interest in STEM (Diekman et al. 2010; Diekman et al. 2021; Diekman and Steinberg 2013; Diekman, Steinberg, and Clark 2017; Lippa

1998; Schwartz and Rubel 2005). Similarly, politics is traditionally associated with independence, conflict, and power, which helps explain why women are less attracted to political engagement. But when the presence of women politicians signals the communal aspects of politics, such as working collaboratively or helping people (Eagly and Crowley 1986), women are more likely to seek out the political arena (Schneider et al. 2016).

Context is important. Reminding group members of negative stereotypes about their group (e.g., "girls aren't good at math")—what psychologists call "stereotype threat"—can generate a range of physiological, cognitive, and emotional responses that lead to worse performance. Yet when stereotype threat leads individuals to think in terms of a shared group identity ("we" rather than "I"), exposure to role models helps minimize stereotype threat, and test scores improve (Marx, Stapel, and Muller 2005). In politics, we might expect contexts such as a political Year of the Woman to have a similar effect. The very fact of needing a special year to advance women's representation reinforces negative stereotypes ("politics is for boys") and may dampen girls' political engagement. But when that reinforcement is combined with prominent political role models who challenge those stereotypes (e.g., pathbreaking women candidates), STEM research leads us to expect that those role models may counteract stereotype threat and spur greater engagement.

Previous research also helps us conceptualize how and why we might expect women politicians to be role models for young people in particular. In the broadest sense, role models are central to human development: The idea that children, in particular, learn how to behave by observing the behaviors of those around them is foundational to social psychology (Bandura 1977). Although humans are natural experimenters, we do not have to try everything ourselves to deduce the consequences of actions; we learn what is possible, and how to do it, by watching and emulating other people. Role models are likely most effective in those stages of life—childhood and adolescence—when people are most open to learning and new information.

Finally, we need to ask what impact we expect role models to have. STEM role models have been associated with everything from improved test performance to greater interest in STEM majors or careers. In some cases, people seek to emulate the role model by doing what they do—becoming an, athlete, artist, or scientist for example. But even role models with seemingly unattainable accomplishments can move others to action. I may not win a Grand Slam, but I can pick up a tennis racket and play a game at the local court. I don't expect to win a Nobel Prize, but seeing an accomplished woman scientist gives me confidence that I can do well in my science classes. I may never be president, but seeing a woman run for that highest of offices makes me think I too can have an impact in politics as a voter or activist. One key contribution of this book is to consider a range of possible effects of political role models: Perhaps women political role models simply demonstrate that women belong in politics, and thus change beliefs about women's political capacity or encourage other women to try politics for themselves. Or perhaps women politicians inspire other women to consider entering politics as candidates—a direct role model effect.

In sum, our theory of political role models, developed more fully in chapter 2, highlights the ability of women politicians—by virtue of their presence in the political arena—to challenge stereotypes about women and politics, engender greater faith in representative democracy, and inspire political action among girls in particular

Uncommon Women

Recent high-profile candidates might make it seem counterintuitive to suggest that women are uncommon in politics. Most recently, Nikki Haley challenged Donald Trump for the Republican presidential nomination and Kamala Harris was the Democratic presidential nominee in 2024. In 2016 Hillary Clinton was the first woman major-party nominee; while she lost the election, she won the popular vote. In the 2020 presidential race, there were six women among the candidates for the Democratic nomination, three of whom who were eventually considered to be in the top tier: Elizabeth Warren, Amy Klobuchar, and Harris, who went on to be Joe Biden's running mate and vice president.[3] That same year twenty-one women ran in a general election for the Senate, just two shy of the record of twenty-three set in 2018; nearly as many women ran in 2022. In House contests, 2020 was a record year for women, with 298 female candidates running as major-party nominees; those numbers dropped only slightly in 2022. In the eleven states that held an election for governor in 2020, only three women ran; but two years later, in 2022, far more states had gubernatorial elections, and twenty-five women ran for governor across thirty-six states—a new record.[4]

In light of these numbers, are women candidates common? It depends on one's standard of comparison. Yes, women candidates are setting records, but even those numbers are underwhelming when we consider that women are slightly more than half of the overall population. For example, those six women participating in the 2020 Democratic primary debates were outnumbered by the twenty-three men in the race. In the end, Biden won the nomination, despite poor results in early primaries, and the two 2020 presidential candidates were both white men over the age of seventy. Similarly, in congressional elections, even in the record year of 2020, women were nowhere near parity with men: The twenty-one women candidates for Senate were competing for thirty-five seats and represented just 30 percent of all candidates, while in the House of Representatives they were only slightly higher at 34 percent. In 2020 women were vastly underrepresented in races for governor (13 percent), and in the historic year of 2022 women were still only 34 percent of the field.

Women politicians in the United States are also underrepresented when compared to other nations. When we compare women in national legislatures, the United States is only "in the middle of the pack" (Paxton, Hughes, and Barnes 2020, 254), alongside Bulgaria and Egypt. Even when compared to countries with similar cultures and without mandatory gender quotas, the United States ranks relatively low, falling behind Canada, Australia, and the United Kingdom.[5]

Women are even less common in executive offices. The United States has never had a woman president, while, as of May 2024, twenty-eight other nations have a woman as an elected head of state or government.[6] Women are also less likely to run for the executive office of state governor than men. Over the entire course of American history, only forty-nine women have served as state governors (Paxton, Hughes, and Barnes 2020, 261). Even after the record year for women gubernatorial candidates in 2022, only twelve states are led by a woman.

The persistent underrepresentation of women in positions of political leadership sends a message to men and women alike: Women are not fully included in the political system. Many will infer that politics is a man's game, and they may even conclude that women are less competent to lead.

A Role Model Preview

What, then, might happen if more women served as political role models? In this book we build a theory of political role models that leads us to expect that when people are exposed to women politicians, we will see a change in whether they envision women as leaders, in their assessment of American democracy, and even in whether they choose to be engaged in politics. Beliefs and behaviors are hard to move, so we look for role models among those whose attitudes are most malleable—the young, rather than the old.

Evaluating our theory requires data. To examine the potential impact of women as political role models, we take advantage of the fact that because women are underrepresented in American politics, in every election there are some places where women run for office and many others where they do not. In some places a lone woman might run, while in others multiple women may be on the ballot. Stripped down to its essentials, our analysis explores whether people in places with more women candidates develop different attitudes and behaviors than those where few or no women run.

We do not expect role models to affect everyone in the same way. As we have suggested, we anticipate that age matters: The role model effect is likely greater among young people, adolescents specifically, than their elders. Also, we expect that partisanship matters. The heightened state of political polarization suggests that women in politics may be viewed through a partisan lens. Among both politicians and the public, women are more likely to be Democrats than Republicans. Democrats also are less likely to hold traditional views on gender. Do these partisan gaps in identification and attitudes about gender roles mean that Democrats and Republicans view women candidates—of either party—differently? Similarly, do Democrats or Republicans react differently to women candidates from their own party? We suspect that race matters too. Women of color are especially underrepresented as political leaders; do pathbreaking minority women candidates inspire girls of color in particular?

We will not keep you in suspense: Women role models matter for adolescents. In contrast, role models have less consistent effects on adults, which helps explain the varying findings in previous research on the subject. However, the way role models matter depends on the effect in question: Republican boys and girls, who are generally less supportive of women leaders than their Democratic counterparts, become more positive when exposed to women role models. Regardless of party, girls become more optimistic about the quality of American democracy when they live in a district or state where women run for high office. Democratic girls and Republican boys become more politically engaged in the presence of women role models, but for opposite reasons. The fact that most women candidates are Democrats shapes the role model effects we observe. When, in an experiment, we highlighted Republican women candidates, Republican girls were more likely to respond. Women of color role models have particularly strong effects on adolescents, as does a framing that emphasizes how novel women candidates really are.

Perhaps most important, role model effects persist. Adolescents exposed to role models are more likely to vote as adults.

Road Map

Chapter 2 sets out our theory of political role models. Drawing from democratic theory, political science, and social psychology, we propose a theory of role models attuned to the specific political and gender dynamics associated with women politicians. Our theory highlights three kinds of potential effects and our specific expectations for each. We provide a framework for understanding previous work on political role models and map a way forward for our own research and research to come.

The next three chapters test our theory across the three possible effects. We begin, in chapter 3, with the question of whether the presence of women candidates affects people's attitudes about women's capacities—women acting as role models in an indirect sense. By defying sexist stereotypes about women in the public sphere, women politicians are exemplars, subtly changing attitudes about gender roles in politics and beyond, particularly for those whose views have the most room to move.

Chapter 4 then turns to attitudes toward democracy. It seems plausible that the scarcity of women in the political arena might lead young people to have little confidence, even subconsciously, in democracy as a system of government. Seeing more women in politics, however, bolsters perceptions of democracy among girls, regardless of party, in particular. In this sense, women politicians are role models not only for empowering individuals to get involved in the political system and changing their attitudes about women's capacity to lead, but for promoting the legitimacy of the system as a whole.

Chapter 5 focuses on the gender gap in political engagement and examines whether women candidates for political office motivate young girls to be more politically engaged, efficacious, and ambitious. This sort of inspiration is the most direct effect a political role model might have, and it is what most people mean when they use the term. We find that both Democratic girls and Republican boys become more interested in political participation when they observe women candidates, but for different reasons.

In our final chapters we move beyond our core theoretical expectations to consider additional implications. Chapter 6 broadens our understanding of role models beyond gender to include the intersection of gender and race. How do young people, including (but not limited to) girls of color, react when women of color run for office? We find that the intersectionality of gender and race accentuates the role model effect, especially among girls of color. By overcoming multiple disadvantages, minority women help mobilize (doubly) marginalized groups into politics.

To this point, we will have presented evidence about the role model effect in the "real world," where Democratic women candidates outnumber Republicans. Because we know that party matters, chapter 7 considers what would happen in an "alternate universe" in which there was as much emphasis on Republican women candidates as Democratic ones. To construct this parallel world, we employ experiments embedded in a survey in which we control the information about women candidates that respondents receive, including an emphasis on Republican women.

Because respondents are randomly assigned the information they receive, the analysis in this chapter demonstrates a true causal effect. In general, we find evidence that Republican women role models do indeed cause a change in perceptions of women in politics, and in Republican girls' interest in political engagement, including running for office.

From there, chapter 8 tests two of the assumptions underpinning the very idea of a role model, neither which has been subject to much, if any, empirical evaluation: First, that role models have a bigger impact on young people than on their elders; and second, that the imprint made on youth endures into adulthood. At the risk of giving away the ending, both turn out to be true.

Finally, chapter 9 considers a potential irony in the study of women as role models. To what extent does the role model effect rest on women candidates' being unusual? Do women cease to be an inspiration when they are more common? Or is it that as women candidates become more prevalent, we no longer observe a role model effect—not because women have no impact on attitudes, but because, in reaching parity with men, the gender gaps have closed? We explore this question directly in chapter 9. Spoiler alert: While novelty does matter in a world where women candidates are still unusual enough to generate headlines about being "historic," this does not mean that as women candidates become more common, they will cease to be role models. Rather, their role modeling will be pervasive. And what is true for women role models is likely to be true for other marginalized groups as they also come to be better represented in the political arena.

We are fortunate that many researchers have long been at work on this topic, offering important theoretical insights on the how, what, when, and why of political role modeling. But all these studies have produced a dizzying array of findings both for and against the role model effect, often focusing on different outcomes, definitions of role models, populations, and time periods. Anyone consulting this body of scholarship is likely to be confused by the clatter of seemingly contradictory conclusions and conclude that role model effects are seemingly rare and contingent. Chapter 2 tackles the challenge of finding a melody or two amid this cacophony, and thus the motifs to be repeated in the chapters to follow.

2 * A Theory of Political Role Models

Women being in politics matters.
        Former Australian Prime Minister Julia Gillard (2022)[1]

Women candidates and officeholders must do everything men politicians do, from campaigning for office to legislating public policy. On top of all that, they are widely expected to serve as role models. From 1992 through 2021, for example, political pollsters asked Americans about Hillary Clinton as a role model (in general, for women, for mothers, for professional women, for children, and for wives) more than thirty times. And it's not just Hillary Clinton. In 2018 the Pew Research Center conducted a survey of Americans in which they asked whether "men or women in high political offices are better at . . . serving as a role model for children." Ten times as many people said that women were better role models than said the same about men (41 vs. 4 percent; the rest said there was no difference). Interestingly, the belief in women as role models is held equally by women and men; views on this question do not differ by gender.[2]

  The popular folk theory of role models, as represented in the press, in public discourse, and even in polling questions, views women politicians as pathbreakers who challenge stereotypes and inspire others, especially women and young people, to greater political engagement and even to run for office themselves. Women politicians often embrace this role. In the words of then vice president–elect Kamala Harris, "While I may be the first woman in this office, I will not be the last, because every little girl watching tonight sees that this is a country of possibilities."[3]

  Yet while women politicians are often depicted—and describe themselves—as role models, the term can have different meanings depending on who is using it and in what context. Most members of the general public probably give the precise meaning little thought. However, scholars from various disciplines have given it a lot of thought, leading to different definitions of what it means to be a role model. It is thus important that we be clear about how we conceptualize role model effects. In this chapter we offer our own general theory of *political* role models. Drawing from research in multiple disciplines, we identify the types of role model effects we expect to observe, among whom, and in which contexts. Our theory helps answer a number of key questions: What attitudes might change as a result of exposure to women politicians? What actions might women politicians encourage or inspire? Who is most likely to shift their beliefs or behaviors in response to women role models? And in what contexts and under which conditions? Our theory of political role models, we argue, helps make sense of a rather disjointed body of literature and provides a guide for the empirical analysis in the chapters to come.

Building a Theory of Political Role Models

Our theory of political role models is grounded in democratic theory, political science, and social psychology rather than intuition and aspiration. We begin by being explicit about what we mean by the term *political role model*: Women politicians are political role models when their presence, as women in a traditionally male arena, affects the attitudes and actions of the mass public. Specifically, political role models, simply by their presence, provide evidence of the capacity of women for political leadership, demonstrate that political leaders are diverse and representative, and model women's capacity to engage in politics. The *presence* of women is key; our theory of political role models does not require that people consciously claim any woman politician as a personal role model, only that they are exposed to women politicians. In this sense, we are focusing on what the democratic theorist Hanna Pitkin (1967) termed *symbolic representation*: "the link between presence and citizens' attitudes and behaviors" (Clayton, O'Brien, and Piscopo 2019, 113–14).

We can break down the composite pieces of our theory of political role models. Borrowing from social psychology, we view social *roles* as widely shared expectations for how people in certain groups should behave (Eagly and Wood 2011). Within a society, any category, such as professor, worker, parent, or Taylor Swift fan, brings to mind a range of expected behaviors and characteristics—stereotypes, in other words. Many of these are fairly superficial and descriptive: Think *professor*, and images of tweed jackets and elbow patches leap to mind, even if we know many professors do not fit that stereotype. On the other hand, many role expectations are profound and prescriptive: The social role of parent includes expectations for how these individuals will love, care, and sacrifice for their children.

Gender roles are among the most defining forms of social differentiation and hierarchy in every society. Simply put, we have different role

A Theory of Political Role Models [17]

expectations for women and men. The key distinction is that women are stereotyped as more communal (caring, collaborative, warm), while men are commonly expected to be more agentic (independent, decisive, and competent). Other characteristics typically associated with women include emotionality, dependency, weakness, and softheartedness, while men are expected to be logical, strong, authoritative, and clear-eyed (Eagly and Koenig 2021).

The roles of "woman" and "man" are stereotyped with specific characteristics, but it is also the case that many social and occupational roles are stereotyped as male or female. Nurses, teachers, and secretaries are women; doctors, leaders, and managers are men. These occupational roles are not unrelated to gender stereotypes about characteristics: Roles typically held by women are usually stereotyped as caring, helpful, and supportive—the same characteristics we typically assign to women. Traditionally male occupations tend to be viewed as requiring leadership, decisiveness, and power, stereotypes also associated with men (Koenig and Eagly 2014). Women who take on a role (such as that of scientist) not traditionally associated with women can challenge stereotypes—about women and about scientists (Fuesting and Diekman 2017; Herrmann et al. 2016).

A role *model* is an exemplar of a role. Role models indicate what is possible for a role and how it might be achieved. By showing what is possible, role models can shape people's understanding of the characteristics and types of people associated with that role. For those who share characteristics (such as gender) with the role model, the presence of a role model may generate increased feelings of self-efficacy and interest in the role and provide a behavioral model that other people might follow (Morgenroth, Ryan, and Peters 2015; Peters, Steffens, and Morgenroth 2018).

We often think of role models as embodying the highest aspirations of the role—a person who fulfills the role in particularly laudable or successful ways. A championship athlete may be a role model for other athletes of how hard work, dedication, and talent translate into success. A business leader might exemplify strategic decision-making and ethical leadership to others in her profession.

In this book, however, we are interested less in role models that personify the highest achievements of the role and more in role models who are members of groups not traditionally associated with the role—someone who fulfills or excels at the role who is not typically expected to do so. For example, we associate athletes with youth. An older person who runs a marathon is a role model of the potential to overcome the barriers of age in athletic ability for other older people. Importantly, if enough older people manage such feats, the stereotypes around athletes might be less rigidly tied to youth. These kinds of role models are often members of marginalized groups (such as racial minorities, the economically disadvantaged, and immigrants) who have traditionally been excluded from specific opportunities and expectations (Ziegler and Cheryan 2017).

The type of role models that interest us are explicitly *political*. As a social role, political leaders are stereotyped as masculine—after all, "politics is a man's game"—while the private world of home and family is stereotypically "women's place." These expectations are deeply rooted in American political culture. The same liberal and republican political theories that informed the Declaration of Independence and the US Constitution generally assumed the exclusion of women from public life (Pateman 1980, 1994). These concepts undergird our foundational political documents, practices, and traditions (Kerber 1976, 1988; Kerber et al. 1989). The Declaration of Independence, after all, says that all *men* are created equal. No woman participated in the creation of the American political system at the Constitutional Convention. Instead, we have the famous demand of Abigail Adams, to her husband John, a participant at the convention: "Remember the Ladies." John Adams's response—"I cannot but laugh"—summarizes the views of the Framers and their contemporaries about women's place in politics (Rossi 1973).

Much has changed since 1787, but the association between political leadership and masculinity persists. As one supporter of the 2024 GOP presidential candidate Nikki Haley put it, "She's the only woman out there against all these other guys, and it's always been a man's world" (Wells and Reston 2023). That said, observers today have much more evidence of the political leadership capacity of women than Abigail or John Adams had in the late eighteenth century. A central principle of our theory is that political role models are, to use Jane Mansbridge's (1999) term, *contingent*, meaning that their effects depend in part on a specific historical context in which exclusion of women from politics has been the norm (see Dovi and Wolbrecht 2023). What makes women politicians exceptional, and thus role models, is that it is uncommon for women to fill the role of politician. As women become more common in this role, they will be less exceptional, a dynamic that we explore explicitly in our analysis.

By taking on a role not traditionally associated with women, women politicians challenge traditional stereotypes about both women and politics. Women's presence in politics thus suggests a different set of expectations for women (and for politicians), a more equitable and inclusive politics, and a kind of political engagement and participation that others can emulate. Specifically, our theory of political role models expects that women politicians have three kinds of effects on the public. First, by providing an example of the political capacity of women, political role models challenge stereotypes and make people more positive about the abilities of women as political leaders. Second, by demonstrating that the political system is inclusive and open to diverse voices, political role models foster greater support for democracy and greater faith in the representativeness of the political system. And finally, by offering exemplars of women political leaders and generating political interest, the presence of women politicians inspires women in particular to greater political engagement.

The presence of women politicians, whether or not they are identified as role models, challenges stereotypes about women's capacity for politics, makes the political system seem more representative and legitimate, and encourages greater political engagement. People who can name a political role model are more engaged in politics (Sweet-Cushman 2023)—indeed, it may be the political engagement that leads them to identify political role models—but our theory of political role models encompasses effects for those who may not consciously choose someone in politics to admire and emulate.

Instead, we conceive of a process akin to Zaller's (1992) influential receive-accept-sample model of public opinion. The presence of women politicians sends a message about who fulfills that role—that is, that women can be and are political leaders. People exposed to women politicians *receive* that message and *accept* it by storing that information in their memory. They may not remember the woman politician's name or even her existence, but the lesson learned remains. Then, when asked to consider the suitability of women for office or how representative the political system is or whether they themselves are interested in participating in politics, they *sample* from the messages in their memory storage. The more examples they have stored of women in public life, the more that women politicians will come to mind when such people are asked about politics. As a result, people will be more likely to agree that women have the capacity for political leadership (they've seen the evidence), describe the political system as representative (their memories include women politicians, not just men), and, for women in the public who see themselves in women politicians, participate in politics (they are inspired to follow in their footsteps).

In the sections that follow, we lay out our theoretical and empirical arguments for each of these effects, grounded in previous research on role models, even if other scholars have not always used that term. American culture is replete with what we will call a *folk theory* of role models, as politicians and the press often proclaim the ability of glass ceiling–breaking women politicians to challenge stereotypes and inspire others. We call this a folk theory to acknowledge that these ideas are widely held but are based on a hunch or even wishful thinking; they do not represent what scholars would consider an elaborated theory based on clear assumptions, facts, and logic. What we seek to accomplish in this chapter is to put these ideas, and others, on firm theoretical ground in a way that permits us to identify the specific expected effects of women politicians and the conditions under which various role model effects are most likely to occur.

We also use our theory of political role models to understand and organize previous work in this field. Table 2.1 is a summary of empirical research on the impact of American women politicians on beliefs about women leaders, democratic attitudes, and political engagement, including ambition for political office, in the mass public. In other words, research included here models the relationship between the presence of women politicians and some measure(s) of popular attitudes or behavior. Although this table represents our best effort, we do not doubt that we have missed a few relevant papers and books. Our goal is nonetheless to offer a sense of the state of the field in terms of what has been studied and what has been found.

Few of the authors we have encountered explicitly employ the term *role model* to describe their research, but all of these papers and books report on research that meets our definition of a role model effect: a response to the presence of women politicians. The "Significant outcomes" column in table 2.1 lists those outcomes for which there was a statistically significant effect associated with the presence of women politicians. A substantial body of literature examines these questions in other nations as well, but, owing to some of the unique aspects of the US political system (such as candidate-centered campaigns, plurality elections, single-member districts, and the absence of quotas), we focus in this table on the American case. We will nonetheless refer to research about other countries throughout this book where it is appropriate.

One possible conclusion from table 2.1 is that the overwhelming consensus of this research is that yes, women politicians do serve as political role models, shaping citizens' attitudes and behaviors through their presence as candidates and officeholders. As always, the devil is in the details. While a consensus exists in the broadest sense, previous research varies considerably in the effects studied, in what ways, with what measures, among which groups, and with what kinds of data. As a result, the degree to which women politicians are in fact role models remains very much open to debate, with findings often described as mixed or weak (Dolan 2006; Lawless 2004; Stauffer 2021) and others reporting no effects at all (Broockman 2014; Schneider and Holman 2020). Our theory helps make sense of previous research and will guide our analysis in the chapters to come.

Table 2.1. The impact of American women politicians on mass attitudes and behaviors

Source	Significant outcomes	Woman role model	Who is affected?	Age	Type of representation	Type of data
Beliefs about women as political leaders						
MacManus (1981)	Confidence in women officeholders	Officeholders	Both	Adults	Dyadic	Observational
Democratic attitudes						
Atkeson & Carrillo (2007)	External efficacy	Officeholders	Women	Adults	Collective	Observational
Clayton, O'Brien, & Piscopo (2019)	Legitimacy of antifeminist actions	Officeholders	Both, but esp. men	Adults	Collective	Experimental
High-Pippert & Comer (1998)	Trust	Officeholders	Men	Adults	Dyadic	Observational
Stauffer (2021)	External efficacy	Officeholders	Both	Adults	Dyadic	Observational
Political engagement						
Atkeson (2003)	Efficacy, discussion, proselytizing, knowledge	Candidates	Women (men for knowledge)	Adults	Dyadic	Observational
Bonneau & Kanthak (2018)	Ambition	Candidates	Women	Adults	Dyadic	Experimental
Broockman (2014)	Null for turnout, officeholding	Candidates	Women	Adults	Dyadic	Observational
Burns, Schlozman, & Verba (2001)	Knowledge, interest, efficacy, candidate knowledge	Candidates	Women	Adults	Dyadic	Observational
Campbell & Wolbrecht (2006)	Participation	Candidates	Women	Adolescents	Both	Observational
Costa & Wallace (2021)	Ambition	Candidates	Women	Adults	Collective	Experimental
Deckman & McDonald (2022)	Participation	Candidates	Women	Young adults	Dyadic	Experimental

(*continues*)

Table 2.1. (*continued*)

Source	Significant outcomes	Woman role model	Who is affected?	Age	Type of representation	Type of data
DeMora et al. (2023)	Ambition	Candidates	Educated white women	Adults	Dyadic	Experimental
Dolan (2006)	Participation	Candidates	Women	Adults	Dyadic	Observational
Dolan (2008)	Knowledge	Candidates	Women	Adults	Dyadic	Observational
Ferreira and Gyourko (2014)	*Null for officeholding Senator knowledge,*	Officeholder	Women	Adults	Dyadic	Observational
Fridkin & Kenney (2014)	Participation	Officeholders Candidates (1992 only)	Women	Adults	Dyadic	Observational
Hansen (1997)	Proselytizing		Women	Adults	Dyadic	Observational
High-Pippert & Comer (1998)	Interest, participation, efficacy, competence	Officeholders	Women	Adults	Dyadic	Observational
Jones (2014)	Knowledge	Officeholders Candidates (1992 only)	Women	Adults	Dyadic	Observational
Koch (1997)	Interest, candidate recall		Women	Adults	Dyadic	Observational
Ladam, Harden, & Windett (2018)	State legislative candidates	Officeholders	Women	Adults	Dyadic	Observational
Lawless (2004)	MC knowledge	Officeholders	Women	Adults	Both	Observational
Manento & Schenk (2021)	State legislators	Officeholders	Women	Adults	Collective	Observational
Mariani, Marshall, & Mathews-Schultz (2015)	Participation	Candidates	Women	Adolescents	Both	Observational

Palmer & Simon (2008)	Women candidates	Officeholders	Women	Adults	Dyadic	Observational
Reingold & Harrell (2010)	Interest, discussion, proselytizing, knowledge	Candidates	Women	Adults	Dyadic	Observational
Safarpour et al. (2022)	Turnout	Candidates	Both, esp. young & in 2018	Adults	Dyadic	Observational
Sapiro & Conover (1997)	Participation, attention	Candidates	Women	Adults	Dyadic	Observational
Schneider, Sweet-Cushman, and Gordon (2023)	Ambition	Officeholders	Women	Adults	Collective	Experimental
Stauffer (2021)	Null for efficacy	Officeholders	Women	Adults	Collective	Observational
Stokes-Brown & Dolan (2010)	Proselytizing, voting	Black officeholders	Black women	Adults	Dyadic	Observational
Stokes-Brown & Neal (2008)	Proselytizing	Candidates emphasizing economic issues	Women	Adults	Dyadic	Observational
Uhlaner & Scola (2016)	Turnout	Officeholders	(White) women	Adults	Collective	Observational
Wolak (2015)	Intention to vote	Candidates	Men less likely	Adults	Dyadic	Experimental
Wolak (2020)	Candidate recall	Officeholders	Both (women more)	Adults	Both	Observational
Wolak & McDevitt (2011)	Knowledge	Officeholders	Both, but opposite directions	Adolescents	Collective	Observational
Wolbrecht & Campbell (2017)	Discussion	Candidates	Women	Young adults	Dyadic	Observational

CHAPTER 2

The Effects of Women Political Role Models

Our theory of political role models predicts that the presence of women politicians challenges stereotypes about women leaders, increases perceptions that government is representative, and inspires people to political engagement. In this section we further articulate and differentiate among different ways in which political role models may shape political beliefs and behaviors.

BELIEFS ABOUT WOMEN AS POLITICAL LEADERS

A role model demonstrates what a group member can do, and a political role model demonstrates what group members can do in *political* roles. Demonstrating the capacity of groups previously excluded from a role is a common expectation of role models in general; indeed, this is one of many motivations for those who seek greater representation of women in politics. In her classic work, Mansbridge (1999, 628) argues that descriptive representation can create "a social meaning of 'ability to rule' for members of a group in historical contexts where that ability has been seriously questioned." The presence of women politicians is a symbol of women's inclusion, capacity, and power. When people observe women in positions of political leadership traditionally held by men, they may conclude that women do in fact have the temperament and ability for politics, contrary to the long-held stereotype of women as too emotional, weak, and irrational for political roles. The expectations for politicians may become less masculine and more open to characteristics traditionally associated with women.

Social psychology, and social role theory in particular, provides one rationale for why we expect political role models to change people's beliefs about women's capacity for political leadership. Associated with the work of social psychologist Alice Eagly and her many collaborators, social role theory posits that key biological differences—specifically women's childbearing and men's typically greater physical strength—historically led women and men to adopt distinct roles: women as caregivers, men as protectors and hunters. Gender stereotypes arise from the social division of labor—in other words, from observing women's and men's actual roles in society. Women thus are associated with care, emotion, dependence, and the home, while men are associated with strength, protection, and independence. Even as physical strength has become less important to economic and social power, and as childbirth and early childhood have consumed less of women's adult lives, these gender stereotypes are still operative. As people see women and men in distinct social (caregiver/

leader) and occupational (e.g., nurse/doctor) roles, they come to understand those roles, and the characteristics related to them, as naturally associated with one or the other gender.

The resulting gender stereotypes are widely shared throughout society, enforced via the policing of social behavior, and reproduced through childhood socialization. Those who act contrary to gender stereotypes—think assertive women or timid men—are punished by social sanctions ranging from exclusion or disdain to bullying and violence. This process of differential treatment and gender role socialization begins before birth and continues throughout childhood (Lips 1989). Social norms and internalized expectations lead women and men to conform to these stereotypes in their behaviors and life choices (Eagly and Wood 2011).

American politics largely confirms traditional gender stereotypes about women and leadership. Any observer could easily draw the conclusion that politics is the domain of (white) men. Although much has changed, American women remain dramatically underrepresented as political leaders and legislators. The United States, of course, has never had a woman president and did not elect a woman vice president until 2020. As of 2023, women held 25 percent of US Senate seats, 29 percent of seats in the US House of Representatives, 24 percent of governorships, and 33 percent of state legislative seats (CAWP 2023a). Dominant gender stereotypes continue to view politics as a masculine endeavor. The characteristics associated with women, such as care, emotion, and dependence, do not fit with our expectations for the role of political leader—what social scientists call role incongruity. This mismatch between stereotypes about women and the expectations for political leaders limits both the supply of women politicians (by making politics unattractive to women) and the demand for them (by making elites and voters uncomfortable with women in the role; Eagly and Karau 2002; Schneider and Bos 2019). Indeed, men are so strongly associated with leadership that they often overlap in the minds of citizens; when one thinks "leader," one also thinks "male" (Eagly and Karau 2002; Koenig et al. 2011).

For social role theory these two things—women's underrepresentation in politics and gender stereotypes about politics—are causally related: The dearth of women in political roles and the overrepresentation of men and masculinity both communicates that politics is not appropriate for women, and reinforces the idea that the characteristics associated with men (power, rationality, independence) are also those associated with politics (Eagly and Karau 2002; Koenig et al. 2011). Dominant gender stereotypes—men are naturally agentic (independent, strong, powerful) and women essentially communal (caring, soft, emotional)—have clear implications for politics, with the former far more consistent with conventional political expectations than the latter. To the extent that women seek out opportunities to fulfill communal goals, they are less likely to select a career path (like politics) when it is largely framed in agentic terms (Diekman and Steinberg 2013; Diekman, Steinberg, and Clark 2017; Eagly and Wood 2011; Schneider and Bos 2019).

The result is a vicious cycle: The lack of women in politics contributes to stereotypes about women's inappropriateness for political leadership. Those stereotypes in turn contribute to women's exclusion from political leadership (Eagly and Koenig 2021). The incompatibility of stereotypes about women and those about political leadership—role incongruity—generates negative responses as citizens view women as a bad fit for the job (Eagly and Karau 2002; Koenig et al. 2011). Research shows that people tend to attribute traditionally feminine qualities (such as compassion and collaboration) to women in politics but are more likely to describe men politicians in terms of masculine traits (leadership and competence) and masculine issues (economics, foreign policy) (Alexander and Anderson 1993; Bos, Schneider, and Utz 2017; Holman, Merolla, and Zechmeister 2011; Schneider and Bos 2014). These stereotypes help explain why women are less likely to be recruited or nominated by parties, must be extraordinarily qualified to compete with less qualified men, are evaluated differently than men by voters, and necessarily develop campaign tactics to address and mitigate those stereotypes (Bauer and Carpinella 2018; Schneider and Bos 2019). The resulting exclusion of women from political office once again reinforces traditional gender stereotypes that women are incompatible with political leadership. And so the cycle continues on (for a discussion, see Dolan 2014; Sanbonmatsu 2002).

Can the presence of increasing numbers of women in politics challenge gender stereotypes and change attitudes? Social role theory expects that as women's roles shift, stereotypes about women should change as well. For example, in recent decades women's increased presence in traditionally male occupations, such as doctors, lawyers, and managers, has upended some stereotypes about women and about those roles (Diekman and Eagly 2000; Eagly et al. 2020; Koenig and Eagly 2014). Yet, stereotypes are not altered quickly or easily. Rather, it is a long-term process, requiring visible and consistent change in a group's relationship to a role over time. As Eagly and Koenig (2021, 348) argue, "The presence of a few highly successful role occupants from a formerly excluded social category does not produce an updating of the category's stereotype until more persons from that category enter the role." One male nurse does not change gender stereotypes about the nursing occupation. Our own take is similar: A single or a few women politicians are exceptions who prove the rule.

But when women become more common as politicians, beliefs about the appropriateness of politics for women can begin to change. The timing and broader context are critical, factors which we address throughout this chapter and book.

We are aware of just one paper about the US case that examines the impact of women politicians on beliefs about women's capacity for political leadership (see table 2.1): In a 1979 survey of 399 registered voters in Houston, Texas, MacManus (1981) reports that one-third of respondents indicated that the presence of the first woman city controller, Kathy Whitmire, changed their "views of women serving in city government." Ninety-four percent of those said their views changed in a positive direction. Consistent with our theory of political role models, MacManus (ibid., 91) describes these findings as "evidence of the extent of Whitmire's ability to help break down sex-role stereotypes." Because Whitmire was the first woman to "occupy an atypical female job," her performance was "generalized by the population to women as a collectivity." Other work speaks more indirectly to the issue of changing attitudes toward women: research in the United States shows that the recent increase in the presence of women in political roles has resulted in more positive evaluations of women politicians and less conflict between expectations for political leaders and stereotypes about women (van der Pas, Aaldering, and Bos 2023).

The impact of women politicians (and/or gender quotas) on beliefs about women as leaders has received more attention in research outside of the United States (Coffé and Reiser 2021; Evans 2016; Kim and Fallon 2023). Alexander's (2012) twenty-five-nation study finds that when the share of women members of parliament increases, women in the public become more positive about the capacity of women to govern. In more recent work covering forty-eight countries, Allen and Cutts (2018) also find the share of women in parliament (as well as the presence of gender quotas) correlates positively with support for women as political leaders. On the other hand, in nineteen Latin American countries, Morgan and Buice (2013) find no effect for the percentage of women in the legislature, but report that men are more likely to support women as political leaders where there are more women selected for leadership in the cabinet. Women's attitudes, however, do not change. Using the randomized assignment of women to local councils in India, Beaman and colleagues (2009) report that exposure to female council heads undermines traditional stereotypes about women's capacity to lead and willingness to vote for women. Others are less sanguine. Comparing the United States and Sweden, Matland (1994, 287) concludes that "broad representation of women does not eliminate the use of gender schemata."

DEMOCRATIC ATTITUDES

We also expect that the presence of political role models will lead people to view politics as more open and inclusive and thus to express greater satisfaction with democracy and representation. This expectation is common in popular role model rhetoric. Consider the tweet sent by Senator Patty Murray (D-WA) when she became the first woman to serve as president pro tempore of the US Senate in early 2023: "It's not lost on me the significance of what it means to be the first woman to serve in this role. This is another sign that slowly but surely, Congress is looking more like America."[4] By this logic, the more women candidates and officeholders, the more Americans will have reason to believe that their government is representative of—and effectively represents—all Americans.

Scholars have long theorized that the presence (and absence) of women politicians can have important effects on citizens' views of the political system and of political representation in general. Why? The concept of political equality is central to the ideals of liberal democracy. If group members are not visible as political leaders and legislators, citizens may question whether groups are equal in political power, influence, and status and thus question the legitimacy of the state itself. On the other hand, a political system in which members of previously excluded groups (e.g., women) are able to contest elections and serve in office may be viewed as more representative, fair, equitable, and open (Phillips 1998).

Members of the previously excluded group may be particularly likely to factor descriptive representation into their evaluations of government and democracy. Mansbridge argues that descriptive representation can increase "the polity's de facto legitimacy in contexts of past discrimination" (1999, 628). The presence of fellow group members, she goes on to say, can make "members of historically underrepresented groups . . . feel as if they themselves were present in the deliberation" (ibid., 650). In other words, diverse representatives can lead fellow group members in particular to perceive the political system as more responsive to the people as a whole.

Previous research suggests that the absence of women from politics is at least partially responsible for women's perceptions of the political system as biased and inaccessible. For example, the long-standing finding that women are less likely to report that they feel personally capable of affecting or understanding politics (personal efficacy) is often attributed to the persistent image (and reality) of politics as a "man's game" (Atkeson and Rapoport 2003; Bennett and Bennett 1989; Burns, Schlozman, and Verba 2001; Campbell et al. 1960; Conway 1985). Evidence that bias is being successfully challenged and overcome—such as by a historic number of traditionally underrepresented candidates—might move those attitudes in the other direction.

That said, it is not only the excluded group that may value the representation of previously excluded voices. In an important recent paper, Clayton, O'Brien, and Piscopo (2019) found that the presence of women in decision-making bodies increases the legitimacy of, trust in, and acquiescence to policy decisions, regardless of the topic. When decisions appear to go against the interests of women, men in particular are more likely to accept those decisions as legitimate and fair if women are part of the decision-making body. The authors argue that this pattern reflects men's lesser capacity to judge women's issues on their own, and thus their reliance on cues, such as the presence of women, to evaluate the quality of policy choices.

Evaluations of government have received more attention than beliefs about women leaders but still lag behind engagement as an impact of interest, as table 2.1 shows. External efficacy is a common approach to measuring this potential impact; respondents are more likely to say that government is responsive to citizens when women serve in government (Atkeson and Carrillo 2007; Stauffer 2021).[5] Other research finds that being represented by a woman increases political trust, but only among men (High-Pippert and Comer 1998).

In studies outside the United States, women are associated with less corruption and greater honesty (Barnes and Beaulieu 2014, 2019). Research demonstrates a positive association between the presence of women politicians and women's confidence in the legislative process (Schwindt-Bayer and Mishler 2005), trust in elections, confidence in democratic institutions, and democratic support (Hinojosa and Kittilson 2020); greater satisfaction with democracy in their country and confidence that elections reflect voters' views (Karp and Banducci 2008; but see Burnet 2011); and enhanced external efficacy (Oser, Feitosa, and Dassonneville 2023).

POLITICAL ENGAGEMENT

By far the most common expectation of political role models is that they inspire other women to follow in their actual footsteps by becoming more actively involved in politics and perhaps even running for office themselves. In some ways this is the most consequential potential impact of role models: Attitudes about women as leaders or the quality of American democracy are clearly important, but it is political action that most directly brings about political change. More women voting, protesting, donating, and advocating for candidates and causes has the potential to influence election results and policy decisions. Why would we expect that people exposed to political role models become more politically engaged? We suggest several different possible paths, each of which informs (but does not determine) our expectations.

Stereotype change. As we discuss above, social role theory expects that gender stereotypes develop from observing the actual presence of women and men in various roles. These gender stereotypes guide our understanding of how women and men are expected to behave. Expectations are not only internalized, but enforced through social sanctioning, mate selection, and even law. The rewards for acting in ways consistent with gender stereotypes are many, while the punishments for violating those expectations can be significant. This means that both women and men hold similar gender stereotypes (even when those stereotypes evolve), but the implications for their own behaviors diverge. Men are expected to behave in ways consistent with gender stereotypes about men, taking on leadership and managerial roles consistent with masculine stereotypes (assertive, competitive, and dominant). Women, on the other hand, are expected to follow the gender stereotypes for women—that is, to be self-sacrificing, emotionally expressive, and other-oriented, and to fulfill caretaking roles (Eagly and Wood 2011).

As women increasingly enter a role (such as politics) from which they had previously been excluded, gender stereotypes about that role—and who is allowed to fill it—may change. As gender stereotypes change, then so should the behavior of those for whom the stereotypes are updated. When they observe women in political roles, we expect both women and men to update their stereotypes about women to reflect their new roles in society; that is, both women's and men's *attitudes* about the appropriate roles for women should change. Yet it is only stereotypes about women that are changing; there is no expectation that men have become less associated with politics and power than in the past. For that reason, only women's *behavior* should change, not men's (Diekman and Eagly 2000; Eagly et al. 2020; Koenig and Eagly 2014). In short, social role theory provides one reason to expect women, and only women, to be more politically engaged when they observe women politicians.

Interest and attention. Our focus is on women as political role models, but we recognize that there may be other mechanisms whereby women politicians can spark political engagement. Interest, attention, and knowledge are key predictors of political participation (Delli Carpini and Keeter 1996). While political interest is a basic predisposition, people, events, and issues can encourage interest, draw attention, and enhance knowledge in politics, which should in turn translate into more political engagement and participation.

The presence of women candidates and officeholders may be sufficiently unusual and eye-catching to stimulate greater attention to and interest in politics. Note that, like our theory of political role models, this mechanism relies heavily (but not of necessity exclusively) on the relative rarity of women in these roles. Both women and men might have their attention drawn to politics by the novelty or curiosity of women in a traditionally male field. Social psychology provides mixed evidence: Under some conditions counter-stereotypical actors attract more attention, but in others it is the stereotype-consistent actors who draw the most focus (e.g., Asgari, Dasgupta, and Stout 2012; Plaks et al. 2001).

Alternatively, we might expect women in the general public—who may identify with other women, share the interests and priorities of other women, or have a natural interest in people like them in politics—to be particularly attentive to and interested in women politicians. Previous empirical work is more consistent with this second hypothesis; women, and only women, become more interested in and knowledgeable about politics and candidates when a woman is running (Atkeson 2003; Burns, Schlozman, and Verba 2001; Dolan 2008, 2011; High-Pippert and Comer 1998; Koch 1997; Lawless 2004; Reingold and Harrell 2010; Wolak 2020). Indeed, some research outside the United States suggests men may become *less* interested in politics when exposed to women politicians (Kittilson and Schwindt-Bayer 2012).

Women's attention might also be drawn to female politicians because women candidates and officeholders are more likely to raise issues of particular relevance to women in their campaigns (Dabelko and Herrnson 1997; Dolan 2005, 2008; Kahn 1993) and legislate on them when in office (Dittmar, Sanbonmatsu, and Carroll 2018; Swers 2013, 2020). This mechanism departs more directly from the political role model path we have been describing but again relies on the novelty of women politicians and the issues they may raise. While women generally lag behind men in traditional measures of political knowledge, research has repeatedly shown that when knowledge questions focus on issues of particular interest to women or in areas related to women's experience, the gender gap in knowledge is eliminated or even reversed (Hutchings 2001; Miller 2019; Stolle and Gidengil 2010). (Another factor is men's higher propensity to guess rather than admit not knowing [Lizotte and Sidman 2009; Mondak and Anderson 2004]). Delli Carpini and Keeter (1996) argue that "domain-specific" information—information particularly relevant to specific groups—can help close knowledge gaps and encourage interest and attention to politics. Following from this logic, to the extent that women politicians are relevant to women, or raise issues that are relevant to women, we can expect women to be more attentive, interested, and engaged when women run and serve.

There have been few direct tests of this specific effect. Herrnson, Lay, and Stokes (2003) report that women who run "as women" (emphasizing women's issues and reaching out to women's groups) are more likely to win election; similarly, emphasizing feminine issues, but not feminine traits, helps women candidates succeed (Bauer 2020). That said, a direct test of role model effects did not directly support this hypothesis. Stokes-Brown and Neal (2008) found that women candidates who highlighted economic issues—*not* women's issues such as abortion, political reform, or social welfare issues—were associated with more political proselytizing among women. The study's authors suggest that although economic issues are always central to campaigns, women candidates may frame economic issues differently and in ways relevant to women, helping to explain the effect.

Whether or not women's issues are the cause, we have good reason to expect that women politicians' exceptionalism draws greater attention and interest to politics, especially for women. Theoretically, we view enhanced attention and interest as another path to greater political engagement for women exposed to women political role models.

Backlash and threat. We have identified several reasons to expect that women should be attentive to and inspired to political engagement by political role models. However, we hold out the very real possibility that men may become more politically active when women politicians are present owing to a sense of backlash or threat. As with the other mechanisms we have described, the key is that women are in a role stereotypically reserved for men. As a result, some men may view women politicians as trespassing against social norms or taking away status or power that should be reserved for men. Thus far we have described the impact of political role models in largely positive terms: The presence of women politicians minimizes gender stereotypes, strengthens democratic faith, and/or makes political engagement more attractive or accessible. For some groups, however, that same challenge to stereotypes that women politicians represent may generate a backlash, because these groups view women politicians as contrary to their own interests—or even a threat.

We know that, in general, perceived threats to current status or preferred policies can encourage political activism (Campbell 2006; Krosnick, Visser, and Harder 2010; Miller and Krosnick 2004). Threats to group identity and interests can be particularly mobilizing. In recent years, for example, anti-immigrant policies and candidates (such as Donald Trump) have spurred voter mobilization among Latinos (Gutierrez et al. 2019; Pérez 2015; White 2016). Similarly, Trump's racist rhetoric stimulated

Black turnout (Towler and Parker 2018). On the other hand, some white Americans perceive increasing racial and ethnic diversity as a threat, inciting greater engagement and support for racially conservative candidates (Major, Blodorn, and Major Blascovich 2018; Stewart and Willer 2022).

We expect a similar backlash to spur political activism when women are on the ballot. As we have argued, the presence of women candidates represents a break with the past, shifting gender roles, and greater equality and power for women in American politics. Political leadership is viewed as a masculine endeavor, so the presence of women in such positions leads to role incongruity: "A potential for prejudice exists when social perceivers hold a stereotype about a social group that is incongruent with the attributes that are thought to be required for success in certain classes of social roles" (Eagly and Karau 2002, 573–74). While many may view these as positive developments, others may view the shift as a threat to preferred hierarchies and proscribed social roles, or even to their own political and social power.

In recent years social scientists have documented a widespread perception of gender identity threat among men, and white men in particular, in response to this and other challenges to traditional masculinity. As women have increasingly caught up with men in terms of educational attainment, income, and professional status, and as traditionally male occupations such as manufacturing have declined, some men perceive a loss of status, power, and authority and express a preference for more traditional gender roles (Cassino and Besen-Cassino 2021; Clark, Khoban, and Zucker 2023). This sense of gender threat is observed in indicators such as hostile sexism, attitudes that favor men's dominance, or strength of identification with masculinity (Glick and Fiske 1996, 1997). Perceptions of threatened masculinity are linked to a range of behaviors and attitudes, including religious traditionalism, consumption of pornography, and gun ownership (Cassino and Besen-Cassino 2021; DiMuccio and Knowles 2021).

Threats to traditional masculinity also have political consequences (Clark, Khoban, and Zucker 2023; DiMuccio and Knowles 2020). Seeing women in perhaps the most masculine of roles—that of a political leader—can contribute to a sense of gendered threat that mobilizes political action. In the 2016 presidential election, for example, masculinity as an identity and sexism as a belief system were more relevant to engagement and vote choice than had been the case in previous presidential elections. Not only was Hillary Clinton a woman in what was traditionally the male role of presidential nominee, but she also had a long history as a foil to those with more traditional gender views. Her opponent often derided her, and other women, in distinctly gendered terms (Conroy, Martin, and Nalder 2020). Among other things, Trump disdained women who accused him of harassment as too unattractive to pursue, criticizing the looks of his Republican primary opponent Carly Fiorina ("Look at that face!" [Solotaroff 2015]), and saying, after a debate with Hillary Clinton, "When she walked in front of me, believe me, I wasn't impressed" (McCaskill 2016). In that same debate, Trump dismissed Clinton as "such a nasty woman" (Stockman 2015). Not surprisingly, then, hostile sexism and masculine identity are associated with greater support for Trump and/or other Republican candidates in recent years (Carian and Sobotka 2018; Cassese and Holman 2019; Cassino and Besen-Cassino 2021; Deckman and Cassese 2021; Gidengil and Stolle 2021; Valentino, Wayne, and Oceno 2018). They are also associated with increased political engagement (Banda and Cassese 2022). Highlighting that women candidates are "firsts" or claiming that women candidates are trading on particular qualities unique to their sex appears to trigger backlash as well (Cassese and Holman 2019; Cassino and Besen-Cassino 2021).

Unlike previous rationales for a role model effect, a sense of threat applies largely, but not exclusively, to men. Women candidates and officeholders can trigger a sense of gender threat among men, cueing feelings of status loss and identity threat. To counter this perceived threat and assert their rightful place, we might expect that men and boys would become more engaged in politics in response to the presence of women candidates. While we do expect backlash to be a more common reaction to women politicians among men, we emphasize that one of the key measures of gender threat, hostile sexism, is an attitude that can be (and is) held by women as well as men and shapes their political choices (Cassese and Barnes 2019). Men, however, are more likely than women to express hostile sexism, so it is among men where we are most likely to see such effects.

Previous research. The overwhelming focus of previous research has been on engagement with politics. In some cases, the engagement is psychological, such as interest in and knowledge about politics. A propensity for political discussion is another key way to gauge political interest and attention. In other cases, scholars examine measures of activity ranging from the most basic (voting) to the more intensive (such as contacting members of Congress, working on campaigns, or engaging in protest) to the most elite (running for office).

Why has previous research focused on engagement specifically? It probably helps that engagement questions are standard on most political surveys, providing multiple opportunities to examine the impact of women politicians. More important, political engagement is an area in which women have historically lagged behind men. Women were historically prohibited from participating in most formal political roles (e.g., that of voter), and strong social norms against women in politics discouraged (but did not entirely prevent) them from participating in others ways both before and after they achieved suffrage (Cott 1990). Women in the electorate have long been less likely to report personal efficacy, that is, the feeling that they personally are capable of affecting or understanding politics—beliefs that contribute to women's lesser political participation (Atkeson and Rapoport 2003; Bennett and Bennett 1989; Campbell et al. 1960; Conway 1985). However, although this has long been viewed as a shortcoming of women, Baxter and Lansing note that "instead of interpreting the difference [in personal political efficacy] as an inadequacy of women, we suggest that given the very limited number of issues that citizens can affect, the lower sense of political efficacy expressed by women may be a perceptive assessment of the political process. Men, on the other hand, express irrationally high rates of efficacy" (1983, 51).

Gender differences in political participation, once "one of the most thoroughly substantiated [facts] in social science" (Milbrath and Goel 1977, 116), have in recent years narrowed or disappeared (Burns, Schlozman, and Verba 2001; Schlozman, Brady, and Verba 2018; Burns et al. 2018). At the same time, men continue to outpace women in campaign donations (Burns et al. 2018) and, at the highest levels of engagement, running for and serving in political office (Lawless and Fox 2010).

Women's lesser political engagement and activism raises serious concerns about democratic legitimacy and representation. If women were less likely to participate in elections, contact officeholders, or engage in protest, their interests and values would not be heard as clearly or emphatically as men's (Burns, Schlozman, and Verba 2001; Hinojosa and Kittilson 2020). Political engagement also strengthens the bonds between government and citizens, conveys key information between the represented and their representatives, and advances the legitimacy of democratic systems.

One solution to the problem of women's lesser engagement—proposed by both scholars and activists—is to increase the number of women in prominent political positions. That is, a major motivation for previous research on the impact of women politicians on women's engagement has been a fundamental concern about representation, political voice, and democratic legitimacy. One might hypothesize that the fact that women closed the campaign activism gender gap in recent years might be in part attributable the increasing numbers of highly visible women political role models in the same period.

The profusion of role model scholarship represents the efforts of social scientists to evaluate these claims systematically. One reading of table 2.1 is that these expectations were correct: In the United States, the presence of women politicians is positively associated with a range of engagement measures. We see evidence of women politicians encouraging enhanced interest, knowledge, discussion, proselytizing, participation, and even interest in running for political office. Research beyond the United States generally tells a similar story (Barnes and Burchard 2013; Carreras 2017; Castorena 2022; Clayton 2015; Foos and Gilardi 2020; Fraile and Gomez 2017; Gilardi 2015; Hinojosa and Kittilson 2020; Liu 2018; Liu and Banaszak 2017; Pereira 2019; Zetterberg 2009).

A closer look at table 2.1 (and the non-US literature) tells a more complicated story. We have listed the outcomes for which the presence of women politicians is a *statistically significant* predictor. In most cases, however, researchers examined multiple behaviors and reported only occasional, and sometimes only null, effects for many of those outcomes. (Those null findings are not listed in the table.) A few studies systematically examine and report on a broad range of dependent variables and conclude that in most cases, there is no effect or that the effects found tend to be somewhat scattershot (Dolan 2006; Lawless 2004). Other studies find no effect at all (Broockman 2014; Schneider and Holman 2020).

How to interpret those findings is less clear. One possible conclusion is that there is not really much of a role model effect at all, and the effects we observe are closer to exceptions than the rule. Another possible conclusion, and the one we find persuasive, is that the outcomes scholars examine (such as interest and participation) are fundamental predispositions that are difficult to move. Indeed, given the many factors that shape an individual's propensity to pay attention to politics or participate in elections, the idea that exposure to women candidates might move the needle may seem improbable.

Under what conditions, then, do we expect the presence of women politicians will move attitudes or behaviors? We take up that task next. In the section that follows, we expand our theory to identify important factors that help determine whether, when, and to what extent role model effects occur. Table 2.1 outlines some of the variation in the conditions under which previous scholars found evidence of role model effects. By considering these factors systematically, our goal is to make sense of those apparently scattershot findings.

Who Responds to Political Role Models?

So far our theory has specified what sorts of effects role models will have on both beliefs (about women as leaders or about democracy) and behaviors (political engagement). Many questions remain, however: Who responds to role models? Which women are role models, and in what contexts? We identify those most likely to respond to political role models, giving particular attention to age, gender, race, and partisanship.

AGE

A key argument of this book is that role model effects are more likely among younger people than older. That role models inspire children is often a key claim of the folk theory of role models. Women politicians frequently highlight their potential impact on young people in particular. To take just two recent examples, Kamala Harris proclaimed her vice presidency as proof that all possibilities are open to girls, while GOP presidential candidate Nikki Haley trumpeted the importance of her special efforts to reach out to "strong girls."[6]

These politicians are not wrong to focus on children and adolescents. Pre-adulthood is the key life stage for socialization about gender stereotypes, as well as for learning about the broader political world. Scholars describe childhood and adolescence as the "impressionable years," a period in which people are particularly open to political learning and develop the political attitudes and behaviors that will guide them through adulthood (Beck and Jennings 1982; Campbell 2006; Jennings, Stoker, and Bowers 2009; Oxley et al. 2020; Wolak 2009). Many important political predispositions, such as partisanship, are traced to childhood (Sears and Valentino 1997), and many key gender differences in politics, such as political knowledge (Wolak and McDevitt 2011), and gendered attitudes, such as on abortion (Pacheco and Kreitzer 2016), are developed in childhood and adolescence as well.

Importantly, children understand politics as gendered—specifically, that politics is for boys—from a very young age (Diekman and Schneider 2010; Schneider and Bos 2019). In an innovative recent study, Bos and colleagues (2022) asked students in grades 1–6 to draw a political leader. The majority of girls and boys drew men as political leaders, although at younger ages, boys were more likely to draw men than were girls. While the likelihood of boys drawing male leaders was consistent across the children's ages (about 70–75 percent), girls became *more* likely to draw male political leaders over time (to the point that older girls were as likely to draw men as older boys were), consistent with their expanded exposure to political reality. As girls learn about politics, they increasingly understand it as a male domain.

In comparison, shifts in political attitudes and behaviors become less likely as people age and develop habits and experience. Of course, people change their minds about many things—including politics and policy—all the time. But our core inclinations and values are established early in life and, short of dramatic events or experiences, tend to stay fairly consistent across our lives. Partisanship is the prime example. Although scholars debate exactly how stable partisan identification is and under what conditions it might change, there is little question that most people identify with the same party in their sixties as they did in their twenties or even their teens (Erikson, MacKuen, and Stimson 2002; Green, Palmquist, and Schickler 2002; Jennings and Niemi 1981).

For these reasons, we expect political role models to more consistently and significantly impact young people compared to older people. As table 2.1 shows, the vast majority of studies have examined adult samples. The privileges of adulthood mean that adults' views and actions can have a more direct impact on political outcomes. Adults are not difficult to survey, and political surveys of them abound. Minors, however, require parental consent to participate, which means surveys of this population are costly in terms of time, effort, and money. Those surveys that do poll adolescents on political matters tend to focus on political activities in which they *expect* to participate, because many standard political activities are either unavailable (e.g., voting) or unlikely (e.g., campaign donations) among young people. Yet, while less immediately consequential, many of the political preferences and habits developed in childhood can and do shape citizens' behavior throughout their life, making adolescents' exposure to female role models likely of considerable long-term impact (Beck and Jennings 1982; Jennings, Stoker, and Bowers 2009; Campbell 2006). Given younger people's declining interest in politics, we might also consider the potential of role models to encourage trust, engagement, and ambition to be normatively pressing as well (Lawless and Fox 2017; Shames 2017).

The few studies that have examined the impact of women politicians on adolescents and children generally support the impressionable years hypothesis. Our own work on adolescents and younger people (under the age of thirty) finds that the presence of viable and visible political role models is associated with greater political engagement, with increased discussion of politics playing a particularly key role (Campbell and Wolbrecht 2006; Wolbrecht and Campbell 2017). We report similar effects for the presence of women in parliaments cross-nationally (Wolbrecht and Campbell 2007). Deckman and McDonald (2022) find that young women become more interested in political engagement when exposed to candidates who do not fulfill the "old white guys" stereotype. Randomly assigned gender quotas in India narrow the gender gap in the career aspirations, educational attainment, and household chores of girls and boys (Beaman et al. 2012). Requiring college students to interview women politicians increases political ambition among young women, but not young men (Greenlee, Holman, and VanSickle-Ward 2014; see also Doherty 2011). The defeat of the first woman presidential nominee to a misogynistic opponent in 2016 led to both disillusionment about democracy and an intent to engage in political protest among Democratic adolescent girls (Campbell and Wolbrecht 2019).

While we expect young people to be particularly susceptible to role model effects, only a small number of previous studies examine this population, and none have directly compared adolescents to adults. In this book, we do both.

GENDER

Our theory of political role models is concerned with the impact of women politicians *as women*, and thus attention to gender is essential. We use the term *gender* purposively. It is common to view sex as a biological marker that distinguishes females from males, while gender is the social meaning we give to sex; that is, gender is the set of stereotypes, norms, and expectations that society assigns to the biological categories of woman and man. We are centrally concerned with the latter, but we also use the term *gender* to emphasize that we are concerned with "men and women as social groups rather than biological groups" (Sanbonmatsu 2008, 109). That said, we fully recognize the important limits of these two categories. As a set of characteristics, masculinity and femininity are two distinct dimensions that can and do describe both men and women (individually and as a group) to differing degrees (McDermott 2016). Moreover, while we focus on women/girls and men/boys as our subjects of analysis, we recognize that this dichotomy does not reflect the full complexity of gender, including nonbinary and trans identities. As social norms have changed, increasing numbers of citizens express gender identities not well captured by the male-female dichotomy. When possible, we recognize those distinct identities in our research.

In popular role model rhetoric, politicians and the press almost always expect women and girls to be inspired by pathbreaking women in politics. The very language of role models—a group member who demonstrates to other group members how they should act—suggests women politicians are demonstrating to other women and girls that politics is a place for them. When we step back and consider role models theoretically, however, the story is more complex and depends upon the outcome we are examining. Our theoretical expectations for the impact on beliefs about women's capacity for political leadership are that both women and men will be affected, which is also consistent with previous research (MacManus 1981). Gender stereotypes are widely held and understood by both women and men. A shift in the distribution of women and men in a role (for example, more women in politics) should thus shift the stereotypes held by both (young) women and (young) men (Koenig and Eagly 2014).

What about evaluations of government? As we have discussed, seeing members of previously marginalized groups stand for and hold elected office may lead citizens to view government as more representative, responsive, fair, and legitimate (Mansbridge 1999; Phillips 1998). Members of those marginalized groups in particular may both prioritize descriptive representation and feel more confident that their interests are being represented when their fellow group members seek and hold office. Moreover, women are more likely to express egalitarian views than are men, suggesting they put a premium on those values (Blinder and Rolfe 2018). Thus, we expect that both women and men likely understand government as more representative when women are present, but we also expect that such effects will be stronger and more consistent among women who are experiencing descriptive representation directly, who may pay more attention to women politicians, and who are generally more egalitarian in their attitudes. The work on evaluations of government so far is mixed, with some studies finding effects for both women and men, some only women, and even one article with only men responding (Atkeson and Carrillo 2007; Clayton, O'Brien, and Piscopo 2019; High-Pippert and Comer 1998; Stauffer 2021).

When it comes to political behavior, we expect women and girls to be more interested, attentive, and engaged with politics when women politicians are present, but we are less inclined to expect changes in interest or engagement among men. Through socialization and social sanctioning, people tend to act in ways consistent with gender stereotypes (Eagly and Wood 2011). As stereotypes change, people may act in new ways, reflecting the new stereotypes. The presence of women candidates and officeholders, we have argued, challenges stereotypes about *women*, and thus, while both women and men should update their *beliefs* about women in politics, only women should actually change their *behavior*. Similarly, we have argued that women and girls are more likely to be interested in and attentive to the presence of women in politics, and that women politicians are more likely to prioritize issues of interest to women and to frame issues in ways that speak to women's interests and values.

As table 2.1 demonstrates, in the vast majority of cases, scholars find that the presence of women politicians increases political engagement among *women*, with no or uneven effects among men. That said, we expect that there may be conditions under which some men shift their behavior in response to the presence of women politicians. As we argue above, those men who perceive women politicians as a threat to traditional gender hierarchies may become more engaged, particularly in purposeful activities, such as campaigning or voting. A sense of gendered threat among men is a pathway to increased political engagement among men that is distinct from the more direct role model effect we expect among women and girls.

RACE

When adolescents observe women role models in politics, they see not just gender, but race as well. The exclusion of women of color from political leadership has been both more extreme and longer-lasting than that of white women. No woman of color served in the US Congress until 1964, and in the sixty years since, just over a hundred minority women have ever served in federal elected office. Given both their success in overcoming both gender and racial bias and their ability to demonstrate the political-leadership potential of women of color, our theory of political role models expects that minority women politicians should be particularly effective role models in general, and especially for adolescents of color.

Just as scholars have explored the impact of women political role models, researchers have examined role models of color as well. For example, in terms of changing stereotypes, whites who experience African American officeholders are more favorable toward African Americans, more liberal on race-related issues, and more likely to vote for Black candidates in the future (Chauchard 2014; Hajnal 2007). With regard to democratic attitudes, Blacks and Latinos report more satisfaction with government, more trust, and more efficacy when they are represented by co-racial members (Bobo and Gilliam 1990; Bowen and Clark 2014; Box-Steffensmeier et al. 2003; Kaufmann 2003; Pantoja and Segura 2003; Sanchez and Morin 2011; Tate 2001; but see Marschall and Shah 2007). However, while extensive, research on the impact of minority candidates and officeholders on political engagement, especially turnout, is more mixed (Barreto 2007, 2010; Bobo and Gilliam 1990; Clark 2014; Clark and Block 2019; Fairdosi and Rogowski 2015; Fraga 2016; Gay 2001; Gilliam and Kaufmann 1998; Griffin and Keane 2006; Henderson, Sekhon, and Titiunik 2016; Kaufmann 2003; Keele et al. 2017; Keele and White 2019; Lublin and Tate 1995; Marschall and Shah 2007; Rocha et al. 2010; Spence and McClerking 2010; Tate 1991; Vanderleeuw and Liu 2002; Washington 2006; Wolak and Juenke 2021).

Black, Latina, and other minority women are exemplars of the political potential of not just women or minorities but of their specific intersectional identities. Just as masculinity has long been associated with political power in the United States, so has whiteness. Women of color are excluded from both of those categories, and thus we expect that their presence in politics challenges stereotypes, evinces broad representation, and inspires political engagement in unique ways. For this reason, we expect to find that minority women engender distinctive political role model effects among co-racial, other-racial, and white adolescent girls and boys. We articulate those specific expectations in chapter 6. We have little previous research to guide us, because few researchers have examined women role models of color specifically—in part because until recently, minority women candidates and officeholders were so rare (for exceptions, see Montoya et al. 2022; Stokes-Brown and Dolan 2010).

PARTISANSHIP

We can recognize someone as a role model, even if we do not agree with everything they stand for or share their partisan allegiance. When the Canadian city of Medicine Hat, Alberta—Campbell's hometown—elected its first woman mayor in 2021, her (male) opponent conceded graciously, saying that "she's an inspiration for everyone, including my own daughter, and I wish her all the best."[7] The losing candidate's daughter might have preferred her father's policies and party, but that doesn't mean that the presence of a woman candidate didn't also provide her evidence of the capabilities of women in politics, improve her view of representation, or inspire her to political action herself.

At the same time, we live in an historically polarized era. Parties organize our politics and shape our political views, from evaluating candidates to willingness to receive the COVID-19 vaccine (Gadarian, Goodman, and Pepinsky 2022). The rise of affective partisanship means that Americans often view out-partisans in the public and in office with suspicion and even hostility (Abramowitz and Webster 2018). Partisans are increasingly sorted into opposing camps where overlapping identities—party, race, religion, region, social class, occupation—reinforce and reproduce each other, shaping a range of political views and actions (Huddy and Bankert 2017; Huddy, Mason, and Aarøe 2015; Mason 2015, 2018; Mason and Wronski 2018).

Partisanship also interacts with sex and gender in important ways. Women candidates and officeholders are significantly more likely to be Democrats than Republicans (Thomsen 2015); in the current US House, 43 percent of Democrats are women, compared to just 16 percent of Republicans; in the US Senate, those numbers are 31 percent and 18 percent respectively (CAWP 2024). Women in the electorate are more likely to identify with the Democratic Party than are men (Wolbrecht and Corder 2020). Democratic policy positions are more closely aligned with feminist policy goals, while Republicans are associated with more traditional roles for women (Wolbrecht 2000). Respondents use more female-related words to describe the Democratic Party and more male-related words to describe Republicans (Winter 2010).

What might all this mean for a role model effect? One possibility is that Democrats in the public are more likely to change their attitudes or actions in response to the presence of women politicians; those women politicians are likely to be Democrats, after all. The Democratic Party is associated with civil rights and inclusion (Gerring 1998), so we might expect Democrats to be more inclined to view women politicians as an inspiration or to value the presence of women in politics. On the other hand, given the dearth of Republican women politicians, women politicians may be more attention-grabbing or stereotype-challenging to Republican respondents, and thus more likely to have an effect. Or perhaps it is co-partisanship that matters, with respondents more likely to pay attention to and be impacted by women politicians of the same party.

Our expectations for the role of party may depend on the outcome in question. Perhaps Republicans who see mostly Democratic women in politics will not update their evaluations of women in politics, but Democrats will. Alternatively, Democratic respondents already have a more favorable attitude toward women politicians, so perhaps role models have less of an effect; Republicans, less likely to endorse the idea of women as political leaders, may have more room to move. Given their party's focus on civil rights and inclusion, Democrats may be more likely to view government positively when women are present; Republicans may simply not value women's presence in a way that influences their evaluations of government. Should party matter at all for engagement, or should women, but not men, regardless of party identification, be inspired by the model of visible women in politics? Previous research does not consistently control for party or co-partisanship, but some studies find the impact of women politicians on the engagement of women is stronger or even only found between co-partisans (Reingold and Harrell 2010; also Dolan 2006; Lawless 2004; Stokes-Brown and Neal 2008; Wolak 2015).

We expect partisanship is also key for young people. Can we really speak of teenagers, who are too young to vote, as identifying with a party? In a word, yes. Partisan affiliation among teenagers is hardly a new idea in American politics, because political socialization was an integral part of the seminal work on party identification. In *The American Voter*, first published in 1960, Angus Campbell and his colleagues found that party identification—a psychological attachment to either the Republicans or Democrats—is formed while one is young, long before one develops a clearly defined set of policy preferences (Campbell et al. 1960). In the decades since then, a robust body of literature has developed to explain the partisan development of youth and how party identification is often passed from parents to their children (Achen 2002; Greenstein 1974; Hatemi and Ojeda 2021; Jennings and Markus 1984; Jennings and Niemi 1968, 1981; Jennings, Stoker, and Bowers 2009; Kroh and Selb 2009; Ojeda and Hatemi 2015). Even work questioning the claim that partisanship is a long-term disposition by describing it as a running tally of the incumbent's performance in office nonetheless acknowledges that the tally's starting point is a product of childhood socialization (Fiorina 1981). Scholars who argue that party identification should be thought of as a social identity also highlight the importance of childhood socialization (Green, Palmquist, and Schickler 2002). Political scientists interested in partisan polarization again find that partisan attitudes develop in one's youth. The same partisan animosity—known as affective polarization—found among adults is observed in adolescents (Tyler and Iyengar 2022). If past research on the childhood origins of party identification is not convincing, we also point to the fact that, across the many analyses we report in the pages to come, there are sensible, sizable, and statistically significant differences between teens who identify as either Republicans or Democrats. In our polarized times, partisanship matters, even among teenagers.

In an extension of a paper we published in 2006, Mariani, Marshall, and Mathews-Schultz (2015) report that since the early 2000s, role model effects among adolescents have become more partisan. While all girls were inspired to political engagement by the nomination of Geraldine Ferraro in 1984 and the first Year of the Woman in 1992, the 2008 presidential campaign of Hillary Clinton, the first Speakership of Nancy Pelosi, and the vice-presidential nomination of Sarah Palin were more likely to impact co-partisan girls, rather than girls in general. We take partisanship into account in all of our role models but are less confident in predicting the direction of the effect.

When Are Women Political Role Models?

Does the presence of women politicians *always* generate role model effects? We think not. We expect that some women politicians, in some contexts, are more likely to have an impact on citizens' beliefs and behaviors than others. In this section we detail the contexts and characteristics we expect to be most likely to generate any role model effect.

VISIBILITY

One key factor is visibility, following from the basic logic that women politicians who are not visible to people are unlikely to impact them (see

Hinojosa and Kittilson 2020 for a thorough discussion). The more visible the candidate or officeholder, the more likely we are to find a role model effect. Scholars have accounted for visibility in a number of ways. The vast majority of the research described in table 2.1, for example, considers women candidates for or officeholders in the US House, the US Senate, and/or a governorship as potential role models. These higher-profile offices are more likely to produce significant campaigns and generate substantial press coverage than lower-profile offices, such as state legislator, city council member, or statewide offices such as controller. Work outside the United States similarly highlights the importance of visible offices for role model effects (Liu and Banaszak 2017).

A dramatic increase in women's representation (and the attendant press coverage) is another form of visibility. For example, previous work found that women politicians affected political engagement during the 1992 Year of the Woman but not in surrounding years (Hansen 1997; Koch 1997). In Latin America, Hinojosa and Kittilson (2020) show that substantial jumps in women's representation generate attention and knowledge that facilitate role model effects. Another gauge of visibility is viability—the competitiveness of the candidate (Atkeson 2003; Dolan 2006). If a contest is noncompetitive, it is unlikely to draw much press attention, and a candidate who trails considerably behind the winner is unlikely to be well-known.

NOVELTY

Related to, but nonetheless distinct from, visibility is the impact of novelty, the extent to which the presence of women politicians is new and uncommon. Ironically, role models are particularly consequential when the press draws attention to how unusual women politicians are, such as in the 1992 Year of the Woman (Hansen 1997; Koch 1997). Safarpour and colleagues (2022) report that women candidates generated higher turnout in 2018 (the second Year of the Woman) but not in 2014, an election far less characterized by attention to women candidates *as* women. Similarly, in earlier work we find that it was not the number of women candidates per se, but rather the extent to which press coverage emphasized their novelty and status as pathbreakers, that was associated with higher political engagement among adolescents over time (Campbell and Wolbrecht 2006).

We can also conceptualize novelty as a woman running for or holding an elected office previously held by a man. As women politicians have become more common, a woman running for reelection, or for a seat already held by a woman, may not generate much attention to her gender per se. A woman running for a seat held by a man, on the other hand, stands out as a challenge to the status quo. In a 2017 paper, we found a role model effect for political discussion among younger people, but only for women candidates running for seats currently held by men (Wolbrecht and Campbell 2017). In a survey experiment in Brazil, however, novelty did not have an impact separate from the presence of women candidates (Schwindt-Bayer and Reyes-Housholder 2017). We address novelty directly in chapter 9.

PERCEPTION

The issues of visibility and novelty raise an important question: How much awareness of women politicians is necessary to induce a role model effect? Knowledge of candidates may be considered a role model outcome, and a number of papers have found that candidate recognition is higher when women candidates are on the ballot (Burns, Schlozman, and Verba 2001; Fridkin and Kenney 2014; Jones 2014; Koch 1997; Lawless 2004; Reingold and Harrell 2010; Wolak 2020). Alternatively, if respondents' knowledge of women politicians—such as name recognition or accurately estimating the share of seats held by women—is missing or faulty, other role model effects may be less likely. For example, many citizens over- or underestimate the extent to which women are represented in legislatures. Research suggests that those inaccurate estimates of women's collective representation, not the actual level, are what drives movement in trust in government and efficacy (Burden and Ono 2020; Stauffer 2021).

That said, we expect that role model effects may occur without conscious recognition of women's presence in politics. A woman candidate may draw attention and interest in politics even when respondents cannot recall her name. Absent accurate knowledge of women's presence in a given race, a general sense that there seem to be more women campaigning or that issues of interest are being raised (by women politicians) may well be sufficient to spark interest or shape attitudes and behaviors. The presence of women might also impact the behavior of others and facilitate a role model effect in that way; in our earlier work, for example, the reason girls became more interested in political activity when women candidates were present is that they experienced more discussion in their homes (Campbell and Wolbrecht 2006). This enhanced discussion may have been generated by the girls, but was just as likely driven by the behavior of the adults in their households. Nevertheless, it remains an open question whether conscious recognition of the presence of women politicians is a necessary condition for a role model effect.

TIME AND THE PRESENCE OF WOMEN IN POLITICS

Thinking about novelty and visibility also draws our attention to questions of time and context. Should we expect to see the same role model effects in every time period? The answer is clearly no. We expect women to have an impact on mass attitudes and behaviors because they challenge gender stereotypes, draw attention to politics, and represent a threat to traditionally masculine power. The extent to which women politicians have such an impact likely varies over time, largely as a function of the position of women in politics as well as other social and economic changes. The twentieth and twenty-first centuries have witnessed not only a dramatic increase in the visibility of women in politics, but also widespread changes in women's roles in the family, work, and society. The attendant shifts in socialization and context surely mean that a woman politician is viewed far differently in 2024 compared to 1924.

When there are very few women, or just one, their presence may not challenge gender stereotypes so much as cue them; as a result, women in such situations are judged to be less capable and a poor fit for traditionally male jobs (Biernat et al. 1998; Heilman 1980). Consider Rep. Clare Booth Luce (R-CT), who in 1944 was one of only eight women in the US House of Representatives. In a *Los Angeles Times* article titled "Rep. Clare Booth Luce Sees Women Taking Leading Role in Postwar Politics," the writer nonetheless describes Luce as wearing "a pale blue wool shirtmaker dress . . . a corsage . . . and sturdy black alligator oxfords," noting that Luce "honestly admits being 40 years of age. She looks about 22!"[8] Such coverage does little to convince anyone that women belong in politics. Women from Egyptian Queen Cleopatra through British Queen Victoria, and Prime Ministers Indira Gandhi (India), Golda Meir (Israel), and Margaret Thatcher (United Kingdom), were viewed as exceptions that did not in fact invalidate the rule that women do not belong in politics (Steinberg 2008).

As women's presence in politics moves beyond the truly exceptional, role model effects become more likely (Eagly and Koenig 2021). Women politicians remain novel, but there are sufficient numbers that their presence challenges persistent stereotypes about appropriate roles for women. Firsts remain plentiful and notable, but not entirely isolated. Our theory most clearly expects role model effects under these conditions, and indeed, the vast majority of empirical scholarship on role models examines just such a period (the 1970s to present) in American history. During this era women made important gains while remaining dramatically underrepresented in American politics: Women comprised just 3 percent of Congress in 1980, a figure that doubled to 6 percent in 1990 and doubled again to 12 percent in 2000. As late as 2010, women still occupied just 17 percent of all congressional seats (CAWP 2023d). Given these low levels of representation, we should not be surprised that research in this period finds that woman candidates and officeholders do in fact influence the general public's attitudes and actions. Scholars have been looking for political role models in the period during which we might most expect to find them.

In recent years, however, women politicians have become more common. In the US Congress today, 151 women hold 28 percent of the seats in the US House and Senate combined (CAWP 2024). After an almost twenty-five-year gap since Geraldine Ferraro, Sarah Palin was the Republican vice-presidential nominee in 2008. Nancy Pelosi served as the Speaker of the House from 2007 to 2011, and again from 2019 to 2022. In 2016 Hillary Clinton was the Democratic nominee for president, and in 2021 Kamala Harris became the first woman vice president of the United States.

What does the greater visibility and prominence of women in politics mean for role model effects? On the one hand, women remain unusual and noteworthy, consistent with the conditions necessary for role models. On the other hand, however, we expect that as women's presence continues to expand and normalize, role model effects may diminish, for several reasons. Women politicians may not command as much attention. As gender stereotypes are updated to include politics as an appropriate venue for women, there may simply be less room for any one women candidate or officeholder to impact attitudes and behaviors. While perhaps not there yet, we may expect role model effects to diminish as women politicians become more "normal," a possibility we consider directly in our concluding chapter.

CANDIDATES VERSUS OFFICEHOLDERS

Role model theory expects that women in politics challenge stereotypes and inspire political action. As such, we can expect (and research has found) women in a variety of political roles to have this kind of effect, ranging from women judges and justices (Badas and Stauffer 2018; Shortell and Valdini 2022) to political activists; for young people in particular, we might think of environmentalist Greta Thunberg or girls' education advocate Malala Yousafzai (Wahlström and Uba 2023). Our own research, for example, finds that women activists after the 2016 election of Donald Trump provided a model of response to loss and inspired increased interest in protest among Democratic girls, especially those most disillusioned with politics (Campbell and Wolbrecht 2019).

For the most part, however, scholars have focused on women running for and holding elected political office as potential role models in American politics. We limited table 2.1 to only such research. Given our emphasis on visibility, should we have different role model expectations for candidates versus officeholders? Candidates are far more in the public eye, especially in their own states and districts, than are officeholders. A candidate's central goal is to put themselves in front of their constituents to build name recognition, favorability, and political mobilization. Officeholders, on the other hand, certainly seek to maintain communication with their constituents, but constituents are less likely to be exposed to the day-to-day work of governing. (That said, we recognize that the line between campaigning and governing is extremely blurred [Mayhew 1974]). Women candidates are particularly relevant as role models when the expected effects are related to elections, such as interest, attention, activism, and turnout.

REPRESENTATION

As we have argued, the study of role models is fundamentally an evaluation of one possible consequence of descriptive representation. But what form of representation should generate a role model effect? As table 2.1 demonstrates, the vast majority of role model research has focused on dyadic representation: the relationship between specific representatives and their own constituents. Yet, it is also possible to conceive of representation in collective terms, as the extent to which a political institution as a whole provides representation to citizens. From a normative point of view, both forms of representation are relevant: the degree to which the legislator you have a hand in choosing represents you, as well as the extent to which the legislature or political system writ large represents you. Indeed, given that most government action is collective—that is, it requires the coordinated action of the body as a whole, not just one's own representative—citizens have strong incentives to care about collective representation (Stauffer 2021; Weissberg 1978).

The argument for focusing on dyadic representation is that politicians in one's own district and state are more visible to citizens, through local media coverage, outreach to constituents, and personal networks. While the nation's capital may seem distant and inscrutable, local candidates and officeholders may be more familiar and visible to many citizens. Normatively, the representatives that citizens themselves have a hand in selecting bear a particular representational burden: These are the people who are expected to stand and act for citizens in their district or state, and thus may be where citizens look for their understanding of government, their evaluations of women as political leaders, and their inspiration to political engagement.

This does not mean that collective representation is unimportant. Particularly in our discussion of political engagement (chapter 5) and in an experiment we conducted (chapter 7), we analyze adolescents' responses to women's collective representation. We also view collective representation as an important background to any dyadic effects. As we saw most clearly in the two Years of the Woman (1992 and 2018), the presence of women candidates nationwide can heighten attention to gender and politics, emphasize women's underrepresentation, and frame women candidates and officeholders as pathbreakers who are upending traditional gender stereotypes (McDonald, Porter, and Treul 2020; Safarpour et al. 2022; Wilcox 1994). Such a context (heightened collective representation of women) is associated with the strongest dyadic role model findings (Hansen 1997; Koch 1997; Safarpour et al. 2022).

How Should We Study Role Models?

Our theory of role models suggests a set of outcomes (beliefs about women as leaders, democratic attitudes, engagement and activism) and a number of key characteristics describing respondents (sex, race, partisanship, age) and women politicians (viability, visibility, novelty, role, type of representation). What sorts of evidence should we use for our analysis? Table 2.1 shows that research on role models has been largely observational—a snapshot of political attitudes and actions at a specific moment of time. Observational data have the advantage of capturing people's attitudes in their "natural habitat." This means that respondents had sustained exposure to real-world political campaigns, complete with news coverage, advertising, campaign outreach, social media, and conversations within their social network. In these analyses, researchers compare respondents in districts and states that had women candidates or officeholders to respondents in states who did not. At the most basic level, a difference between these two groups can be attributed to the presence of women politicians.

The shortcoming of observational data is the inability to definitively determine causality. One problem is the possibility of selection effects: Perhaps respondents with and without women politicians are different not because of those politicians, but because women politicians are more likely to run and hold office in particular kinds of places with particular kinds of constituents. And indeed, we know that this is the case (Ondercin 2022; Palmer and Simon 2008). Scholars can and do account for these differences by including controls in their models, but it is unlikely that any model can control for every way in which places with women candidates are different from those without them. As a result, we should be concerned that it is not the presence of women politicians that generates the change in political beliefs or behavior, but rather some third factor that both makes a place amenable to women's representation and is associated with specific political attitudes and actions, such as the heightened political engagement of women. We might even have the direction of causality wrong. Perhaps it is those places where people are more positive about women leaders, more likely to trust in government, and more engaged in political affairs where women are more likely to run and to win.

The gold standard for determining causality is randomized experiments. By eliminating all other factors and isolating the one variable of interest (in this case, the presence of women politicians), we can be more confident that any observed effects are due to the treatment, and thus causal. In such experiments, then, respondents are assigned at random to be exposed (or not) to women candidates. Any difference between the two groups *must* be a function of the exposure to women candidates; there are no other differences between the two groups other than exposure to that treatment. Since it is beyond our ability to randomly assign women candidates to different districts (something about the democratic process and representation), experiments in this case must largely be within the survey itself. As a result, the ability to pinpoint causation comes at the price of external validity—exposure to women candidates is brief and happens within the artificial setting of an experiment.

A third approach is a panel survey, in which the same respondents are interviewed both before and after exposure to women politicians, such as prior to and following an election. This allows the researcher to compare not just group (with women candidates) to group (without women candidates), but within individuals over time. Do we observe a change in the attitudes or behaviors of respondents from their initial responses to their responses after their exposure to women politicians? This approach goes a long way toward addressing the problem of selection bias: Individuals reside in the same place for both surveys, so any change after the exposure to women politicians can be attributed to that treatment and not to the characteristics of the location.

Panel studies are rare, however. Conducting robust public opinion surveys has always been difficult and is becoming more so. A panel design requires researchers not only to identify and persuade people to answer a survey once, but also to find and persuade them to answer a second survey, several months (or longer) later. As we detail in the following chapters, several panel surveys comprise the primary evidentiary basis for the findings reported here. We also describe findings from several observational sources and report on a set of survey experiments in chapters 7 and 9. By triangulating a number of datasets with different characteristics, we can be more confident in our conclusions.

Summarizing the Theory

As summarized in table 2.2 (arrows indicate we expect a positive effect), our theory of political role models expects women politicians to influence (1) beliefs about women's capacity for politics, (2) evaluations of representational democracy, and (3) political engagement and activism. These effects are not simply interesting; they actually suggest that women politicians can help bolster and advance democracy. In a robust democracy, citizens believe in the equality of all citizens, trust their representatives to serve the public good, and actively engage in politics. Undermining bias against women politicians helps advance the cause of political equality in American democracy. Increased trust and satisfaction with representative institutions bolsters the legitimacy of democratic government. Encouraging political engagement, especially among those who have long been excluded, advances popular sovereignty, the expectation that government is truly of and for the people (Hinojosa and Kittilson 2020).

We focus the bulk of our analysis on adolescents, the group most likely to be affected by role models, as their political views and intentions are still developing and for whom exposure to women politicians may have long-lasting impact. We examine this expectation directly in chapter 8, comparing the presence and size of the role model effect among adolescents compared to adults. We look for role model effects among both girls and boys, but our expectations vary with the effect being examined. In our theory of political role models, both girls and boys are expected to update their stereotypes about the political capacity of women, but it is girls who are expected to change their behavior to match the changing stereotype. Boys may also change their behavior, but it may be threat that is driving that response, not changing stereotypes per se. Partisanship is both central to American politics and to our analysis; we consider how both partisanship and co-partisanship may shape any role model effect. A unique survey permits us to examine the impact of race, and women political role models of color specifically, in chapter 6.

Not all (potential) role models are created equal. We focus our analysis on exposure to women *candidates*, rather than officeholders, in American politics. Our logic is that political campaigns serve to make candidates (incumbents and challengers) visible to the public, including to adolescents, who are generally less attentive to politics. Continuing with that logic, we

Table 2.2. Expectations of women as political role models

	Women as leaders	Faith in democracy	Political engagement
Girls	↑	↑	↑
Boys	↑		↑

further focus our analysis on women candidates who are viable (i.e., who win or come close to winning their seat). At some points we also examine women candidates who are novel, meaning they are running for a seat currently held by a man. All of these candidate characteristics increase the likelihood of observing a role model effect.

We focus largely, but not exclusively, on dyadic representation. In doing so, we assume that candidates in one's own district and state are more visible to citizens and thus more likely to shape their engagement. Previous research suggests that knowledge of women's presence in collective bodies—that is, legislatures—is poor and unreliable (Burden and Ono 2020; Stauffer 2021). We also might expect that attitudes and behaviors are most directly shaped by one's own candidates for those positions. That said, a dyadic approach is in some ways a departure from the social role theory which has informed our theory of political role models. Social role theory expects changes in stereotypes and behavior in response to changes in the *collective* gender composition of particular roles (such as that of scientist or CEO) over a significant period of time (Eagly et al. 2020). We emphasize that our theory of political role models is informed by the insights of social role theory, but our research does not test it explicitly. That said, we do not see our expectations for dyadic representation as necessarily in conflict with social role theory. Rather, we view exposure to women politicians in one's own district or state as a cue or reminder of the presence of women in politics. Specific election campaigns with women candidates generate repeated exposure to women in politics, but we expect that information is received within (and reinforces the sense of) the growing numbers of women politicians overall.

Our empirical analysis is grounded in multiple original opinion surveys gathered around the 2020 national US elections. Every election is unique, and 2020 perhaps particularly so. The incumbent president had already been prosecuted for impeachment once, and the January 6, 2021 attack on the Capitol generated a second impeachment trial, which took place around the time of our post-election surveys. Perhaps most important, a global pandemic and widespread lockdowns transformed the 2020 campaign. Traditional campaigning was dramatically circumscribed, with likely impacts on exposure to political information among the mass public. Yet, voters perceived the election as having incredibly high stakes and expressed historically high levels of interest and attention, as well as concerns about their ability to cast their ballot during the pandemic (Gilberstadt et al. 2020). As we have argued, context is often important for realizing any role model effects.

The unique context of 2020 may raise concerns about the generalizability of our findings. We suggest that no election is "standard"; other recent presidential election years have been characterized by the first-ever woman major-party nominee (2016) or a former president who faces dozens of active criminal indictments (2024). If we wait until a "normal" election to gauge role model effects, we will be waiting a very long time. If anything, the lack of direct attention to women candidates specifically (compared to say, 2016 or 2018) means that 2020 offers a conservative test for role model effects. All that said, we certainly hope that scholars will continue to investigate potential role model effects in other years and in other kinds of elections.

Having outlined our theory of political role models, we now turn to the task of using these data to put our expectations to the test in the chapters that follow. We start by asking whether women politicians change adolescents' minds about whether women can be effective leaders.

PART II
Testing the Theory

3 * Faith in Women

Whenever I meet a little girl, I tell them "I'm running for president, because that's what girls do."

Senator Elizabeth Warren (D-MA)[1]

During her 2020 campaign for the Democratic presidential nomination, Elizabeth Warren had a special tradition for when she met young girls, linking pinkies—which everyone knows means an unbreakable pinkie promise—so that they would not forget that girls can be leaders too. She even published a children's book called *Pinkie Promises*, in which a young girl named Polly goes to a rally and meets a woman named Elizabeth who is running for president. After making a pinkie promise with Elizabeth, Polly summons the courage to attend a new school, kick the winning goal at a soccer game, find a missing dog—and run for class president. Polly gives a campaign speech to her classmates in which she echoes Elizabeth: "I can be a leader, because that's what girls do."

Historically, of course, running for president has most certainly *not* been something that girls do. Prior to 2020 a total of nine women had pursued the presidential nomination of a major American party, with a few others running as minor-party nominees (CAWP 2023c). This dearth of women candidates matters. Stereotypes about women and men develop from what people actually observe, and if there are few women political leaders, people conclude that political leadership is something men—but not women—do (Koenig et al. 2011; Koenig and Eagly 2014). Combined with stereotypes that frame women as naturally compassionate and dependent (instead of having characteristics associated with politics, such as power and strength), people have reason to doubt the ability of women to succeed in political roles.

On the whole, Americans today say they believe women *are* capable of political leadership. Since 1937 the Gallup Poll has periodically asked Americans whether they would vote for a woman running for president if she was qualified and had been nominated by their party. In 1937 the idea

Figure 3.1. Elizabeth Warren tweet highlighting her "pinky promises" to encourage girls to run for office

of a woman being elected to the highest office in the land was so preposterous that the question specified: if "she qualified *in every other respect*" to be president. A full 64 percent of Americans said that they would not vote for a woman—even if nominated by their own party. By 1971 the numbers had flipped: Sixty-six percent of Americans said that they would vote for a woman as chief executive. Moreover, the wording of the question no longer required the qualifier that—no, really—a woman could be qualified for the presidency. By 2019 virtually every American—94 percent—said that they would vote for a woman for the highest office in the land (see figure 3.2).

Similarly, we found nearly universal support for women as political leaders, at least in the abstract, when interviewing parents and teens from across the country. We conducted interviews of roughly an hour in length with teen-parent pairs, all of whom were also respondents to the nationally representative Family Matters 2 survey, described in more detail below. Our teens and parents came from all across the country and all walks

Faith in Women

of life. The adolescents spanned a wide range of interest in politics, from highly engaged to apathetic. Ideologically, some were conservative, others progressive. Most were somewhere in between. Because we suspected that, owing to a desire to give a socially desirable response, adolescents and adults alike might be reluctant to admit having reservations about women political leaders, we asked both parents and teens whether they know other people who might not vote for a woman because of her gender. Typical was Andrew,[2] a high school junior from Texas. When asked whether people he knows "see a difference between men and women when they run for office," he responded: "No. I don't think so, because, when you're running for office . . . gender limitations aren't really a role in something like that."

Anna, a conservative mother from rural Maryland, spoke of her general support for women in office, even though she was opposed to Hillary Clinton in 2016. She assured us that her dislike of Clinton was not because of gender, and that she impressed this upon her daughter. Speaking of Clinton, Anna said, "as much as I am pro-woman and support females in what is generally a male role, I did not feel she was the right person for it, so I wanted to make sure that my 10-year-old understood that we weren't against her because she was a female. We were against her because of things that she had done in the past."

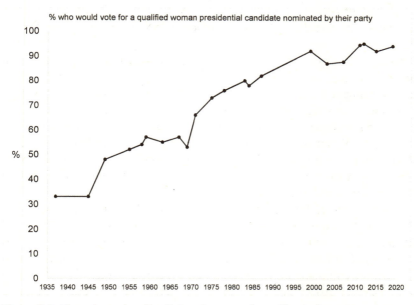

Figure 3.2. These days, virtually all Americans say they will vote for a woman president

In this day and age, respondents might be reluctant to admit they harbor doubts about women in office due to social pressure. One way to get around the problem of respondents giving the answers they think are socially acceptable, rather than their true opinion, is a list experiment. In this kind of study, people are randomly assigned to two groups. Group 1 gets a list of, say, four statements like "Professional athletes getting million-dollar-plus salaries." Group 1 is then asked *how many* of these statements make them "angry or upset," but—and this is important—they are not asked *which* statements specifically anger or upset them. A second group gets the same list of statements, plus one more; in this case, the additional statement is "A woman serving as president." Group 2 is also asked how many of these statements make them angry or upset. Because these two groups should be identical in every way, *except for the statements they read*, we should expect that each group will be as likely as the other group to be upset by the first four statements. Any additional anger or upset among Group 2 (compared to Group 1) *must* reflect their feelings about a woman running for president. The advantage of this approach is that since the question is about the list as whole, and not about individual statements, it allows respondents to report anger about women candidates for president without having to actually admit that response to the interviewer (Streb et al. 2008).

One such study conducted in 2006 reported that a little more than a quarter of respondents felt angry or upset about the idea of a female president, despite the fact that recent polls showed that more than 90 percent of survey respondents indicated they would vote for a woman for president (Streb et al. 2008). Interestingly, and as predicted by our theory of political role models, attitudes shifted as the presence of women politicians changed. In the next ten years, Americans witnessed a woman as a serious contender for the presidency (Clinton in 2008), a nominee for the vice presidency (Palin in 2008), and a Speaker of the House (Pelosi, 2007–11). When scholars conducted the same list experiment again in 2016, they found that the percentage of respondents who were angry or upset about the idea of a woman president had dropped by half, to just 13 percent (Burden, Ono, and Yamada 2017).

Democrats and Republicans differ on this score. In the list experiments, Republicans were more likely to be angry or upset about the idea of a woman president than were Democrats. In fact, the reduction in hostility between 2006 and 2016 was driven almost entirely by Democrats, who by 2016 showed no anger or upset about a woman president (Burden, Ono, and Yamada 2017). Similarly, in recent Gallup Polls Republicans have been roughly 5 percentage points less likely to say that they would vote for a woman presidential candidate (remember, the question specifies that she is both qualified and nominated by their party). The Pew Research Center reported in 2018 that 63 percent of Democrats hope to see a woman president in their lifetimes, compared to only a quarter of Republicans (Thomas 2019). A recent meta-analysis of dozens of experiments finds that both independents and Democrats express a slight preference for women candidates, while Republicans reveal a slight preference for men (Schwarz and Coppock 2022).

Since 1974, the nationally representative General Social Survey has asked Americans whether "most men are better suited emotionally for politics than are women." As with the Gallup question about a woman presidential candidate, this query about emotional suitability for politics reveals persistent partisan differences. In 1974 roughly 60 percent of Republicans, both women and men, agreed that men are better suited emotionally for politics, compared to 40 percent of Democrats. By 2021 Democrats and Republicans alike became far less likely to say that only men have the emotional mettle for public life, but the partisan gap remains. Among Democrats, only 4 percent of women and 8 percent of men give the nod to men over women. Among Republicans, it is 18 percent of women and 27 percent—over one in four—of men. In other words, when we scratch the surface of the apparent widespread acceptance of women in elected office, resistance remains. That resistance is mostly found among Republicans, and Republican men in particular.

A few of our interviews provided reasons to suspect that our interlocutors were more resistant to women in office than they let on. Above we quoted Anna, the mom who opposed Hillary Clinton for reasons other than her gender. Interestingly, she also spoke of her concerns about Kamala Harris, specifically calling out her gender. In Anna's words, "When the vice president was given the position that she was given this time, I did talk a lot about people getting the positions that they earn and not being appointed because of their gender." Claiming that Joe Biden only chose Harris as a running mate because she is a woman is not necessarily the same as objecting to women in general, but at the very least it suggests that Anna does not see Harris in particular—the first woman to serve as vice president—as qualified for her position.

We also had a few parents and teens describe "people they know" as resistant to women in elected office. One is Alexa, a liberal teen from California's Bay Area. Even though Alexa herself says that she would "love to see" a woman president, because "that would be amazing," she reports that this attitude is not shared by all of her peers: "I would say that people at my school, like a portion of them, they would prefer a man to run for office rather than a woman." Her mom, Marcy, a diehard Democrat who works at a local university, agreed: "I've got into arguments with colleagues who feel like, oh, I could never—they've actually openly said 'I would never vote for a woman, a female president.'"

The most overt opposition to women serving in any position of leadership came from Heather and Emily, a mother-daughter pair who live in rural Minnesota. Emily is the oldest of ten children, all of whom are homeschooled. They are theologically conservative Christians; the husband and father is a pastor who leads the family in daily devotionals and scripture reading. While they were coy about their partisanship, it became clear that they are Republicans, as are virtually all the members of their church. (They spoke of the controversy that erupted when one congregant said he was supporting Biden). In this interview, there was no concern that social desirability bias prevented them from sharing their real views. When asked point-blank whether she thinks "it matters whether it's a man or woman who's running for office," Heather responded with an opinion that would have been far more common in 1937:

> We kind of believe that men should rule because that's also according to the scriptures. We would like to see men in office instead of women. Women are easily swayed by emotions and easily deceived, as Eve was at the beginning. That's what the scriptures say. We generally would vote for a man. We would vote for a man instead of a woman.

Nor was there a generation gap, as Emily agreed with her mother:

> I would say as well, I vote for men because I think God created men for leadership and women to be the helper. There's so many examples in the Bible of men who are in leadership being corrupted or taken down by the women in their lives. Even today, I think men are just naturally stronger leaders. That's what God created them for.

Here we have both a parent and teen express not just reservations but outright opposition to women in leadership roles, on biblical grounds. While such views are not as common today as in the past, hearing them expressed so unequivocally is a reminder that a nontrivial number of Americans do not see politics as a place for women. These views are held by both women and men, young and old, but are concentrated among Republicans.

These patterns begin in adolescence. In a survey we conducted of American teens aged fourteen to eighteen (more detail below), we asked respondents to indicate their agreement with the statement: "If we had more women in elected office, America would be. . . ." As with all of the attitudes we discuss in this chapter, respondents' opinions were measured on a sliding scale that ranges from 0 (worse) to 10 (better), with a neutral opinion equal to 5.

We also inquired about women's ability, relative to men, to undertake the tasks associated with high political office. Specifically, we asked respondents about four different leadership traits. The order of traits was randomized, and respondents used a slider to place their attitude on a 0–10 scale. They were given the list below of leadership traits and asked to indicate whether "men are generally better" (0) or "women are generally better" (10) at each.

A. Working out compromises
B. Being honest and ethical
C. Being a strong leader
D. Working well under pressure

We included both traditionally feminine (A and B) and traditionally masculine (C and D) characteristics. While factor analysis shows that all four traits are highly correlated (suggesting they all tap an underlying belief about women's relative capacity for political leadership), we have nonetheless analyzed them separately, as it could be that women candidates are more likely to affect perceptions of one type of trait than the other.[3]

Figure 3.3 displays the average responses for four groups defined by both gender (girls/boys) and party (Democrats/Republicans) in the order we employ throughout this book: Republican boys, Republican girls, Democratic boys, Democratic girls. As we will see throughout this book, understanding the role model effect requires attention to both gender *and* party. Among both Democrats and Republicans, girls are significantly more supportive of women as political leaders than are boys. Among both girls and boys, Republicans are significantly less supportive of women's capacity to lead than Democrats. The combination of gender and party generates clear and consistent patterns. Democratic girls are in a category all by themselves, at least twice as likely as any other group to endorse women's capacity for politics. Similarly, Republican boys are distinctive on the other end, showing little to no endorsement of women's leadership. Democratic boys and Republican girls, however, are strikingly similar in their attitudes, with Democratic boys lagging slightly behind Republican girls.

Although this is slightly removed from politics, we find the same pattern for attitudes regarding gender roles in general. We also asked a series of questions tapping into traditional (men are superior to women and the sexes occupy distinct roles) and hostile sexism (women are trying to take power from men), a form of modern sexism (Glick and Fiske 1997, 2001; Gothreau, Arceneaux, and Friesen 2022; Swim et al. 1995). We combined

CHAPTER 3

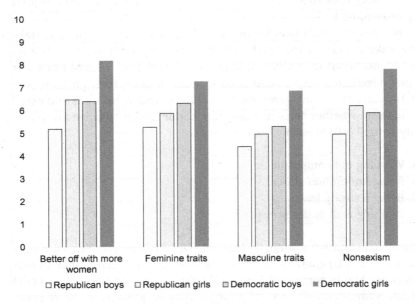

Figure 3.3. Republican boys are the least likely to see women as leaders, hold nonsexist attitudes

these items into a single Nonsexism Index.[4] Respondents were again given a slider to indicate whether they agree or disagree with the following statements:

A. It is usually better for everyone involved if the man is the achiever outside the home and the woman takes care of the home and family. (traditional sexism)
B. Discrimination against women is no longer a problem in the United States. (modern sexism)
C. Most women interpret innocent remarks or acts as sexist. (hostile sexism)
D. Women seek to gain power by getting control over men. (hostile sexism)
E. Women are too easily offended. (hostile sexism)

As shown in figure 3.3, the pattern for these questions about sexism in general is nearly identical to those about women's ability to be political leaders.

To recap what we have seen thus far, the Gallup Poll, General Social Survey, list experiments, survey of adolescents, and our qualitative interviews all paint a consistent picture about Americans' perceptions of women's capacity for political leadership. Although on the surface there appears to be nearly universal acceptance of women in political office, including but not limited to the presidency, a deeper look indicates that not everyone agrees—even among teenagers.

In particular, positive attitudes about women as political leaders are more common among girls than among boys; girls also tend to be less sexist. Our theory of political role models emphasizes that gender stereotypes are widely shared, but this does not mean that other factors do not come into play. Gender stereotypes are indeed overwhelmingly consistent across age, education, employment, race, and marital status, but they are also characterized by "some ingroup favoritism, with women, relative to men, rating women more favorably" (Eagly et al. 2020, 311). Our data are consistent with these established patterns.

Ambivalence or opposition to women as political leaders is also more common among Republicans than Democrats. Many Republican families belong to religious groups that teach traditional gender roles (Putnam and Campbell 2012). Such attitudes are not necessarily as extreme as believing that because the biblical Eve was beguiled by a serpent, women today should not be in elected office. Instead, they are likely to be more subtle—for example, in their faith religious leaders are all men; most women are homemakers. However, religion is not the only potential influence on Republicans' gender attitudes. Another could be the popular culture they consume—books, movies, and television shows that reinforce traditional gender roles. Still another influence could be the political environment, as women candidates are more likely to be Democrats than Republicans. In short, there are still minds to be changed about women as leaders, and we suggest that one potential lever for change is exposure to women as they run for office.

Expectations for Role Models

Can the presence of women politicians change people's views about women's capacity for political leadership? As we saw in chapter 2, democratic theorist Jane Mansbridge (1999) highlights changed perceptions of women's "fitness to rule" as a key benefit of descriptive representation. Similarly, Anne Phillips (1998, 63), in *The Politics of Presence*, calls this function the role model argument—the expectation that women candidates and officeholders "dislodge deep-rooted assumptions about what is appropriate to women and men." In her classic statement on women's interests, Virginia Sapiro (1981, 712) writes: "Increased representation of people who 'look like' women will effect powerful symbolic changes in politics. Women and men continue to think of politics as a male domain because the empirical truth at this moment is that politics is a male domain.... More women in office will increase the acceptability of women in government." With these words—written more than forty years ago—Sapiro lays out the logic of our analysis: If people do not see women as fit to rule because few women are in the political arena, then seeing more women credibly competing for office—obviously a precondition to having more women serve in office—will lead people to envision women as capable of leadership.

WHO CHANGES THEIR MINDS?

Girls and boys. If seeing women run changes minds about women as leaders, whose minds will be changed? Gender stereotypes are widely shared among all members of a society or culture. When the actual presence of women in a role changes, both women *and* men should update their beliefs. Both women *and* men have become more likely to see women as stronger on traditionally masculine traits as women's roles have changed (Diekman and Eagly 2000; Eagly et al. 2020; Eagly and Wood 2011). That said, "in-group favoritism" means women respondents rate women more favorably on dimensions such as competence. As we saw in figure 3.3, girls and boys start from very different baselines, with girls being consistently more favorable toward women leaders than are boys.

This in-group favoritism means that when it comes to the perception of women's capacity to lead, it is the boys who lag behind the girls, and thus the boys who need to catch up. Previous work on role models has focused on political engagement and activism, where women historically lagged behind men. Women role models are expected to help women catch up to men and close the gender gap in engagement and ambition. When we talk about gender stereotypes regarding women's capacity for political leadership, however, it is men who hold more traditionally stereotypical views; in this case, then, men need to catch up, not women. Recall that Mansbridge (1999) argues that members of underrepresented groups, including women, are role models not only for those who share their identity. Role models can potentially change the attitudes of those in the dominant group, who might be the most resistant to members of new groups' "fitness to rule." Indeed, Mansbridge makes the case that, normatively, we should be more concerned about changing the minds of the dominant group, since they hold the power.

As we saw in chapter 2, there has been relatively little research on the effect of American role models on attitudes toward women's leadership capacity, and the work that has been done has produced mixed results. In the single US paper on this topic, MacManus (1981) finds that a significant minority of Houston respondents believed the first woman city controller made them more positive about the potential for women to serve in elected office. Research in countries other than the United States (Coffé and Reiser 2021; Evans 2016) finds that women politicians shift only men's views of women as political leaders (Beaman et al. 2009; Morgan and Buice 2013), both women's and men's views (Allen and Cutts 2018), or only women's views (Alexander 2012).

Our theory of political role models expects that women politicians will affect the attitudes of adolescent girls *and* boys. However, given that boys are less enthusiastic about women as political leaders to start with, we suspect we may find that it is boys' minds who will be most likely to change, as they have the most room to move.

Political party. Our theory also expects party identification to shape the impact of women politicians on the public. Since 1992, long before our adolescent respondents were born, the majority of female candidates for the House and Senate have been Democrats (Thomsen 2015). This was even true in 2020, the high-water mark for Republican women running for office. In that year—the focus of our analysis—women candidates were still more likely to be Democrats than Republicans. Across the country, in 2020 two-thirds of all women candidates were Democrats—*even* in a record year for Republican women. In 2018, another year that will feature in our analysis (see chapter 4), the gap between the parties was still greater, as Democrats made up over three-quarters of all women on House, Senate, and gubernatorial tickets.[5] Not surprisingly, as of 2024, in the US House, 44 percent of Democrats are women, compared to just 15 percent of Republicans (CAWP 2023b).

It is not only that women candidates are more likely to be Democrats. Women in the electorate are also more likely to identify with the Democratic Party (Wolbrecht and Corder 2020). Democratic policy positions are more closely aligned with feminist policy goals, while Republicans are associated with more traditional roles for women (Wolbrecht 2000). Respondents use more feminine words to describe the Democratic Party and more masculine words to describe Republicans (Winter 2010). Not surprisingly, Democrats express the most support for women as political leaders (Horowitz, Igielnik, and Parker 2018), perhaps more evidence of "ingroup favoritism."

Since most women candidates are Democrats, and voters tend to assume that woman candidates are liberals and Democrats (Dolan 2014; Sanbonmatsu 2002), we may expect Democrats to be more open to updating their views of women as political leaders. Moreover, the overrepresentation of Democrats among women candidates may make Republican boys and girls less likely to view women candidates as exemplars of the leadership potential of women.

On the other hand, Democratic respondents in 2020 may not view women candidates as anything new or novel, minimizing their effect on Democrats' views of women's fitness to lead. We argue in chapter 2 that novelty is likely an important factor in generating role model effects. Given the comparatively small numbers of Republican women candidates in recent decades (in other words, their novelty within the GOP), Republican respondents may be more surprised, and therefore affected, by the presence of women candidates than are Democrats. We have already seen that Democrats are more supportive of women leaders; as a result, Democratic girls and boys may be at their limit for support for women politicians. Republicans, on the other hand, have plenty of room to move their views in the direction of their Democratic sisters and brothers. For these reasons, we suspect that exposure to women candidates will be associated with more positive evaluations of women as political leaders among Republican respondents, more so than among Democrats.

Co-partisanship. We have proposed that women candidates are probably most likely to affect the views of boys and Republicans, given that girls and Democrats already express high opinions of the leadership capacities of women. It may also be the case that girls and boys, regardless of party, are more likely to pay attention to and be affected by candidates who share their partisan identity, especially during a period of extreme partisan polarization. Party identification is a lens through which citizens see and understand the world. Affective polarization means that Americans often view out-party politicians with suspicion and even hostility (Abramowitz and Webster 2018). As we explore further in chapter 5, in recent years the impact of women politicians on the engagement of women tends to be stronger or even only found between co-partisans (Reingold and Harrell 2010; also Dolan 2006; Lawless 2004; Mariani, Marshall, and Mathews-Schultz 2015; Stokes-Brown and Neal 2008; Wolak 2015). If co-partisan women candidates lead to greater political engagement, it seems plausible that they would also be more likely to alter attitudes toward women as leaders.

Putting Role Models to the Test

In its essentials, our research answers a straightforward question: Do teens in places where women candidates run for office have different attitudes from teens in places where few or no women run? For all of the statistical methodology we employ to guard against threats to causal inference, the fundamental logic of our analysis is comparing changes among young people in places with women candidates to changes among young people in places where fewer or no women run.

Faith in Women [69]

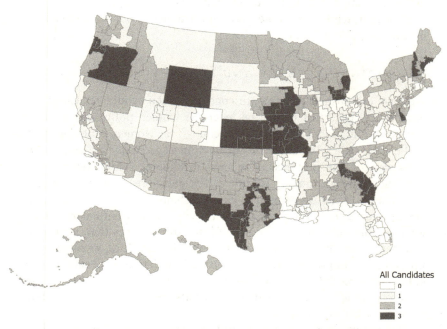

Figure 3.4. The distribution of women candidates for House, Senate, and governor, 2020

WHERE WOMEN RUN

We are assisted in this endeavor by the considerable geographic variation in the presence of women candidates. Figure 3.4 displays the distribution of women candidates around the United States for three high-profile offices circa 2020.[6] Each state is shaded for the number of women candidates running for the two statewide offices of senator and governor. Specifically, the map shows whether at least one woman ran for either office in the most recent election, which, owing to varying election cycles, ranges from 2016 to 2020. Each congressional district is then shaded further if at least one woman ran for the House of Representatives in 2020. In some places there are multiple women running for office, while in others there are none. We display 2020 because our individual-level data are from this year.

These patterns are not random. Different states and congressional districts have distinct records when it comes to women candidates. Eighteen states have never had a woman governor, for example (Dittmar 2022). Until 2022 Vermont had never sent a woman to Congress (Shivaram

2022). A small handful of state legislatures have reached gender equity, or close to it, while other states have fewer than one out of five seats held by women (CAWP 2023b).

MEASURING PRESENCE AND PERCEPTION

We have established that the presence of women candidates varies geographically, but must people be aware of women politicians for us to observe a role model effect? Or is it enough for women politicians to be in the ether? We think about this distinction as *perception* versus *presence*.

Presence. The presence of women candidates simply refers to the number of women running for office. The mere presence of any woman candidate may not be enough to cause a change in attitudes, especially among teenagers, who are unlikely to pay much attention to politics. We therefore only count candidates for the three offices that, next to the presidency, are the most prominent in American politics: member of the US House of Representatives, US senator, and state governor. We are not accounting for women who run for other high-profile offices, such as mayor, which only means that any results we find are over and above those for other salient women candidates.

Why not count presidential candidates? Our analysis depends on comparing adolescents who live in different states and districts and thus on observing different numbers of women candidates. The national context is more or less a constant. While there is obviously more presidential campaigning in some places than others, in 2020 everyone in the country received some exposure to the vice-presidential campaign of Kamala Harris and to the candidacies of multiple women in the Democratic presidential primaries. As well, there might be legacy effects of Hillary Clinton's 2016 presidential candidacy. Any results we find are in addition to whatever impact these women candidates may have had. Because the national context is not a factor in our analysis, we have stacked the deck against finding any sort of role model effect at the local level, since time-series analysis suggests that moments when women have national prominence stimulate greater engagement, at least among some girls (see chapter 5 for examples).

To further ensure that we are capturing women who are visible, we focus on candidates who meet a minimum threshold of electoral viability. Our assumption is that only viable candidates garner the resources to run a campaign that can break through the background noise of people's everyday lives, especially for teenagers, who are even less likely than adults to pay attention to politics. Likewise, viable candidates receive far more media attention than long shots and sacrificial lambs. Previous research, including our own, finds that women candidates are more likely to be role models when they are visible (Dolan 2006; Hansen 1997; Koch 1997; Wolbrecht and Campbell 2017), which is more likely when they are viable. Following from our own and previous research, we count a candidate as viable if she either wins her race (the ultimate validation of viability) or comes within ten percentage points of winning (Atkeson 2003; Wolbrecht and Campbell 2017). For example, in our own congressional district (Indiana's 2nd), the 2020 race for the House of Representatives featured two women, a Republican incumbent and a Democratic challenger. The most basic measure of women's presence would be a tally reflecting those two candidates. However, this 2020 House race had a relatively low profile, as ours is a district gerrymandered to favor the Republican incumbent. Consequently, the Democratic challenger was considered a long shot, with few resources for her campaign and little news coverage. Not surprisingly, the Democrat lost in a landslide, with only 38.5 percent of the vote, compared to 61.5 for the Republican. Accordingly, our local Democratic candidate in 2020 was not coded as viable.

Our theory of political role models also expects that women candidates are more likely to have an impact when they are *novel* (Broockman 2014; Gilardi 2015; Mariani, Marshall, and Mathews-Schultz 2015), specifically when they are running for a seat currently held by a man. Our logic is that seeing a long-term incumbent woman run for reelection may not draw attention or encourage young people to rethink gender stereotypes. A woman running for a seat held by a man, on the other hand, may make gender more salient and draw attention to the persistently unusual nature of women's campaigns. Previous research suggests that women candidates who are both viable and novel are the most likely to affect the behaviors of young people (Wolbrecht and Campbell 2017). We expect the same to be true for a change of attitudes toward women as leaders.

Seventy percent of our respondents live in a community with at least one woman candidate. That figure falls to 47 percent if we consider only viable women candidates, and to 22 percent if we focus only on women running to replace a man. For the purposes of our analysis, this Goldilocks type of distribution is ideal: neither too many nor too few. If there are too few women, there is not enough statistical power: detecting an effect would be like finding a needle in a statistical haystack. On the other hand, too many women would mean not enough variation. If there were women candidates in every district and state, their presence could not account for any differences across communities. It would be all needles and no haystack.

Perception. The fact that one or more women is running—viable, novel, or neither—does not mean that people in that community are *consciously* aware of their presence. Even if the voting (or soon-to-vote) public is not consciously aware (or does not even remember the names) of women candidates, their presence may generate excitement and attention to the campaign, change the image of what a politician looks like, or encourage greater discussion of political issues where women are perceived to have expertise. But perhaps that's not always enough to change people's attitudes about women. Thus, we are also interested in whether people, particularly young people, perceive that there are women running, and whether they meet the even more stringent criteria of knowing whether women are running for a specific office and, if so, representing which party. *Perception* refers to whether people are able to recall the presence of women candidates. It is measured with a question that asks all respondents whether any women ran for the House of Representatives in their district and, in states where it was relevant, whether there were women candidates for the Senate or for governor.[7] Adding up the perceived number of women competing for each office produces a tally comparable to our measure of women candidates' presence. To again return to the example of our own congressional district, we suspect that many people living in our district would not have been able to recall the Democratic candidate off the top of their heads. If they could not, their perception would not match the actual presence of two women candidates. In fact, given that our Republican representative kept a low profile (e.g., did not hold town hall meetings), it is likely that she too would not have been top of mind for many.

Just how well-known are women candidates? As we saw in chapter 2, women candidates may be better known than male candidates because of their gender (Burns, Schlozman, and Verba 2001; Fridkin and Kenney 2014; Koch 1997; Lawless 2004; Reingold and Harrell 2010; Wolak 2020). Keep in mind as well that the issue may not be how accurate respondents are when asked about the presence of women candidates, but simply whether they perceive women candidates at all (Burden and Ono 2020; Stauffer 2021).

Importantly, the ability to correctly (or almost correctly) answer questions about the number of women running for major offices in your district and state requires exposure, and probably interest in and attention to, the political world. Many Americans are exposed to political information as part of their daily lives, including through their personal networks; one can learn a great deal about politics without really trying. That said, political knowledge is strongly related to both political interest and attention, suggesting that those who can answer questions about the presence of women candidates are likely distinguished in these other ways as well (Delli Carpini and Keeter 1996).

Throughout this book, we examine the effects of both presence and perception, as each might have an effect on the various outcomes we will investigate. In fact, whether one or the other impacts teens' views suggests the mechanism by which role models operate for that particular attitude. If the perception of women candidates has an effect, it implies that the role model effect operates through the conscious awareness of women candidates. If, however, it is the presence of women candidates that matters, it suggests a subliminal process of attitude change.

BELIEFS ABOUT WOMEN AS POLITICAL LEADERS

To gauge these young people's attitudes toward women as political leaders, we did not ask whether women are capable of serving as political leaders, because we feared that responses to such a question would be subject to social desirability bias and thus inflated. Instead, we asked a series of questions meant to tap views about women as political leaders. As we detail above (see fig. 3.3), we instead ask respondents whether the country would be better off with more women in office and whether they perceive women or men as more likely to demonstrate specific feminine and masculine leadership traits. Because these refer most directly to politics, they are our focus. However, scholars and activists have long expected women politicians to transform views of women's capacities in general. Indeed, this rhetoric is often framed expansively: Women leaders show girls that they can do *anything*! Exposure to women candidates may affect stereotypes about women candidates, so we consider whether they might also impact respondents' fundamental attitudes about women and gender. We thus ask: Does exposure to women candidates make adolescents less sexist?

Family Matters 2 Study

To conduct our analysis, we rely on a national survey called Family Matters 2 (FM2), the details of which are described in table 3.1.[8] Family Matters 2 has a number of features that make it unique. First, it is a scientific survey of 820 teenagers (age thirteen to seventeen), a notoriously difficult population to survey. They were surveyed online, the most natural mode for this generation of digital natives. FM2 provides a window into the political and social attitudes of American teens, a population about which there is far more speculation than data.

Second, Family Matters 2 also includes a survey of one of our teen respondents' parents. Independently of their children, parents answered an online survey with a set of questions nearly identical to those asked

CHAPTER 3

Table 3.1. Family Matters 2 study

Population	National sample of adolescents (age 14–18) and one parent
Mode	Online
Description	2-wave longitudinal survey
Sample size	Wave 1: 820 adolescent-parent dyads
	Wave 2: 654 adolescent-parent dyads
Dates	Wave 1: October 7–27, 2020
	Wave 2: February 5–March 22, 2021
Details	512 households recruited from probability sample
	308 households recruited from nonprobability, opt-in sample
	Data weighted to match national population parameters for age, sex, education, race/ethnicity, Census region, and marital status (based on the American Community Survey)
Firms	Probability sample: SSRS Opinion Panel
	Nonprobability sample: Dynata
	SSRS conducted the survey and prepared the dataset for analysis.

of their adolescent child. The parent survey is informative as a source of data on the parents of American teenagers, another important population. Even more significant, the data on parents mean that, for any outcome we examine, we can control for the influence of the home. For instance, it should come as no surprise that parents who are highly engaged in politics often have children who are also politically engaged. There are many potential reasons for parent-child congruence, including the direct transmission of political attitudes, shared genetics, and a common social context, all of which can act together (Alford, Funk, and Hibbing 2005; Hatemi, Alford, and Eaves 2009; Jennings and Niemi 1981; Jennings, Stoker, and Bowers 2009). Whatever the explanation, we want to be sure that we can distinguish between the influence of parents (who of course might themselves be influenced by the presence of women politicians) and the more direct influence of the women politicians themselves. As a consequence, our statistical models always control for the parent's value of whatever outcome we are testing. Put another way, any effects we find for either the presence or perception of women candidates cannot be explained away as owing to parental influence, but are above and beyond whatever influence parents might have.

Third, Family Matters 2 is also a panel, or longitudinal, survey, meaning that the same people (both teens and parents) were surveyed twice. The first survey took place in the fall of 2020 (October), prior to the election, while the second was following the election, in February and March of 2021. It is the panel feature of the survey that is especially important, for it enables us to examine each outcome (political engagement, gender attitudes, and so on) *after* the election while controlling for that very same attitude *before* the election.[9] In other words, we are modeling what changes over the course of the election campaign.

The reason that the pre- and post-election surveys are so critical is that they help us deal with the obvious question arising from any statistical relationship between women candidates and people's attitudes. Could it be that women candidates are more likely to run where voters—and their teenage children—are more politically engaged? That may very well be the case. Because our survey is a panel, our analysis focuses on the *change* in beliefs from before versus after the election. If a place is conducive to women's candidacies, that will be true both before and after the election; the context stays the same. It is far less likely (and not even very logical) that women candidates are more likely to emerge in places where, over the course of a campaign, teenagers *change* their attitudes. Any relationship we discover between women candidates, either the presence or perception, and any political attitude is relative to the baseline attitude held prior to the election. In this chapter, this means that any relationship between women candidates and beliefs about women leaders accounts for respondents' attitudes prior to the election.

Some skeptical readers may still wonder whether the places where women run are just different, and that whatever makes them different also leads to greater engagement among some people who live there, for some unexplained reason. As much as we would like to, we are unable to randomly assign women candidates to some races. Instead, we control for an array of variables that previous research has shown to predict women-friendly districts. These characteristics include region, geographic size, urbanicity, immigration, racial and ethnic composition, household income, education, occupation, presence of children, and party (Ondercin 2022; Palmer and Simon 2008).[10]

We also include a host of other control variables. For example, our analysis always controls for the educational aspirations of the teen as a proxy for their social class and for their age, since political interest may rise as teens mature. We also account for their race, in case there are racial differences (see chapter 6 for our test of whether women candidates of color are role models for young people). And, of course, we always account for the teen's gender, either as a control variable or by comparing effects for adolescent girls versus boys.

As we present results for the relationship between either the perception or the presence of women candidates, keep in mind that any such relationship is over and above the influence of respondents' homes, pre-existing attitudes, demographic characteristics, and friendliness of their communities to women candidates (not to mention the national context).

To show any effect, women candidates have a high bar to clear. Of course, however, even with all these features, the word "effect" is not truly accurate, as it implies causation. These data are observational—people in their natural habitat—which means that we cannot definitively determine causation. In chapter 7 we employ experiments that do pass the causality test, but they have their own trade-offs. Our philosophy is that no single methodology can be definitive, and so we draw on both observational and experimental data. Like a prosecuting attorney collecting evidence from as many witnesses as possible, we rely on testimony from multiple sources.

A Role Model Effect for Republicans

Do minds change when women run? Yes, they do. Not all minds and not for all women candidates, but, in broad strokes, we find consistent evidence for the role model effect—and, for the most part, where, when, and for whom we would expect to see it. As we expected, the effect of role models on attitudes toward women as leaders requires only that someone be in a community where women run; it is the presence of women candidates that leads to attitude change. Changing beliefs about women's capacity for leadership thus do not depend on the conscious recall that women were running (perception). Since these results are for women candidates' presence only, we display and discuss those findings only. (In a later chapter we will see effects for the perception of women candidates.) Furthermore, these effects are strongest for women running to replace men. Accordingly, we will focus on novel (and viable) candidates. The results for all viable candidates, novel or not, are similar, albeit weaker.

Whose minds are changed? Republicans', both boys' and girls'. Our results are shown in figures 3.5–3.8. Since these figures are in a format that we will repeat throughout the book, let us take a moment to explain what they display. Our objective with these figures is to satisfy two types of readers. One type is deeply interested in statistical nuance and wants to know all the details. The other type is less interested in nuance and simply want to know the main point. Our hope is that we have given enough information to provide clear answers for both kinds of readers.

These figures isolate the impact of women candidates while holding constant the other potential influences on political engagement described above. We employ ordinary least squares regression with robust standard errors clustered by congressional district, which will be the case for every model of observational data we display throughout this book.[11] Along the horizontal axis (x-axis) is the number of viable, novel women candidates while the thick bars on the vertical axis (y-axis) show the value of the outcome in question. All of the control variables have been set to their observed values (Hanmer and Kalkan 2013). As will be our practice throughout the book, the results are divided into four gender-party groups, which vary in size: Republican boys (186 respondents), Republican girls (129), Democratic boys (216), and Democratic girls (219). The fact that these subsets of our respondents are small in number means that it is difficult to detect statistically significant differences. In other words, we have limited power. As a result, ours is a conservative analysis, as we will have statistical certainty only for results that are relatively substantial in magnitude.[12] Throughout this book we will present a lot of results, some of which clearly meet the conventional standard for statistical significance of a p value of .05—which means that we would expect this outcome by chance only five times out of a hundred. In other cases, the results do not meet that cutoff, but are nonetheless in the expected direction and close to significance, say a p value of .12. Because statistical significance is relatively difficult to achieve, even when results do not meet the conventional (and arbitrary) threshold for statistical significance, they can still be informative—suggestive, if not conclusive. We err on the side of inclusion and let readers judge for themselves whether the results are notable or not.

In order for the reader to see whether any of our findings are statistically significant, the thin bars display the confidence interval (sometimes loosely referred to as the margin of error). If those bars do not overlap, we can have confidence that the difference between two values is significant, or in other words did not happen by chance. Careful readers will note the use of 85 percent confidence intervals in the figures. Others have shown that 95 percent intervals are too conservative for a conventional test of differences with a type 1 error probability of .05 (Maghsoodloo and Huang 2010; Radean 2023). This literature recommends an 83.5 percent interval, which we have rounded up to 85.

Figures 3.5–3.8 display results for four outcomes: whether the country would be better off with more women in office (fig. 3.5); whether women possess feminine (fig. 3.6) and masculine (fig. 3.7) leadership traits; and nonsexist attitudes (3.8). For example, in figure 3.5, Republican boys score an average of about 4.5 on the "better off with more women" scale (remember, it is coded 0 to 10). Where there are two candidates, their score rises to a little over 6.4, with the value for one woman candidate being in between (5.4). Notice also that the error bars between 0 and 1 women candidates do not overlap, while the error bars for 0 and 2 candidates are even farther apart. The non-overlapping errors bars mean that, for Republican boys, the relationship between the number of women candidates and their attitude toward women in office is statistically significant.

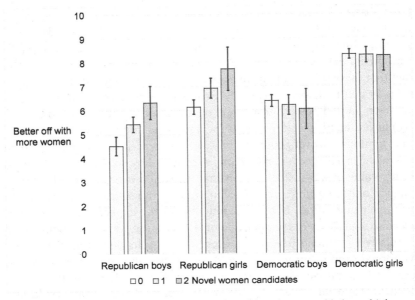

Figure 3.5. When women run, Republican girls and boys are more likely to think America would be better off with more women in office

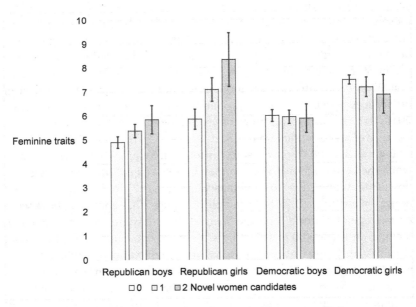

Figure 3.6. When women run, Republican boys and girls are more likely to associate women with feminine traits

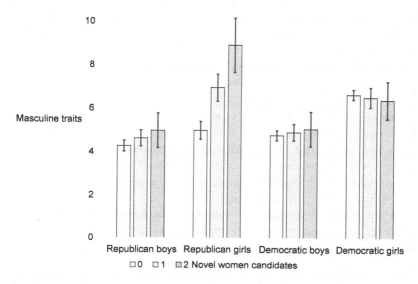

Figure 3.7. When women run, Republican girls are more likely to associate women with masculine traits

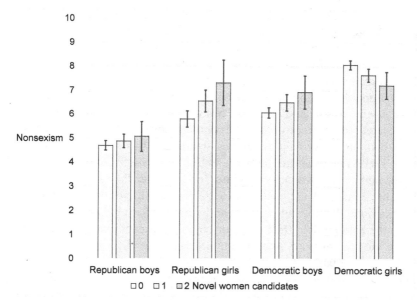

Figure 3.8. When women run, Republican girls are also more likely to hold nonsexist attitudes about women in general

Before discussing each of these four groups, remember that they have different baseline values. As the figures show, in communities with no women candidates, Democratic girls are far and away the most likely to score highly on each of the four gender attitudes, while Republican boys are the least likely.

Even though the girls and boys start from different baselines, we see nearly the same patterns for Republicans regardless of gender. Where women run, Republican girls and boys become more supportive of women in elected office and more likely to say that women have those leadership traits stereotypically associated with women (working out compromises, being honest and ethical)—in other words, the association clearly meets the conventional threshold for statistical significance. For GOP-identifying girls, we also see a significant increase in their perception that women possess masculine traits and in nonsexist attitudes in general.

Recall that we hypothesized that Republicans have the most need to catch up, and so this is where we are most likely to see role models affect their perception of women, both as political leaders and more generally. We see the most consistent results for Republican girls, because living in a community with women candidates is associated with a change in all four attitudes we have examined, so much so that they catch up with Democratic girls. Among Republican boys—the group whose views lag furthest behind—we see movement on whether there should be more women in office and on the perception of feminine traits. As for Democrats, we generally do not see a role model effect. One notable exception is for Democratic boys' nonsexism, which, as with Republican girls, rises in the presence of women candidates—partial support for our hypothesis that women candidates would change the minds of all boys.[13]

Do Republicans' minds change when women run, or only when they see *Republican* women candidates? To test the possibility that adolescents are more likely to be attentive to and have their views shifted by candidates of their own party, we employ models identical to those already presented, except with two separate candidate tallies, one with the number of viable, novel Democratic women candidates, and another the same count but of Republican candidates, matched to the partisanship of the adolescents— for example, Republican women candidates for Republican girls.

Is the role model effect only for co-partisan candidates? To our surprise, the answer is no. Republican girls react similarly to women candidates of either party. Republican boys' minds only change, however, when Democratic women run. This could be because of something unique about Democratic women candidates. Perhaps they are more likely to emphasize their gender, or their campaigns are more visible to young people and thus draw the attention of Republican boys who would not normally be

Table 3.2. The takeaway: Women role models and attitudes about women's capacities

	Better off with more women in office	Women's feminine leadership traits	Women's masculine leadership traits	Nonsexism
Republican boys	↑	↑		
Republican girls	↑	↑	↑	↑
Democratic boys			↑	↑
Democratic girls				↓

Note: An upward or downward arrow indicates a positive or negative and statistically significant relationship between the presence of viable, novel women candidates and the attitude in question.

inclined to note a woman running for office. Another possibility is that there are relatively few places where Republican boys were exposed to Republican women candidates. Overall, only 10 percent of our respondents live in a community with at least one viable, novel Republican woman running for office—and remember, 2020 was a record year for Republican women candidates. More Republican women on the campaign trail might produce a stronger signal.

This chapter contains a lot of data, and so it is worth pausing to summarize what we have discovered and which of our hypotheses were supported. Going into the analysis, we suspected that we would find that women candidates have the biggest impact on Republicans and boys. Of the two, we find the most consistent evidence that Republicans' minds are most likely to change, whether boys or girls. When we focus on boys only, it is mostly Republicans whose views shift, but for one type of attitude—sexism—we also see also movement among Democratic boys. However, contrary to our expectations, we do not find that young people respond only to co-partisan candidates. In fact, we see more of an effect among Republicans when Democratic women run, but that might only be because there are still relatively few Republican women candidates.

Overall, the takeaway for this chapter (table 3.2) is that when women run, minds change among those whose minds are most in need of changing.

Summing Up

In our interviews of teens and their parents, one father-son pair reflects how attitudes toward women as leaders can change. Living in rural Arkansas, both describe themselves as conservatives and Trump supporters. In the course of our hourlong conversation, we learned that they are also COVID skeptics and regular viewers of Fox News. Given their conservative outlook, one might think that they would have reservations about women in positions of leadership. Actually, though, the opposite is true. Speaking in the spring of 2020, the son, Jared, noted that "a lady," Sarah Huckabee Sanders, was running for governor of Arkansas. He spoke of how she is widely known because "she worked with Trump and stuff." When asked whether it matters if a candidate is a woman, he responded that to his friends, "it would not matter if it's a man or a woman." Upon hearing his son make this comment, Jared's dad observed that during his lifetime there had been a shift in attitudes toward women as political leaders: "Growing up, when I was his age, answering these questions, like it just hit now, like wow, how things have changed. It's not a big deal for a female to run for governor or Senate and all these other things." As he spoke, it was clear that this was the first time he had become aware of the sea change in attitudes about women in positions of leadership.

The findings in this chapter offer some support to those who have expected that the presence of women in political roles challenges stereotypes and expands support for women in politics. Exposure to women candidates leads some adolescents—specifically, Republicans—to have a more positive view of women's capacity to be political leaders, and even to be less sexist in general. Given the relatively low assessments of women's capacity for political leadership among Republicans, and especially among Republican boys, these findings are in the spirit of Mansbridge's (1999) normative goals for descriptive representation: The "haves"—those who most need to update their beliefs about women's "fitness to rule"—are indeed doing so when exposed to women exemplars. What better evidence that women can "do politics" than women doing politics?

Our analysis focuses on the period surrounding the 2020 elections. It is likely that our findings would have been different in the past and will differ in the future. In arguing that descriptive representatives challenge ideas about underrepresented groups' "ability to rule," Mansbridge (1999, 649) clarifies that "this is a historically specific and contextual dynamic." When Sapiro (1981, 712) wrote that "women and men continue to think of politics as a male domain because the empirical truth at this moment is that politics is a male domain," there were two women in the US Senate and 21 (5 percent) in the US House (CAWP 2022). Today, women hold about a quarter of seats in the US Congress.

It is also noteworthy that we find effects for the presence of women candidates, and not only when teens can accurately recall the women running in their community. This is evidence that minds are changed by the subliminal observation of women candidates and explains why Republicans, and Republican boys in particular, have their minds changed by Democratic women candidates. The information they store about women's capabilities comes from what goes on in their environment and does not require them to pay close attention—which they are more likely to do when candidates are of their party. (Think of Jared's awareness of Sarah Huckabee Sanders, a fellow Republican.) Rather, they absorb the message that women can be capable leaders from their casual, even incidental, exposure to women of either party running viable, visible campaigns for office—including advertising, news coverage, conversations with parents and friends, and even comments made by teachers at school.

The fact that we find effects for Republicans, including Republican boys, runs counter to most research and popular rhetoric on women as role models. As we saw in chapter 2, previous scholarship on the impact of women politicians on mass behavior and attitudes—on interest and knowledge, engagement with politics, sexism and stereotypes, democratic attitudes, and ambition to run for office—has largely focused on women and girls as the target. That is, women politicians serve as role models who inspire *other women* to interest, action, efficacy, and ambition. Elizabeth Warren's pinkie promises are made with young girls, after all. And, given that Warren is a Democrat, it is fair to assume that these promises are largely with girls who either do or will think of themselves as Democrats.

However, we should not assume that all role model effects work the same way. A theme of this book is that women role models have varying effects, for different reasons, depending on the outcome in question. As we explained in chapter 2, our theory of political role models expects that changes in the presence of women in a role (such as that of a political leader) should change stereotypes for women and men. As stereotypes about women change, women should change their behavior. Because stereotypes about men's relationship to politics have not changed, their behavior is not necessarily expected to shift. Thus, it is plausible that the presence of women candidates encourages both girls *and boys* to view politics as more equitable (different kinds of people lead, so the system must be fair—a changing attitude), while they help girls in particular become more engaged in politics and even interested in running for office themselves (people like me do this, so can I—a change in behavior). Chapter 4 takes up the first of these topics, chapter 5 the second.

4 * Faith in Democracy

After the winner of the 2016 election was announced, I was not only disappointed but grief-stricken . . . I'm a 15-year-old girl. In our society, I don't have much of a voice at all. And if you're a young person who's upset about the election results, I'm sure powerless is one of the many emotions you're feeling too. But right now is not the time to turn cynical. . . . Now is a time to step up.

Jamie Margolin, in an essay for *HuffPost* after the 2016 election[1]

To this point, we have said little about one of the most famous woman candidates of all: Hillary Clinton, the first woman to run as a major-party candidate in an American presidential contest. Other women had sought their party's nomination—Shirley Chisholm in the 1970s, Elizabeth Dole in the 1990s, and even Clinton herself in 2008—but it was Clinton in 2016 who finally broke the gender barrier. In doing so, she did not shy away from the historic nature of her candidacy. On the night that she accepted the Democratic Party's nomination, she wore an all-white outfit, a nod to the color worn by women's suffrage advocates a century earlier. During the speech, she referenced her place in history: "Tonight, we've reached a milestone in our nation's march toward a more perfect union, the first time that a major party has nominated a woman for President. Standing here as my mother's daughter, and my daughter's mother, I'm so happy this day has come. Happy for grandmothers and little girls and everyone in between." She then went on to speak of how her candidacy was not only significant for girls and women: "Happy for boys and men, too—because when any barrier falls in America, for anyone, it clears the way for everyone. When there are no ceilings, the sky's the limit."[2] Nor was this the only time in her campaign that Clinton spoke of breaking barriers and serving as a role model, including speeches, interviews, and tweets. While on the stump she spoke of inspiring "little girls who dream big." Likewise, news coverage of Clinton's campaign often spoke of her as a pathbreaker (Mitchell 2016).

CHAPTER 4

As scholars of women as political role models, we were watching the 2016 presidential election with great interest. Prior to the election, we had an essay ready for The Monkey Cage, a website featuring short articles by political scientists, about Hillary as a role model. Upon reading it, a colleague told us that if Trump were to win, it could be instead be published on a website in Bizarro World.

We all ended up living in Bizarro World. As predicted by the polls, Hillary Clinton won the popular vote handily, but nonetheless lost to Donald Trump in the Electoral College. As she poignantly put it in her concession speech: "To all the women, and especially the young women, who put their faith in this campaign and in me, I want you to know that nothing has made me prouder than to be your champion. I know that we have still not shattered that highest and hardest glass ceiling, but some day someone will and hopefully sooner than we might think right now."[3]

Clinton's stunning loss raises the question of how young people reacted to the 2016 presidential race. On the one hand, our analysis of congressional and gubernatorial races suggests that it is running, not winning, that matters. If that holds at the presidential level, then Clinton's campaign should have been empowering for girls, and perhaps for boys too. After all, it was impossible to miss the fact that Clinton was running for president. Any presidential contest has a very high profile, but Hillary Clinton's campaign may have been even more salient than usual, given that she was the first woman to make it that far in a presidential race, coupled with her longtime presence in American public life. It could be that, even though she did not win, Hillary Clinton nonetheless served as an inspiration for young people, especially girls.

On the other hand, a presidential race seems different than one for Congress or governor, as it is the highest profile election in the country and arguably the entire world. The office of the presidency is imbued with such symbolic and historic significance that the stakes are extremely high in a presidential contest. This race in particular was different from any other. Hillary Clinton did not lose to a run-of-the-mill Republican. She lost to Donald Trump. Whatever you might think of Clinton, one cannot deny that her experience as Secretary of State, senator, and First Lady gave her unprecedented preparation for the presidency, whereas Trump had never held any public office. At least by the standard of past experience in government, here was a well-qualified woman losing a job to a far less qualified man.

It was not only that Trump was inexperienced. He was also widely known for his demeaning comments about and behavior toward women. As just a small sample, he snidely questioned whether anyone would vote for one of his Republican primary opponents, Carly Fiorina, because of her appearance: "Would anyone vote for that? Can you imagine that, the face of our next president?" (Solotaroff 2015). After being questioned by the Fox News anchor Megyn Kelly during a debate, he told CNN that "you could see there was blood coming out of her eyes, blood coming out of her wherever" (Rucker 2015). Most infamously, in 2005 he was recorded while filming the TV show *Access Hollywood* speaking very lewdly about women, even bragging about being able to get away with sexual assault.

> [referring to an actress] I moved on her actually. You know she was down on Palm Beach. I moved on her, and I failed, I'll admit it. I did try and f*** her. She was married . . . I moved on her like a b****. But I couldn't get there. And she was married. Then all of a sudden I see her, she's now got the big phony t*** and everything. She's totally changed her look . . .
>
> I better use some Tic Tacs in case I start kissing her. You know, I am automatically attracted to beautiful—I just start kissing them. It's like a magnet. Just kiss. I don't even wait. And when you're a star, they let you do it. You can do anything . . . Grab 'em by the p****. You can do anything.[4]

The release of this recording of Trump during the 2016 presidential campaign put his misogyny on full display for all the world to hear. Accordingly, we might think that adolescents paying attention to a presidential race for the first time in 2016 would have been highly disillusioned, not just because Hillary Clinton lost her bid to become the first woman president, but because she lost to someone who said such things about women.

Trump did not only disparage women, however. He also demeaned immigrants and Muslims, endorsed violence against protestors, called on Russians to hack his opponent's email, and spoke approvingly of authoritarian leaders around the globe. This is not normal behavior for a presidential candidate, to say the least, and raised alarms among many observers that Trump's style of authoritarian-leaning populism threatened the health of American democracy (Levitsky and Ziblatt 2018). All of this is to say that there are many reasons young people may have been disillusioned by Clinton's loss to Trump, some related to gender specifically but others about his general disregard for democratic norms.

In the Bizzaro World of American politics after the 2016 election, we changed our plans. Instead of studying President Hillary Clinton as a potential role model, we turned to how Trump's electoral win and Clinton's loss affected young Americans' political attitudes. Did Clinton's candidacy lead young people, girls especially, to become more politically engaged, just as some do when they see women run for offices such as a member of Congress or governor? Or did Clinton's loss to Trump lead to disillusionment with America's political system, or perhaps even the idea of democracy altogether? Especially dispiriting was how Clinton lost: She won the popular vote, 48 to 46 percent, or by roughly 2.8 million votes. Yet because of the Electoral College, this comfortable margin nonetheless translated into a loss. Small-d democrats—those who believe that elections should be decided on the basis of who wins the most votes—have long been critical of the Electoral College (Rakove and McConnell 2016). For young people who have little experience with the quirks of the American electoral system, it may have been particularly jarring to see the loser of the popular vote win office anyway.

These are pressing questions in a period in which American democracy is under considerable pressure. There is evidence that American youth are souring on the idea of democracy as a form of governance (Mounk 2018), and that they believe the system is rigged (Rouse and Ross 2018).[5] The question is whether Hillary Clinton's loss has contributed to that disillusionment. If so, it is the height of irony. One reason for the rise of populists worldwide, including but not limited to Donald Trump, is voters' frustration with the current democratic system. It would be paradoxical for the victory of a populist to feed further disillusionment, which contributed to his rise in the first place.

Connecting Role Models and Democratic Attitudes

Just as the presence of women might help shape people's beliefs about women's capacity for political leadership, as we saw in chapter 3, the presence—and absence, or loss—of women candidates might also shape people's evaluations of government legitimacy, faith in democracy, and belief that government responds to people's needs (often referred to as external efficacy). Theories of descriptive representation highlight how the presence of women (and other underrepresented groups) in positions of power can help legitimize democratic systems, signal the openness and fairness of a political system, and assure underrepresented groups in the electorate that they have a voice in political decision-making (Mansbridge 1999; Phillips 1998). Much of the past research on this topic concerns the absence of women candidates, which has been found to be partially responsible for women's perceptions of the political system as biased and inaccessible (Atkeson and Rapoport 2003; Bennett and Bennett 1989; Burns, Schlozman, and Verba 2001; Campbell et al. 1960; Conway 1985).

Previous research suggests that the presence of women politicians can indeed impact evaluations of democratic government. Women express greater external efficacy when their governor is female and as the percentage of women in the state legislature grows (Atkeson and Carrillo 2007). Similarly, women report increased efficacy and feelings of political confidence when represented by women (High-Pippert and Comer 1998). Nor is this limited to the United States, as cross-national research finds that both women and men express greater satisfaction with democracy in their country and confidence that elections reflect voters' views as the percentage of women representatives increases (Karp and Banducci 2008; but see Burnet 2011). Women's descriptive representation is also associated with greater confidence in the legislative process among women (Schwindt-Bayer and Mishler 2005). While this work focuses largely on the impact on women, others find that confidence in policy outcomes is higher when women are part of decision-making bodies, particularly among men when the topic is related to women. For an issue perhaps outside of their expertise, the presence of women enhances policy-making legitimacy among men (Clayton, O'Brien, and Piscopo 2019).

The presidential election of 2016 was not so much a demonstration of the absence or presence of women as it was striking evidence of the bias and exclusion that women politicians still face. Experiences that reinforce group exclusion from politics can have important effects on political attitudes. Perceptions of gender bias in the political arena discourage women from running for political office (Lawless and Fox 2010), for example. In a series of experiments, Bauer, Krupnikov, and Yeganeh (2019) find that the gender gap in office-seeking ambition widens when people are reminded of women's persistent underrepresentation but narrows when respondents are exposed to the advances women have made in politics. Along these same lines, experiences viewed as confirming men's advantages in and women's exclusion from the political arena have been found to discourage interest in political participation among girls (Bennett and Bennett 1989; Croson and Gneezy 2009; Greenstein 1961). This work leads us to expect that women candidates are most likely to have a positive impact when their presence is framed in terms of empowerment and achievement, but may have no or a negative effect when evidence of ongoing discrimination is highlighted.

Democrats' Disillusionment in 2016

The presidential election of 2016 gave American adolescents a prominent and viable role model, as well as considerable evidence of the bias and harassment that women politicians face. How did teens react? To find out, we turn to Family Matters 1, a precursor to the Family Matters 2 data featured in chapter 2. Like the second Family Matters study, the first also includes surveys with both teens and parents. It too is a panel survey, and thus the same respondents were reinterviewed multiple times. The main difference between the two studies is the length of time between the interviews (see table 4.1 for details). In Family Matters 1, roughly a year passed between the first and second interviews. The first interviews were done in the fall of 2016, in the heat of the presidential campaign. At that time, Democratic teens—both girls and boys—had a more positive view toward democracy than did their Republican peers. We asked for their reaction to the statement "The political system helps people with their genuine needs," a question gauging their opinion about the responsiveness and effectiveness of American democracy in general. In 2016 about 40 percent of both Democratic girls and boys agreed that the political system does help people. In contrast, only about a quarter of Republicans felt the same way.

The partisan differences we observe in 2016 are surprising. While we lack earlier FM studies, the Monitoring the Future survey of high school seniors (see chapter 5) does ask something similar: "Would you say the government is pretty much run for a few big interests looking out for themselves or is it run for the benefit of all the people?" In years prior to 2016, there is not a clear partisan difference on this question. For example, in the years in which Barack Obama was president (2009–16), 13 percent of both Democratic and Republican boys saw government as run for the benefit of all the people, compared to 11 percent of Democratic and Republican girls.[6] Since Democrats and Republicans did not differ much in their assessment of democratic responsiveness before 2016, it seems possible—perhaps even likely—that during the heat of the 2016 campaign, Democratic teens' positive view of the political system reflects the widespread expectation that their party's candidate was going to win the presidency and, in doing so, make history with the first woman to hold the office.

Table 4.1. Family Matters 1 study

Population	National sample of adolescents (age 15–18) and one parent
Mode	Online
Description	3-wave longitudinal survey
Sample size	Wave 1: 997 adolescent-parent dyads
	Wave 2: 601 adolescent-parent dyads
	Wave 3: 371 adolescent-parent dyads
Dates	Wave 1: July–October 2016
	Wave 2: July–October 2017
	Wave 3: August 2018–January 2019
Details	Data weighted to match national population parameters for age, gender, education, race/ethnicity, Census region, and years of education.
Firm	YouGov

Faith in Democracy

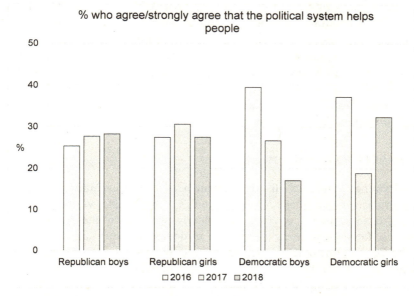

Figure 4.1. After 2016, Democrats became disillusioned with democracy. Democratic girls rebounded, but Democratic boys did not.

Of course, any optimism Democrats might have had was dashed on election night. As seen in figure 4.1, one year later both Democratic girls and boys were much less likely to say that the system helps people with their genuine needs. In 2016, 39 percent of Democratic boys saw democracy as responsive, compared to just 27 percent in 2017. Among Democratic girls, the percentage endorsing a responsive view of American democracy was cut nearly *in half*: 37 percent to 19 percent. There was no similar decline among Republicans, either girls or boys.

We learn at least four important things from the change in Democratic teens' attitudes toward democracy between 2016 and 2017. First, adolescents' attitudes toward democracy in general appear responsive to the political environment. Second, like their elders, young Americans see the world through a partisan lens. While Democrats became more disillusioned, Republicans did not. Third, partisan reactions were not symmetrical. Republicans did not become more likely to see the system as helping people. This could be because Republicans are less likely to be swayed by the immediate political environment, or because young people of either party are more likely to react to an election loss than a win. Or it could be because of Donald Trump himself, perhaps because he did not generate much enthusiasm among Republican-identifying teenagers.

Fourth, we learn from the comparison of 2016 to 2017 that the change in perceptions of American democracy's responsiveness was about both party identification and gender, but the latter more than the former. Democrats, both girls and boys, lost faith in the political system. But that loss of faith was greater among Democratic girls than boys. While these data do not allow us to say for sure, the greater decline among the girls suggests that they were especially affected by Trump's win—perhaps because that meant Clinton lost, perhaps because of Trump's offensive comments about women, or most likely both.

The 2018 Year of the Woman

Did young Democrats' disillusionment persist? Family Matters 1 allows us to answer that question, as it includes a third wave, with interviews conducted in the fall of 2018. After nearly two years of the Trump presidency, Republican teens' perception of democracy still had not budged (see fig. 4.1). In contrast, Democratic boys were even more disillusioned: They went from 27 percent saying that democracy helps people to only 17 percent, essentially matching the views of Democratic girls in 2017.

Democratic girls, though, were unique. In contrast to both Republicans and Democratic boys, their views about democracy rebounded. From 2017's low of 19 percent, in 2018 32 percent said that democracy responds to people's genuine needs—not quite where that figure was in 2016 (37 percent), but close.

This presents an interesting puzzle. Why would we see Democratic girls' views of democratic responsiveness bounce back? The explanation cannot be that something happened to make all Democrats sanguine, as Democratic boys soured even more from 2017 to 2018. Nor can the explanation be focused on all girls, since Republican girls were unmoved. Instead, the solution to the puzzle must center on the intersection of gender and party.

The most likely answer lies in the wave of Democratic women who ran for office in 2018. Dubbed the second Year of the Woman, in 2018 a record number of women ran for the House, Senate, and governor, the vast majority of them Democrats. These women candidates also were historically diverse, including pioneering women of color, indigenous women, and members of the LGBTQ community. Many ran unconventional campaigns, emphasizing their authenticity, experiences, and gender; campaign ads included images of women serving in the military, recounting personal crises, and breastfeeding their children.[7]

Figure 4.2 illustrates how 2018 stands out. The panels display the numbers of Democratic and Republican women running for the House and

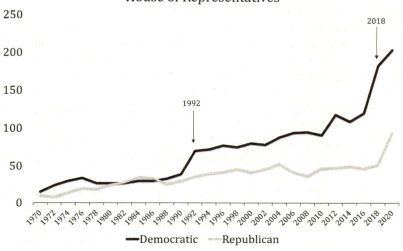
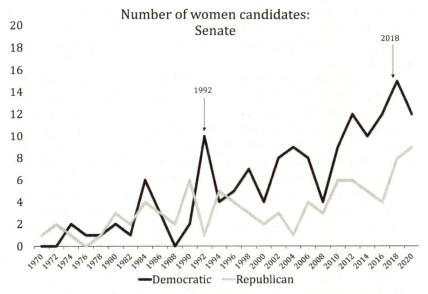

Figure 4.2. In both the House and Senate, a big increase in women candidates in 2018

Senate since 1970. The original Year of the Woman in 1992 also was a mostly Democratic phenomenon, as the sharp increases in Democratic candidates for the House and Senate in 1992 indicate (Wilcox 1994).[8] The upsurge in women running in 2018 far exceeds all previous years by a considerable margin. A total of 476 women ran in a House primary and 53 in a primary for the Senate. Of these, 234 won their primary for the House and 23 for the Senate. To put these numbers in perspective, in 1992, the first Year of the Woman, *half* as many women ran in a general election for the House (117) and Senate (11). Moreover, in 1992 the Year of the Woman was solely a congressional phenomenon, with only three women running for governor. In contrast, 2018 witnessed the largest number of women gubernatorial candidacies ever, with sixty-one women running in gubernatorial primaries and sixteen in general election governors' contests.

In 2018 as in 1992, Democratic candidates far outnumbered Republican ones. In both the House and gubernatorial races, there were more than three times as many Democrats; in Senate races, there were twice as many. There was an even greater imbalance in the candidates who won. When the votes were counted, eighty-nine Democratic women had been elected to the House, compared to only thirteen Republican women. Of the thirty-six newcomers who had won, thirty-five were Democrats. And of the fifteen women candidates who beat incumbents—a relatively rare feat in the incumbent-friendly House of Representatives—every single one was a Democrat.

The circumstances leading to the second Year of the Woman are reminiscent of the first. In 1992 conventional wisdom held that the surge of women candidates—primarily Democrats—was a reaction to the confirmation of Clarence Thomas to the Supreme Court, in spite of Anita Hill's testimony that Thomas had sexually harassed her. Trump's election ignited a similar reaction, but on a greater scale. The day after his inauguration, millions of people in communities across the country participated in the Women's March, the largest single-day protest event in American history. This was followed by the rise of what came to be known as the Resistance as women across the country focused on opposing the Trump administration. Many were becoming politically active for the first time—including running for office (Chenoweth and Berry 2018; Meyer and Tarrow 2018; Skocpol and Tervo 2020). For example, after Trump was elected 26,000 women contacted Emily's List, an organization that trains pro-choice Democratic women to run for office. That compares to nine hundred women between 2015 and 2016—an increase of nearly 2800 percent! Both 1992 and 2018 were also record years for congressional retirements, providing those inspired women with opportunities to

Figure 4.3. A prominent example of how the media covered the wave of Democratic women candidates in 2018

translate their passion into access to nominations and election victories (DeSilver 2016; Wilcox 1994). In both 1992 and 2018 women candidates were the subjects of widespread press coverage (e.g., North 2017; Simon and Lah 2017; Tackett 2017; Wilcox 1994). An especially illustrative case is a 2018 *Time* magazine cover story entitled "The Avengers: First They Marched, Now They're Running" (Alter 2018; see fig. 4.3).

The attention to women candidates in 2018 was not limited to the number of women running but often centered on the memorable stories of the individuals who ran. At twenty-nine, Abby Finkenauer was one of the two youngest women ever elected to the House. The other was Alexandria Ocasio-Cortez, who had become a social media sensation, so much so that she is widely known as AOC, and thus joins the rarefied rank of politicians identified only by their initials. The list of notable women goes on. Alongside AOC in the progressive wing of the Democratic Party were Ayanna Pressley in Massachusetts, Rashida Tlaib in Michigan, and Ilhan Omar in Minnesota. Together, these four came to be known as the Squad. Notably, all four are women of color. Similarly, 2018 saw the first two Native American women elected to the House (Sharice Davids and Deb Haaland) and the first two Hispanic women elected from Texas (Veronica Escobar and Sylvia Garcia).

While evidence of loss and bias can lead to disenchantment with democratic politics (as we saw in 2016), our theory of political role models, and previous research, suggests that narratives highlighting the pathbreaking accomplishments of women may generate confidence in democratic systems and decision-making. In other words, extant research gives us good reason to think that the rebound in Democratic girls' view of democracy is a reaction to the influx of highly publicized women running for high-profile offices. As women, these candidates were especially salient to girls, and as Democrats, to Democratic girls in particular. Furthermore, while the 2018 wave of women candidates certainly highlighted women's continued underrepresentation, women candidates (and coverage of them) largely took on an empowering tone, with popular slogans emphasizing the revolutionary power of women's candidacies. Among the most popular slogans was "The Future Is Female," which encapsulates the goal of greater gender inclusion and empowerment for future generations of women—the essence of the role model effect.

We explore this possibility more systematically by asking how adolescents' attitudes toward democracy are affected by the presence of women candidates in their district and state. To find out, we turn to the 2018 wave of the Family Matters 1 study. Our analysis closely follows what we presented in chapter 3, only in 2018 rather than 2020. Again we have data from both teenagers and parents, and again we include the same host of control variables for individuals, House districts, and states. One small difference is that the data were collected prior to Election Day, and the previous attitude we control for (i.e., the lagged dependent variable) was measured a year, not months, before.[9] As before, because we control for the outcome we are measuring in a previous wave of the survey—that is, democratic responsiveness in 2017—we are really measuring the average change, in this case from 2017 to 2018.

Our key measure is, once more, the number of women running for the House, Senate, and governor. As before, we focus on viable women, those who were either elected or came within ten percentage points of winning. Because of the attention paid to Democratic women—the "Avengers" all

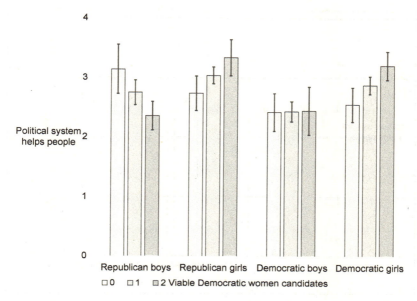

Figure 4.4. In 2018 both Democratic girls and Republican girls saw democracy as more responsive when Democratic women ran

came from one party—we first focus on their potential impact. Family Matters 1 does not have a measure of respondents' perception of women candidates, and so our focus in this analysis is solely on the presence of women running for office in a respondent's community.

Figure 4.4 displays the results. In keeping with earlier evidence for the impact of women candidates, we see that the presence of viable Democratic women candidates leads Democratic girls to say that the political system is responsive to people's needs, an effect that clears the bar for statistical significance. More Democratic women, greater political efficacy—at least for Democratic girls. Democratic boys do not have the same reaction. Their view of democracy remains unchanged where Democratic women run.

Were Republicans also affected by Year of the Woman 2, the sequel? Interestingly, for Republican girls the answer is yes. Like Democratic girls, they too became more positive toward democracy if they lived in a community where one or more viable Democratic women ran for office. Not only is the effect statistically significant but, substantively, the effect is of comparable size to that for Democratic girls. It appears that, in this case, gender trumps party.

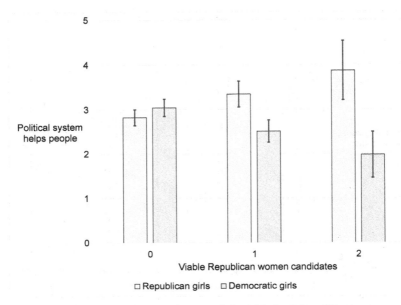

Figure 4.5. In 2018 Republican girls responded positively to Republican women candidates too; Democratic girls reacted negatively

Republican boys respond very differently from everyone else. Unlike Democratic boys' attitudes, Republican boys' attitudes *do* change in the presence of Democratic women candidates. Unlike Democratic and Republican girls, however, their view of the political system becomes more *negative*. While these data do not permit us to determine why Republican boys react the way they do, we can make an educated guess. If, as seems likely, most people—including Republican boys—interpret a question about "people" to mean "people like me," then it makes sense that Republican boys would look at women candidates and conclude that politics was not helping people like them. This negative effect of Democratic women candidates on the attitudes of Republican boys is yet another example of how more gender diversity in American politics is not a development welcomed by everyone.

What about the effect of Republican women candidates? For boys of either party, the answer is none. Republican girls, though, react to Republican women (again, viable candidates) just as they do to Democratic women. The more GOP women who run, the more likely Republican girls are to say that the system is responsive. This is still more evidence that, for Republican girls, it is the candidates' gender, not their party, that matters (see fig. 4.5).[10]

Not so for Democratic girls. When they are exposed to Republican women candidates, they become less likely to view democracy as fulfilling the needs of the people—an effect that is both statistically and substantively significant. We concede that this result was surprising to us, and we do not claim to have a definitive explanation for it. One possibility is that women candidates catch the attention of all girls, thus priming them for attitude change. Having caught the attention of Democratic girls, Republican women lead to attitude change in the direction of questioning the political system. Remember that Democratic girls became less convinced that the system of government helps people with their needs because of their disillusionment with Donald Trump. It makes sense that their perception of democracy would not improve upon exposure to women who are aligned with Trump and his party. In other words, the candidates' gender draws these girls' attention, but it is their party that drives disillusionment.

We have placed a lot of stock in one question about democratic responsiveness. This is simply because Family Matters 1 is a product of its time. The issue of young people's feelings about democracy—or, for that matter, threats to liberal democracy—was not as salient when the survey was designed prior to 2016. By the time of the third, 2018 wave of the study, young people's democratic attitudes were very much a concern. Accordingly, the 2018 survey included a question from the World Values Survey that had recently set off alarm bells about young people's acceptance of democracy around the world: whether it was important to them to live in a democracy. While young people's support for democracy globally seemed to be in decline, the American youth included in the FM 1 study actually score high on this question, as only 3.6 percent disagree that it is important to live in a democracy. In spite of this high overall support for democracy, there is still a hint that Democratic girls place greater importance on democracy when and where Democratic women run in a model that nearly replicates those above (see the online appendix for full details). We say "nearly" because the question about the importance of living in a democracy was only asked in 2018, and thus we cannot control for a baseline attitude at a previous point in time.[11] Using this question, Democratic girls' support for democracy rises along with the number of viable Democratic women candidates. We must be cautious about any conclusions, as the effect does not clear the bar for conventional statistical significance. But the fact that the direction mirrors that for the question about democratic responsiveness gives us some degree of confidence that this result is not merely noise.

Unlike the question about whether democracy meets people's needs, in this case we do not find anything of note for any of the other three gender-party groups. Once again, we do not have a conclusive explanation for the difference, but we suspect it has to do with what is known as a *ceiling effect*. The young people in our study were already likely to place a lot of importance on living in a democracy, and so there is little room for them to move—not unlike the way that, as professors, A is the highest grade we can give, even if one A student performs much better than another A student. Since attitudes about democracy are already so positive, there is little room for anyone to move, so the effect only registers—and faintly at that—among the people most likely to be aware of and agree with the women who are running.

Contested Democracy in 2020

The results from 2018 indicate that teenage girls become more positive toward democracy when women run for office, but we might wonder whether this result is due to the unique circumstances surrounding that particular election: the first national election since Hillary Clinton's loss, the rise of the Resistance, the MeToo movement, and the high-profile candidates (such as AOC) who became household names. Do women candidates have a comparable positive impact on attitudes toward democracy in a year with less attention to women, such as 2020?

Even though women candidates received less media attention in 2020 than 2018, there were actually more women candidates for the House in 2020 (see again fig. 4.3). One reason is that many of the women who ran in 2018 won, which means that they ran again in 2020 as incumbents. Any additional women were on top of the batch of incumbents. As well, while there were still fewer Republicans than Democrats, 2020 set a record for women candidates in the GOP (Dittmar 2020). This spike in Republican women was not by happenstance. After the 2018 midterms, the Republican Party made a concerted effort to muster more women candidates (Bade 2020). In fact, one of these newly recruited Republican women, Ashley Vinson, defeated Abby Finkenauer, whose youth, you will recall, made her one of the more notable victors in 2018.

We can examine the impact of women candidates on teenagers' perceptions of democracy in 2020 with the Family Matters 2 study, using precisely the same methodology as that outlined in chapter 3. Recall that this means we measure democratic attitudes in both the pre- and post-election waves of the survey, control for parents' responses to the very same question, account for "women-friendly" characteristics of respondents' congressional districts and states, and control for individuals' demographics. Remember also that the national political environment is held constant,

Faith in Democracy

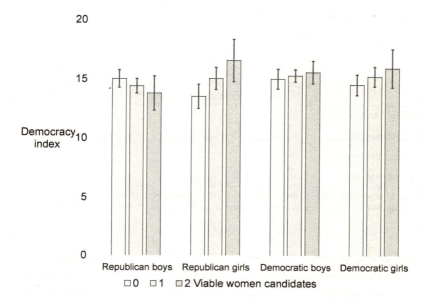

Figure 4.6. In 2020 both Democratic and Republican girls became more positive toward democracy when women ran

and thus any effects for local candidates are over and above the impact of any national campaigns in 2020, including the multiple women who ran in the Democratic presidential primaries and the vice-presidential campaign of Kamala Harris, who was elected as the first woman to serve in that office.

Like its predecessor study, Family Matters 2 asks about the importance of living in a democracy, as well as whether democracy is the best form of government. We combine the two measures to form the democracy index, which ranges from 0 to 20. In addition, FM 2 also replicates the question from FM 1 about whether the political system helps people with their genuine needs. Since it does not correlate very well with the other two questions about democracy, we analyze it separately.[12]

The results show that all girls, Democrats and Republicans, become more positive toward democracy when viable women run for office in their community. The effects are strongest for the democracy index, as they clear the hurdle for conventional statistical significance for both Democratic and Republican girls (fig. 4.6). They are in the same direction for the question about the system helping people but fall short of significance. In spite of our polarized times, this effect is not driven by

Table 4.2. The takeaway: Women role models and attitudes toward democracy

	2018			2020
	Political system helps people (Democratic women candidates)	Political system helps people (Republican women candidates)	Democracy index (all women candidates)	Political system helps people (all women candidates)
Republican boys				
Republican girls	↑	↑	↑	
Democratic boys				
Democratic girls	↑	↓	↑	

Note: An upward/downward arrow indicates a positive/negative and statistically significant relationship between the perception of viable women candidates and the attitude in question.

co-partisanship. That is, girls become more likely to view democracy as responsive when women run, period—without regard for whether they represent one party or the other. Furthermore, like the results for gender attitudes in chapter 3, these effects are observed for the presence of women candidates, so perception is not required.

What about boys? In 2018 we found that Republican boys became more skeptical of democracy when more (Democratic) women ran for office. In 2020 technically there was no effect, as the impact of women candidates did not reach statistical significance for boys of either party for either of our outcomes. Nonetheless, Democratic boys appear less likely to view democracy as responsive when more women, of either party, run for office, although the effect does not reach statistical significance—evidence suggesting that not everyone sees a greater presence for women in politics as a good thing.[13]

The careful reader will have noted a subtle but important difference between the results reported in chapter 3 and those we see here. In chapter 3 the role model effect for attitudes toward women as leaders was greatest for women candidates who were both viable and novel—that is, they were running to replace a man. For democratic attitudes, however, the effect does not rest on the candidates' being novel. Why the difference? One possibility is that views about democracy are particularly shaped by women in office. Women actually governing (not just running) sends signals about the quality of democratic representation. When we limit our candidates to only those who are novel, we exclude the incumbents who are currently sitting in Congress. Stereotypes about women's ability to lead might be more responsive to the attention-getting circumstance of a woman's running for a seat held by a man. This is just post hoc speculation, however, and we will be interested to see whether this distinction holds up in future research.

Summing Up

Hillary Clinton's loss is a counter-example to the usual inspirational stories about women running for office. Demonstrating that role models can cut both ways, her loss to Donald Trump led to disillusionment among Democratic-identifying teenagers, both girls and boys. The downturn among Democrats between 2016 and 2017, however, is not the whole story. The elections of both 2018 and 2020 show us that when women run, adolescent girls are more likely to have a positive perception of the political system.

In light of the concern over young people's attitudes toward democracy, these findings can be read in either an optimistic or a pessimistic way. The pessimist could point to the decline in young Democrats' perception of democratic responsiveness from 2016 and 2017, and to the fact that the decline continued for Democratic boys into 2018 as well. While one could argue that the decline is not so worrying because it was limited to one party, others might suggest that the fact that perceptions of democratic responsiveness are shaped by partisan preference is yet another example of a polarized America and a cause for concern.

An optimist can take a different lesson from recent years. When and where women run viable campaigns for visible offices, girls' attitudes toward democracy become more positive. This manifestation of the role model effect is not necessarily limited to one party, since both Republican and Democratic girls respond to women candidates. When girls look out at a political world in which women play a prominent role, they become more likely to value democracy and to believe that is responsive to people's genuine needs.

Even in this sunny version of things there are still some dark clouds. Not all girls react positively to all women candidates. In 2018 Democratic girls became less supportive of democracy when Republican women candidates ran, and there is evidence suggesting that some of the time, women candidates lead some boys to become less confident in their assessment of democracy's responsiveness. These negative effects are not as pronounced or consistent as the positive ones, but we should not shy away from the possibility that women candidates do not always drive greater confidence in democracy. While girls may welcome a more inclusive democracy, some boys may find it disconcerting or even threatening.

The fact that women candidates can affect teens' confidence in democracy leads naturally to the question of whether they in turn can spur greater political engagement and even a desire to follow in their footsteps and run for office. It seems likely that someone who believes in democracy is more likely to participate in the democratic arena. And when stereotypes change so that politics is viewed as something women do (as we saw in chapter 3), we expect more girls to do politics, or at least intending to do politics as adults. In chapter 5 we turn to the impact of women role models on girls' and boys' active participation in politics.

5 * Doing Politics

Seeing women, who truly demonstrate the diversity that makes America strong, win big in elections across the country makes my dream of one day being President of the United States feel a little bit closer.

Eighteen-year-old Deja Foxx, 2021[1]

The origin story of this book dates back over twenty years. While working as a research assistant in graduate school, one of your authors (Campbell) serendipitously discovered that in a long-running national survey of American high school students, teenage girls' political engagement spiked after both 1984 and 1992, landmark years for women in American politics. In 1984 Geraldine Ferraro was first women to be nominated to run for vice president on a major-party ticket; in 1992 a record number of women ran for Congress. He filed this finding away under "interesting stuff to explore further." Years later, as an assistant professor at Notre Dame, he showed the data to Wolbrecht. Did she think they were interesting? She did indeed. A collaboration was born, and our first paper on role models soon followed (Campbell and Wolbrecht 2006).[2]

Initially we were interested in the question most often implied when politicians tout themselves as role models: Does seeing women run for office lead young people (girls in particular) to be more engaged in politics? The previous chapters have shown that female role models shape attitudes toward women's capacity for political leadership and confidence in democracy itself. In this chapter we return to where our work began, with political engagement. Does exposure to women candidates lead teens to be more interested in activities such as voting, working on campaigns, and contacting elected officials?

The bulk of this chapter focuses on adolescents' attitudes *where* women run for office, but that early discovery about young people's engagement in politics *when* women run for office is revealing and worth updating. Examining change over time provides proof of concept for the role model effect and an opportunity to consider collective representation. We thus start there.

Role Models over Time

Over the past half century, women have increasingly held elected office in the United States. If, like both of your authors, you were born in the early 1970s, women politicians were rare. In the congressional session from 1973 to 1975 there was not a single woman serving in the US Senate, and only sixteen in the House of Representatives—a mere 4 percent. Many young people of the time could be forgiven if they thought of politics as men's domain. By the mid-1980s things had begun to change, but only slightly. Those coming of political age in that era might have been aware that there were two women in the Senate and twenty-two (5 percent) in the House.

Young people were far more likely to be aware of Geraldine Ferraro's candidacy for the vice presidency. When she was announced as Walter Mondale's running mate, Ferraro's picture was on the front page of every newspaper. *Time* magazine put Ferraro on its cover with the headline "A Historic Choice" (fig. 5.1) Many Americans at the time described Ferraro as blazing a trail for others to follow. Mario Cuomo, the governor of New York, said that "one thousand years from now, children of this county and this country will read in their history books how history was made by one person, a lady from Queens, a woman who with all her intelligence and persistence and commitment and dedication in a single stroke created new frontiers for all women" (Weinraub 1984). Ferraro was conscious of being a pioneer, describing her candidacy as "really opening so much more to young women in this country, as well as to older women and working women. If a woman can be Vice President of the U.S., what job is there that a woman cannot do? . . . [I]t creates a whole new role model. There are a lot of women out there saying, when they see me, 'I can do it too'" (Stacks 1984). Nor was it only politicians who spoke of Ferraro as a role model. One delegate to the Democratic National Convention was effusive: "It's like Christmas in July. I didn't think we'd ever be able to tell our daughters they could grow up to be president" (Peterson 1984).

The 1990s brought another milestone for women in American politics. In 1992, dubbed the Year of the Woman, a record number of women ran for Congress and won. As discussed in chapter 4, the narrative at the time attributed the surge of women candidates to outrage over the Senate confirmation hearings for Clarence Thomas to the Supreme Court, during which Anita Hill detailed Thomas's boorish and sexist behavior and, in the opinion of many, was treated disrespectfully by the all-male

Figure 5.1. An example of how the news media portrayed Geraldine Ferraro's vice-presidential nomination as historic

Senate Judiciary Committee. One of those candidates, Lynn Yeakel, said at the time that "in history we're going to see the Hill-Thomas hearings as being the turning point for American women in terms of really stepping forward, taking political power, using the vote, using our money to elect the candidates who represent our values and stand for our rights."[3] Further analysis has shown that the imbroglio over Clarence Thomas was not the only reason for the large number of women candidates in 1992, as there was a perfect storm of other contributing factors—a surfeit of open seats, increased funding for women candidates—but they all converged to make it a groundbreaking year for women in Congress (Palley 1993; Wilcox 1994). Whatever the reason, 117 women ran for a seat in either the House or the Senate. Twenty-four new women were elected to the House of Representatives, bringing the total number of women in the chamber to 47—roughly 10 percent (Chaney and Sinclair 1994). Eleven women ran for the Senate. Five won, bringing the total to seven, more than doubling the three who had previously been serving in the Senate.[4] California also made history, becoming the first state to be represented by two women in the Senate. Although news coverage at the time did not stress this point, every new woman senator was a Democrat.

These newly elected women were often described—by themselves, by others, and by the press—as role models. Among the cohort of newly elected women in Congress was Senator Patty Murray of Washington, who spoke of herself as "a different role model. This Mom in tennis shoes is what I really am."[5] A story in *The Wall Street Journal* included a conversation with a mother of two daughters in Chicago, who said that when voting for Carol Moseley Braun (elected as senator from Illinois), she thought "how wonderful it would be for them to have a role model. A thrill went through me."[6]

In both 1984 and 1992 there was considerable media attention on women candidates. However, there is an irony in the focus placed on women running for office. They were news because they were unusual. More than the actual numbers of women running, what distinguished those election years was the heightened attention to the women's persistent underrepresentation in politics, and thus how pathbreaking the women candidates were. Research shows that potential women candidates became more interested in running for office when exposed to a story about an all-male committee (rather than a gender-balanced committee) making policy related to women's rights (Clayton, O'Brien, and Piscopo 2023). Similarly, we find that in periods of considerable attention to women's interests in the context of the underrepresentation of women (such as in the wake of the Clarence Thomas hearings), adolescent girls become more interested in political engagement.

Figure 5.2 reproduces the original time series from our first paper together, but now updated to 2020. The data are from Monitoring the Future (MTF), a very large, high-quality, nationally representative survey of high school students across the United States. While the primary purpose of the MTF is tracking alcohol, tobacco, and drug use among American adolescents, every year some of the teenagers who take the MTF survey are also asked whether they envision themselves engaging in any of a list of political activities in adulthood. As a result, MTF is a barometer of American teenagers' political engagement, from 1975 to the present. The survey is conducted in the spring and is administered to students in

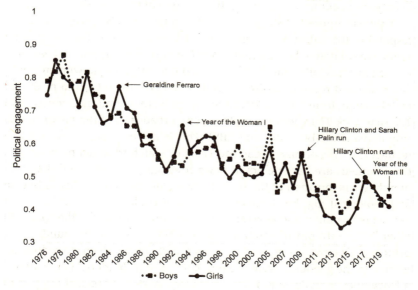

Figure 5.2. Adolescents' political engagement, by gender

school.[7] The figure displays the trend for an index of three political acts, which we will refer to as political engagement: working on a political campaign, giving money to a campaign, and writing to a political candidate. (Remember that the question asks the teen respondents whether they anticipate engaging in any of these acts when they are adults). The eye is drawn to the overall drop in political engagement for both girls and boys. This decline is further evidence of the well-established trend of diminishing political activity (Putnam 2001). Also, note that there are spikes and valleys along the way, as engagement often increases in the wake of presidential election years.

Although the trends for both girls and boys are down over the long run, they do not always move in the same way at the same time. In particular, note the spikes in girls' engagement in 1985 and 1993, the first surveys after Geraldine Ferraro's vice-presidential candidacy and the first Year of the Woman. In both cases, girls became more engaged than boys (these are the two data points that first caught our attention). There is also a spike in 2017, following Hillary Clinton's 2016 campaign for the presidency. In 2017, however, the spike is for both girls and boys, just as after other presidential elections. As we will discuss below, the surge in 2017, and also following the 2018 midterm elections—often described as another Year of the Woman—was as much about party as gender, likely reflecting the more sharply partisan politics of the first two decades of the twenty-first century compared to the last two of the twentieth.

Although figure 5.2 suggests that the spikes in girls' engagement correspond to the public attention focused on women candidates in specific years, we wanted to be sure that it was not only in hindsight that we view women as especially salient. To capture public attention to women candidates, we had research assistants code news coverage, both in print and on television, from 1976 to 2020.[8] Specifically, they examined coverage in *The New York Times* and the nightly news broadcasts of the major television networks (NBC, ABC, and CBS). This is not because we think many teenagers—then or now—read the *Times* or watch the evening news, but these sources are barometers of news coverage generally, and therefore of public conversation at the time. Drawing on media coverage is like an archaeological dig, but instead of tools and cookware the evidence left behind is headlines and news stories, reflecting what was in the "political ether." Our intrepid research assistants read summaries of hundreds of print and TV news stories, coding them for whether a given story drew attention to the gender of women candidates or officeholders.[9] For example, a November 6, 1980 *New York Times* story lauds the "record number of women" to hold seats in the next Congress; in a shift from our present-day politics, all four of the new members of the House and Senate were Republicans.[10] This was hardly the end of record-breaking elections. A *CBS Evening News* story on January 3, 2013, more than thirty years later, highlighted the record number of female senators serving in the upcoming term, noting the first women senators in the 1940s and the fact that only recently (1993) had the ban on women wearing trousers on the Senate floor been lifted.[11] Record years are just one kind of press report highlighting women's novelty in politics; consider a 1976 *New York Times* story about the "Dean" of women members of the House (just nineteen in 1976, with no women senators),[12] a 1995 *NBC Evening News* story on the seventy-fifth anniversary of the Nineteenth Amendment, featuring women senators,[13] or a 2006 ABC interview with Nancy Pelosi, soon to be the first woman to serve as Speaker of the House.[14]

Our hypothesis is that more media coverage of women in politics *as women* corresponds to an increase in teenage girls' political engagement. In other words, when the news coverage spikes, so should the engagement of girls relative to boys. To avoid the distraction of the other trends, figures 5.3 and 5.4 display the difference between girls' and boys' engagement. A positive number means that, in that year, girls were more engaged than boys. Notice that in most years, the gender difference in engagement is negative, meaning that boys were more likely than girls to say that they expected to be engaged in politics. However, there are

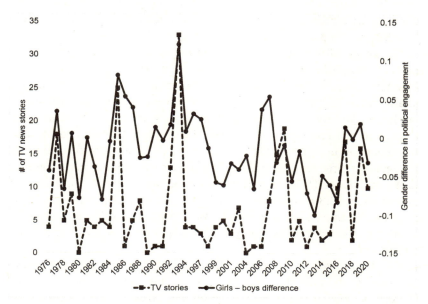

Figure 5.3. Spikes in girls' political engagement correspond to television news stories about women in politics

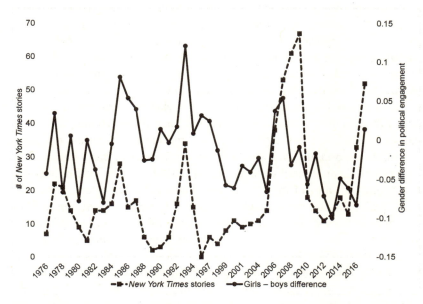

Figure 5.4. Spikes in girls' political engagement also correspond to *New York Times* stories about women in politics

periodic spikes in girls' engagement, where the positive number means that girls are more engaged than boys. In particular, one can see the spikes in 1985 and 1993, the years that first caught our attention.

The gender difference in adolescents' engagement is mapped onto the news coverage of women in politics, television news in figure 5.3 and *The New York Times* in figure 5.4.[15] The scale for this coverage is, of course, totally different from the gender gap in political engagement so the scales on the left and right y-axes differ. Nonetheless, we can still see whether a surge in one corresponds to a spike in another. To take one illustrative example, in figure 5.3 it is clear that 1985's spike in the political-engagement difference between girls and boys corresponds to an increase in the number of TV news stories during the same year. A visual inspection of figures 5.3 and 5.4 shows that whether we count stories on TV or in print, the conclusion is the same: More public attention to women in politics *as women* translates into a bigger gap between girls' and boys' engagement.[16]

We started with 1984 and 1992, but what about more recent years? Specifically, did girls show the same spike in engagement when Hillary Clinton ran for president, both in 2008 and 2016, or after the wave of women congressional candidates in 2018? What about when Sarah Palin was selected as the second woman vice-presidential candidate, or when Nancy Pelosi became the first women to serve as Speaker of the House of Representatives?[17] While these are all historic moments for women in American politics, we might expect that those past spikes in girls' engagement in response to such moments have become a relic of history. For while women remain underrepresented, they are more common than in the past. The coverage of Ferraro emphasized that she was the first woman to be a vice-presidential candidate. In contrast, while Sarah Palin received a massive amount of attention, it was not (entirely) for being first. Nineteen ninety-two was the original Year of the Woman; 2018 was the sequel. Seconds never get as much attention as firsts; just ask Buzz Aldrin, the second man to walk on the moon. When she was nominated as a presidential candidate by a major party, Hillary Clinton was a first—an Armstrong, not an Aldrin—thus suggesting heightened attention to her. Then again, she ran twice, having been in a hotly contested nomination race against Barack Obama in 2008. Also, she had been in the public eye for a quarter of a century, as the First Lady, a senator, and the Secretary of State. Perhaps her enduring presence negated the impact of her 2016 presidential race—more like an Aldrin than an Armstrong after all.

The answer to whether Hillary Clinton's 2016 presidential run corresponds with girl's increased engagement is a qualified yes—*some* girls became more politically active. Specifically, the increase was among girls

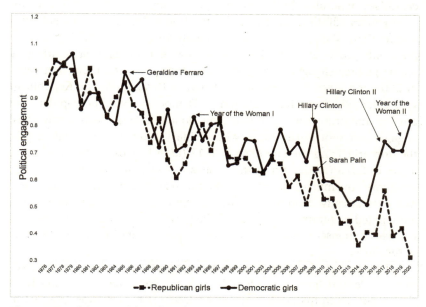

Figure 5.5. Adolescent girls' political engagement, by party identification

who identify with the Democratic Party. Nor is this the only example of a difference by partisanship. Just as in previous chapters we saw that party matters for the influence of role models, the same is true for girls' political engagement. Or, more accurately, it has become true over time. Initially, girls of both parties became more engaged when they saw women run for office. Back in 1985—following the candidacy of Geraldine Ferraro, a Democrat—there was a spike in the anticipated political participation of Democratic *and* Republican girls.

However, since the Year of the Woman in 1992, adolescents' reactions to moments of heightened salience for women politicians have become polarized. That word is often used loosely, but in this case means that in recent years, it has been *Democratic* girls reacting to *Democratic* women candidates (Mariani, Marshall, and Mathews-Schultz 2015).[18] This is no surprise given the extent of polarization in so many facets of American life. We can see this polarization in figure 5.5, which compares teenage girls who identify as Democrats or Republicans. Right after 1992, which could have been called the *Democratic* Year of the Woman, there was a rise in political engagement among both Democratic and Republican girls. Note though that, unlike the Ferraro bump, in this case there was a larger increase among Democratic girls. Republican girls' engagement continued to decline after 1992, with a minor spike in 2009, right after the candidacy of Sarah Palin for the vice presidency on the Republican ticket (and Hillary Clinton's near miss for the Democratic Party's presidential nomination). We observe another Republican uptick in 2017, just after the highly salient 2016 presidential election. In contrast, Democratic girls report greater engagement, with spikes after presidential election years in 2004 and 2008. The widest gap between Democratic and Republican girls emerged when Hillary Clinton—a Democrat—won the popular vote but lost the presidency to Republican Donald Trump. Democratic girls' engagement shot up in 2016 (when Hillary Clinton was competing in the primaries) and even more so in 2017 (after her loss to Trump), rising again in 2018 (in the era of the Resistance—a Democratic movement), and remaining much higher than Republican girls' engagement since then. The dramatically divergent trends in Republican and Democratic girls' anticipated engagement since 2000 likely reflects a range of factors, but partisan responses to prominent partisan women candidates is surely part of the story.

What about gender dynamics within the parties? To find out, we compared girls and boys who identify with the same party, starting with Democrats. Even though Ferraro was a Democrat, there was no spike in engagement among Democratic boys in 1985. Nor in 1993, which is perhaps even more surprising given that this was immediately following the successful presidential campaign of Bill Clinton, a Democrat. Democratic girls and boys generally moved together throughout the 2000s, but after 2018 they diverged. Democratic girls become even more engaged, while there was a precipitous drop-off in engagement among the boys. In short, although Democratic girls' and boys' political activity sometimes moves in tandem, there are also points of divergence, suggesting that their engagement is not driven solely by partisan preference.

What about Republicans? As expected, the post-Ferraro spike in Republican girls' engagement is not matched by Republican boys'. Since then there have been ups and downs, but the pattern is generally one of decline among both. From the late 1990s onward, Republican boys have been more engaged than girls who identify with the GOP. Like Democrats, Republican girls and boys moved sharply apart in 2020, but in this case it was girls whose engagement declined, while boys' engagement moved back to pre-2018 levels. Overall, and as has been a theme in this book, Democratic girls are in a category of their own, ending the series with a level of anticipated political engagement that exceeds that of Republican girls and boys, and of Democratic boys, by at least twenty points.

It is easy to get lost in the details, but the takeaway is that these data suggest a correspondence between the salience of women candidates and surges in girls' engagement. We draw two tentative conclusions. First, the political engagement of teenage girls is plausibly related to historic moments when women in American politics are highly salient. Second, although after 1984 and arguably 1992 as well, the increase in girls' engagement was bipartisan, in more recent years the response has been concentrated among Democratic girls.

These figures are meant only as a plausibility test; skeptics can point to the trends left unexplained and offer alternative explanations for the patterns we highlight. Not every surge in girls' engagement—whether they are Democrats or not—can be readily explained by the prominence of women candidates. But although the evidence is circumstantial, not definitive, there is enough of it to justify further exploring how adolescents, of both parties, respond when they see women, of both parties, run for office.

Role Models Close to Home

The trends over time show what happens in the aggregate when women politicians are salient because they are so unusual. Our expectation that role models affect young people's political engagement, however, is not limited to high-profile women who draw national news coverage. We suspect that teens' attitudes are also shaped, perhaps to an even greater extent, by seeing yard signs, bumper stickers, and campaign ads for candidates who run in their own community—the steady drumbeat of exposure to campaigns closer to home.

As we discussed in chapter 2, roles women perform in the real world help shape gender stereotypes about what women do. Stereotype updating is widespread; we saw in chapter 3 that both girls and boys changed their views about women's capacity for political leadership when exposed to women politicians, although the effect was largely limited to Republican teens, since they had the most room to move. The expectation for behavior is different. For political engagement, we expect to see the most consistent effects among girls, those for whom women role models signal that politics can be women's work. Stereotypes about men and politics have not changed, so we do not expect boys' behavior—that is, engagement with politics—to shift (Eagly and Wood 2011).

Challenging stereotypes is not the only reason to expect the presence of women candidates to inspire political engagement among teen girls in particular. Women politicians might garner greater attention to politics among their sisters in the mass electorate in particular, perhaps owing to the issues women candidates raise, their novelty, and/or their particular outreach to women. And indeed, previous research finds women are more interested in and knowledgeable about politics when a woman candidate is present (Atkeson 2003; Burns, Schlozman, and Verba 2001;

High-Pippert and Comer 1998; Koch 1997; Lawless 2004; Reingold and Harrell 2010; Wolak 2020). Interest and attention are key prerequisites for political engagement (Delli Carpini and Keeter 1996).

At the same time, we also expect that for some people, the presence of women politicians is viewed not as a model of women's capacity for politics or as a source of political interest and attention, but rather as a threat. A growing number of men perceive women politicians as a challenge to traditional masculinity, revealed in, among other ways, heightened hostile sexism and identification with masculinity (Cassino and Besen-Cassino 2021). These beliefs have been linked to rising political participation and electoral support for Donald Trump and the Republican Party (Banda and Cassese 2022; Carian and Sobotka 2018; Cassese and Holman 2019; Deckman and Cassese 2021; Gidengil and Stolle 2021; Valentino, Wayne, and Oceno 2018). Although both women and men can, and do, report support for hostile (and other forms of) sexism, threats to masculinity are of course largely reported by men. We might expect, then, that for some men, the presence of women candidates—women in a nontraditional and powerful role—leads to greater participation, not out of inspiration, but as a form of backlash.

DATA AND MEASUREMENT

We again turn to Family Matters 2 and employ the same type of analysis used in chapters 3 and 4. We predict teens' attitudes measured after the 2020 election, controlling for their attitudes prior to the election, as well as their parent's political activity. As before, we control for the features of each congressional district and state that are associated with the presence of women candidates, as well as individual-level demographic characteristics that might affect political engagement.

Remember also that we have two ways of counting women candidates: presence and perception. Presence is simply the tally of viable women candidates for three high-profile offices: member of the US House of Representatives, US senator, and governor. Perception is measured with a recall question. Respondents were asked whether any Democratic or Republican women were running for the House of Representatives and, where applicable, for the Senate and the governorship. Adding up the *perceived* number of women running for each office produces a tally comparable to our measure of women candidates' presence. Later on we will incorporate the perception of the candidates' party into the analysis.

You might be wondering how well teenagers can recall the women candidates in their community. Not surprisingly, our adolescent respondents are not that accurate, which is consistent with other research about voters' lack of knowledge in general (Delli Carpini and Keeter 1996) and of women politicians specifically (Burden and Ono 2020; Stauffer 2021). But how inaccurate they are depends on how strictly they are graded. As professors who have done a lot of grading, we are well aware that the grade you give depends on the standards you employ. Roughly half of the teenage respondents in our national survey accurately recalled the precise number of women running for the House of Representatives in their district, a number that includes districts with no women (which means that saying no women ran is scored as correct). In districts with a single woman running, only about a quarter could recall that one candidate. For higher-visibility Senate races, accurate recall overall is 75 percent, but since relatively few women run for the Senate, simply guessing "zero" is often the correct answer. When we narrow the criteria down to races with at least one female senatorial candidate, accurate recall is still about 25 percent, just as with House candidates. Conversely, 20 percent of teens who live in a community with no women candidates incorrectly perceived at least one. In some of those cases, though, they were likely recalling a candidate in a district or state close to their own, who would still serve as a role model. Is this level of recall high or low? Before condemning "kids these days" for their lack of political knowledge, ask yourself whether you can accurately recall who ran in the most congressional or gubernatorial elections where you live. It's harder than it might seem.

We begin with the most basic question: Do women candidates have any effect on young people's political engagement? For our purposes, political engagement is operationalized as behavior—things people do. We will examine three types of engagement: voting, political participation, and running for office.

As a form of political activity, voting is sui generis. Not only does it alone determine the outcome of elections, which lie at the heart of a representative democracy, but it is by far the most common way that people participate in the political process (and perhaps the best understood by social scientists). Unlike other forms of political participation, it is also subject to strong social norms—voting is everyone's duty. In the words of the seminal text on political participation, "The configuration of participatory factors—that is, the mix of resources and motivations—required for voting is unique" (Verba, Schlozman, and Brady 1995, 24). Voting stands apart from other forms of political participation (Campbell 2006).

We also examine a series of other political activities: working on a political campaign, participating in a march or protest, giving money to a candidate, and writing to an elected official. Because these forms of activity have long been shown to be driven by similar factors—people who do one of them are likely to do the others—we combine them into a single index (Verba, Schlozman, and Brady 1995; Zukin et al. 2006). This index is similar to the one featured in the trends over time presented above. Compared to voting, these forms of political activity require more time and commitment, are far less common, and are not subject to the same normatively tinged encouragement. On Election Day, voters proudly wear their "I voted" stickers. No one wears a sticker that says "I contributed money to a House candidate" or "I wrote a letter to my Senator."

Third, we also examine running for office—the act that requires the most commitment, is the least common, and has little or no normative expectation. We single out running for office because it is the most direct application of a role model effect. After all, what are political candidates modeling but running for office? Furthermore, the subject of gender and political ambition has been extensively studied (Bonneau and Kanthak 2018; Costa and Wallace 2021; Foos and Gilardi 2020; Holman and Schneider 2018; Lawless and Fox 2010). While much of that literature examines people who are at a stage in life in which they might consider running for office, research on college students and people in their twenties suggests an even lower level of political ambition, because young people increasingly see politics as too contentious and gridlocked to be a productive path for positive change (Lawless and Fox 2017; Shames 2017). Our data look at attitudes even earlier on in life to ask whether teens have any inkling of political ambition. By examining the ambition of youth, we hope our analysis can contribute to that burgeoning literature on why people do or do not choose to enter the political arena.

We are dealing with teenagers, so most of the people we study are not legally eligible to engage in some of these activities (voting, running for office), and are very unlikely to participate in the others (e.g., contributing money). Thus, Family Matters 2 follows the time-series data described above in asking about young people's intentions. Instead of asking for a report of behavior in the past tense—*have* you done X?—our questions are phrased in the future tense: Upon becoming an adult, *will* you do X? Accordingly, we are measuring what teenagers envision themselves doing in adulthood, or their *anticipated engagement*. It is important to note that these measures of anticipated engagement are not the same as asking people about their actual behavior. While all behavioral measures are subject to doubt because of faulty recall, social desirability, or other sources of inaccuracy, such issues are compounded when people are asked to anticipate their future activities. Thus, we do not consider these questions to be an ironclad guarantee of their behavior as adults—we all know about the destination of the road paved with good intentions. Nonetheless, they provide important insight into adolescents' political engagement.

At a minimum, questions about anticipated engagement capture the range of political activities in which respondents might potentially take part. We are not the first to ask people to report their potential participation. Questions like these have been used for over forty years, both for adolescents in the long-running Monitoring the Future study discussed earlier and also for adults (Barnes and Kaase 1979). By asking respondents, whether adults or adolescents, to project into the future, we learn what potential acts are in their repertoire. A skeptic might ask whether these questions are simply a reflection of what our teenage respondents think they are supposed to do. If this is the case, it is still informative, because these activities do not have equal normative value for everyone. Furthermore, knowing the political activities adolescents envision themselves doing captures what Youniss, McLellan, and Yates (1997) call their *civic identity*. In this formative period of their lives, do they consider themselves the sort of the person who votes, works on a campaign, or even runs for office? Are they engaged enough now that they can see themselves participating in politics in the future?

A critic may still reasonably ask whether teenagers' talk is cheap. Does anticipated engagement translate into actual behavior later in life? Using data from follow-up surveys of adolescents in the Monitoring the Future study in the years following high school, previous research by one of your authors (Campbell 2006) does indeed find that young people who see themselves as being politically active often turn out that way, as there is a strong correlation between anticipated engagement in adolescence and reported engagement in adulthood. Furthermore, as shown in chapter 8, we also find that teenagers who live in a community with novel, viable women candidates for high-profile offices become adults who are more likely to vote six to ten years later. Just as partisan identity is often formed during one's youth, so too is a propensity for political participation.

PERCEPTION'S IMPACT

One way to think about our analysis is that the perception and presence of women candidates are in contention with each other. When placed side by side in a statistical model, which one matters most? In our earlier chapters, presence was sufficient; when women politicians are present, they help shape attitudes about women leaders and about democratic governance. Actively perceiving women politicians was not required.

The story for active political engagement is different; only when respondents perceive that women candidates are present do they impact engagement. (For the full models and details, see the online appendix.) In other words, it is the perception of women candidates that has a consistent effect on political engagement, not merely their presence,[19] suggesting that the role model effect for engagement operates through conscious awareness, and perhaps only for those who are attentive to politics. Our theory of political role models suggested at least two pathways for the impact of women role models on girls' political engagement: changing gender stereotypes (about women/girls) and increased interest and attention (from women/girls). The fact that—unlike the impact of the mere presence of women candidates on gender stereotypes (chapter 3)—conscious perception of women candidates is necessary for an impact on engagement lends particular support to the role of interest and attention in facilitating any effect. It is only when teens are consciously aware that women are in their state and local electoral races that their presence is associated with greater political engagement.

We find that the perception of women candidates has a positive (and statistically significant) effect on the most and least common forms of political activity: anticipation of voting and running for office. In other words, when adolescents perceive that there are more women running for high-profile offices where they live, they become more likely to envision themselves as voters and also as political candidates. Although the perception of women candidates has a slight positive effect on the other forms of political participation, the coefficient does not reach traditional levels of statistical significance, so we cannot be confident that this effect is actually greater than zero.

As in earlier chapters, we divide our respondents by party, producing four groups: Republican boys, Republican girls, Democratic boys, and Democratic girls. Among these four groups, women candidates predict greater engagement only among two: Democratic girls and Republican boys. Both become more likely to envision themselves as voters and candidates when they perceive women candidates running in their community. For both groups, the impact of women role models on other forms of political participation is also positive but does not reach the threshold for statistical significance.

INSPIRATION OR THREAT?

While the results to this point indicate that women candidates *do* have an effect and suggest *how*, they leave unclear *why* they elicit greater political engagement. As with any type of political activity, there are two possibilities. Engagement can be motivated either by support for one candidate or by opposition to another. Take voting, for example. When voters mark their ballots for a given candidate, it is either because they prefer that

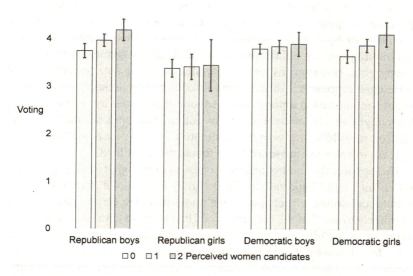

Figure 5.6. When Democratic girls and Republican boys perceive that women run, they become more likely to expect to vote . . .

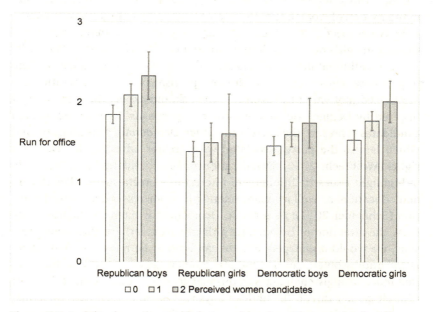

Figure 5.7. And they become more likely to envision themselves running for office one day

choice over the others or because they have an aversion to the opposing candidate. Either way, the ballot looks the same. In the case of women candidates, it could be that greater engagement is driven by either inspiration or opposition. By providing exemplars of what women can do in politics or by drawing attention to politics by their identity, novelty, and framing, women politicians inspire political engagement, particularly among girls. However, as we have argued, it could also be that women candidates represent a threat to traditional gender identity and trigger counter-mobilization among boys. Anyone threatened by women candidates might also be motivated to turn out and vote, not because they are inspired to follow in a woman candidate's footsteps but rather because they are worried about where those footsteps might lead.

The apparently similar reaction of Democratic girls and Republican boys is intriguing, especially given that they have very different views on women and politics. In chapter 3 we noted that Democratic girls are the most likely to say that the country would be better off with more women in office, while Republican boys are the least likely to welcome more women as leaders. Likewise, Democratic girls and Republican boys differ sharply on whether women have the necessary traits to be effective leaders. Republican boys are also the most likely to hold sexist attitudes, including that it is better for women to be homemakers than breadwinners and that women are too easily offended. Why would two groups that differ so dramatically in their views of women leaders both become more engaged when women run? We suspect it is because they are engaged for different reasons—Democratic girls out of inspiration, Republican boys because of backlash.

Two additional pieces of evidence help support this explanation. The first is how teens react to candidates' partisanship. If Democratic girls are indeed motivated by inspiration, we should expect them to be most inspired by Democratic women—their co-partisans. Democratic women candidates represent the party with which Democratic girls identify, and which is also the party associated with greater advocacy for women's rights (Wolbrecht 2000). Democratic women candidates are more likely to highlight issues traditionally of interest to women, such as health care and education, as well as issues relating to women's rights, such as abortion (Schneider 2014). As a result, Democratic women candidates likely draw the attention of Democratic girls in particular. For these same reasons, we would *also* expect Republican boys to be more engaged where Democratic women run. Democratic women, as candidates of the party that more strongly challenges traditional gender roles, represent the most explicit gender threat. Republican boys will be motivated by Democratic (cross-partisan) women—not out of solidarity, but instead because they oppose or even feel threatened by them.

This is precisely what we find. Democratic girls respond only to Democratic women candidates. When we asked whether any women were running for House, Senate, or the governorship, we also asked our respondents if they could identify the candidate's party. When Democratic girls (accurately) perceive that Democratic women are running in their community, they become more likely to say that they will both vote and run for office. As further confirmation, Republican boys' reaction is also limited to when they perceive Democratic women candidates—but we can only have statistical confidence that their likelihood of voting increases (the effect on running for office is also positive but does not clear the bar for statistical significance). It would appear that seeing Democratic women run is enough to mobilize them to vote (a low-commitment act), but not enough to envision themselves running for office, which requires much greater commitment.

For a second piece of evidence, consider how women candidates do and do not affect young people's political efficacy—their sense of personal political empowerment. Our respondents were asked to react to the statement "I can make a difference in my community" on a scale of 0 (disagree) to 10 (agree). Note that this question does not specify *how* they might make a difference, because it does not refer to formal politics. Instead, it asks for the individual's general sense of personal efficacy. Accordingly, it is a good measure of the potential effect of a role model: boosting one's own sense of their own capacity to bring about change in general, not only through political channels.

Figure 5.8 displays how Democratic girls and Republican boys react to Democratic women candidates. The perception of Democratic women candidates leads to a sizable increase in efficacy among Democratic girls but virtually no movement among Republican boys; in fact, Republican boys become slightly less efficacious, although the effect is not significant. Even though it is not shown, Republican boys' efficacy is also unmoved by Republican women candidates. This is what we would expect if Democratic girls were inspired and Republican boys were not. For Democratic girls, seeing women run fosters a sense of efficacy, even empowerment. In contrast, women candidates of either party have no comparable effect on Republican boys, who, recall, have a generally dim view of women's capabilities in general and women political leaders in particular. Rather than fostering greater empowerment among Republican boys, women candidates spark only a greater desire for them to be engaged in politics.

In sum, the question of *why* women candidates lead to greater engagement is answered by seeing *for whom* they spur political activity. The preponderance of the evidence suggests that when Democratic girls see Democratic women run as viable candidates, they become more politically

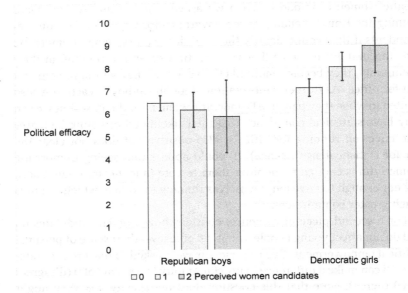

Figure 5.8. When women run, only Democratic girls become more politically efficacious

Table 5.1. The takeaway: Perceived women role models and political engagement, ambition, and efficacy

	Voting	Political participation	Run for office	Political efficacy
Republican boys	↑		↑	
Republican girls				
Democratic boys				
Democratic girls	↑		↑	↑

Note: An upward arrow indicates a positive and statistically significant relationship between the perception of women candidates and the attitude in question.

engaged. Beyond formal politics, they also have a stronger sense of efficacy, the belief that they can make a difference in their community. This is the classic role model effect of inspirational tweets and pinkie promises: Seeing women run leads girls to envision themselves as change makers, voters, and even candidates. For Republican boys, however, the evidence indicates that they become more engaged out of opposition, not inspiration.

Summing Up

We began this chapter with our origin story: the discovery that, over time, adolescent girls become increasingly interested in political engagement at moments of greatest salience for women candidates in national politics. Using data collected at one moment in time—the 2020 election—our analysis in this chapter confirms that the perception of women candidates can engender a heightened level of political activity among adolescents. The consistency between the analysis over time and over space is yet another robustness check for the role model hypothesis. So is the fact that, just like the results for the later years in the time series, the 2020 results also have a partisan inflection.

Careful readers will note that the results for the time series and 2020 do not align perfectly. Over time, the spikes in girls' engagement were for an index of political engagement, while we do not find statistically significant results for a comparable index in 2020. Our previous work (Campbell and Wolbrecht 2006), as well as that of other scholars, also found a positive relationship between women candidates and various measures and indices of political engagement other than voting or running for office (see chapter 2). Why the discrepancy? One explanation might simply be the somewhat inconsistent results across studies: Scholars have uncovered engagement effects in some years, for some candidates, in some data, suggesting the impact is somewhat weak, conditional, and/or difficult to observe. Our year (2020), candidates, and data may just not be among those with discernible positive effects. A closer look at table 2.1 also reveals that many of the positive effects identified are related to interest, knowledge, discussion, and candidate recall, rather than to actual activities such as campaigning, donating, and contacting an elected official. It simply may be that getting people off their couches and out *doing* politics is harder to achieve.

Why, then, the positive effect on an active participation index in the time series? Although we cannot know the reason for certain, we speculate that it is because the time-series data capture the moments when women candidates have extremely high salience nationally, generating enough excitement to move the needle on the most intensive forms of political activity. Local campaigns likely do not generate the same attention and enthusiasm. Instead, they do the quieter work of instilling in young people the desire to engage in "the most basic citizen act" (Verba, Schlozman, and Brady 1995, 9). Unfortunately, the time-series data do not include a question about running for office; but if it did, we predict that it too would spike in those same years where we see an increase in the other forms of participation.

Once again we see evidence that women candidates' salience and novelty are key to any role model effect. In our over-time analysis, we are able to track coverage of women politicians that highlights how unusual and barrier-breaking they are. The examples of Geraldine Ferraro, the Year(s) of the Woman, and Hillary Clinton demonstrate the national media interest drawn by pioneering women—the Armstrongs, not the Aldrins. The same dynamic probably characterizes other races too, even if on a local scale. After all, journalists cover the news—which, by definition, is what is new. Sadly, tracking the news coverage of women politicians in 435 congressional districts is beyond the scope of our research, but we can proxy media attention. For example, in chapter 3 we focused our analysis on women candidates running for positions currently held by men, capturing the same candidate novelty that drives press coverage.

In this chapter salience matters in an additional way: Are women candidates sufficiently salient that our teenage respondents consciously recognized their presence? We have seen in this chapter that when they *perceive* the presence of *Democratic* women candidates, both Democratic girls and Republicans boys become more interested in engaging in politics as both voters and candidates. For Democratic girls, the perceived presence of women candidates enhances their personal efficacy—the sense that they personally can impact the political world—providing the motivation for electoral participation. For Republican boys, those same Democratic women appear to spark greater engagement as well, but as a response to perceived threat, not inspiration. This counter-mobilization is consistent with the findings in the previous chapter that, for some boys in some situations, women candidates can lead to greater disillusionment with democracy. We are reminded once again that more women in politics is not necessarily a positive development for everyone, particularly those who are wary of women holding office. Ironically, however, we have also seen that the presence of women candidates—even Democrats—can subtly work to make Republican teens, girls *and* boys, more accepting of women as political leaders. Opposition in the short term may turn into approval over the long term.

We have now seen, in chapters 3–5, that the presence and perception of women role models shapes adolescents' beliefs about women's capacity for political leadership, evaluations of democratic governance, and level of anticipated political engagement. Importantly, and as our theory predicts, who is affected depends on what the effect is: Republican adolescents become more positive about women as leaders, girls—Democrats and Republicans—report more confidence in democratic politics, and both Democratic girls and Republican boys become more politically engaged, albeit for different reasons.

Case closed, right? Not so fast. These baseline results open up a range of related questions, which often require us to turn to different data and evidence than we have used thus far. Our analysis to this point has considered women candidates, and adolescent girls and boys, as fairly homogeneous, divided only by partisanship. Doing so ignores another key axis of traditional political exclusion: race and ethnicity. In chapter 6 we expand the scope of our analysis of role models to distinguish among white, Black, and Latina women candidates. How does the intersection of gender and race affect how young people react to women candidates?

Political party has been central to our analysis thus far, but all of that analysis takes place in a context in which most women candidates are Democrats. Chapter 7 asks whether we can conclude that women candidates truly cause a change in attitudes by employing an experiment that simulates an "alternate universe" in which we tune out the noise of the real world to ensure that teens focus on the signal: a wave of pathbreaking candidates, of either one or the other party, or both.

We have focused thus far on adolescents, but what about adults? As we saw in chapter 2, most previous research has focused on adults, with mixed results. The impressionable years hypothesis leads us to expect younger people's views and actions to be more malleable than those of older folks. Relatedly, one might wonder if the attitudes of young people have any bearing on what they do as adults. Do role model effects endure beyond adolescence? Chapter 8 answers both of these questions, demonstrating both that women candidates have more impact on the young than their elders and that the role model effect extends into adulthood.

PART III
Extending the Theory

6 * Intersectional Role Models

WITH RICARDO RAMIREZ

But where we once saw closed doors, glass ceilings, and overwhelming whiteness, we now see sisterhood, progressive alliances, and color. This new cohort has done more for transparency, accessibility, and motivating real people to see themselves advocating for their communities since the fireside chats.

Twenty-four-year-old Brea Baker, 2021[1]

In 1964 Brooklyn resident Shirley Chisholm decided to run for a seat in the New York state assembly. A day-care director and child welfare expert, Chisholm had been involved in local Democratic politics for more than a decade but had not previously put herself forward as a candidate. The response was not encouraging. Her local party was reluctant to support a woman candidate, and voters were similarly hesitant. Chisholm later recounted her interaction with an older Black man when she was collecting signatures to run: "Young woman, what are you doing out here in this cold? Did you get your husband's breakfast this morning? Did you straighten up your house? What are you doing running for office? This is something for men" (Winslow 2014, 44).

Chisholm not only convinced that gentleman to sign her petition, she won her primary and a seat in the state legislature. Four years later, redistricting opened up a House seat in Bedford-Stuyvesant, and Chisholm—famously campaigning as "unbought and unbossed"—became the first Black woman elected to the US Congress. (Rep. Patsy Mink [D-HI], elected in 1964, was the first woman of color and the first Asian American woman to serve in Congress.) Chisholm quickly established herself as a national figure, renowned for her outspoken support of feminism, civil rights, and an end to the Vietnam War. In 1972, encouraged by student activists, she declared her candidacy for the Democratic presidential nomination. Continuing the refrain she had heard throughout her political career, observers were skeptical. Wrote one journalist: "U.S. Rep. Shirley Chisholm of New York is a woman and she's black and she doesn't stand a chance of winning the Democratic presidential primary in Florida next Tuesday"

(Fitzpatrick 2016, 146). Chisholm herself recognized the challenges to her position, initially telling student activists, "You must understand, whatever my ability to handle the job and regardless of your belief in me, I am black and I am a woman." When pressed by students, Chisholm recounted that she had realized that the dominance of white men in presidential contests would not be broken "if we don't start now" (Fitzpatrick 2016, 199). Chisholm failed to win the nomination but became the first Black candidate for a major-party nomination and the first woman, of any race, to secure delegates at a Democratic national convention.

More than fifty years later, Chisholm's standing as a barrier-breaking icon is clear from the plethora of Shirley Chisholm T-shirts, mugs, and other items available online, many featuring her iconic "unbought and unbossed" slogan. Since Chisholm's election to Congress, more than fifty Black women have served in Congress. They have been joined by other women of color, including Latinas (thirty-one) and Asian Americans and Pacific Islanders (seventeen) (US House 2023c). In 2018 two indigenous women, Sharice Davids and Deb Haaland, were elected to the US House; Haaland went on to serve as Biden's Secretary of the Interior, another first for Native Americans. Chisholm is widely lauded as a role model who helped open the door for minority women in Congress. In 2018 then-Senator Kamala Harris wrote that Shirley Chisholm's example "spawned generations of Black women determined to and successful at breaking political glass ceilings" (Harris 2018, 2). Chisholm's impact extends beyond Black women, however. During her successful insurgent campaign for the US House, for example, the Latina candidate Alexandria Ocasio-Cortez (popularly known as AOC) tweeted, "Shirley Chisholm broke barriers so the rest of us could too."[2]

Are women of color—like Shirley Chisholm, Kamala Harris, and AOC—role models? By breaking both gender and racial barriers, women of color are uniquely situated to challenge both gender *and* racial stereotypes and, in doing so, to shift both the attitudes and the behaviors of Americans, particularly those who share their gender and racial identities. As suggestive evidence, consider how teens reacted to the candidacy of Kamala Harris for the vice presidency in the 2020 election. In the post-election wave of the Family Matters 2 study, we asked teens how much attention they had paid to Harris. African American girls were far more likely to say that they had read or heard a lot about the vice president—73 percent—than white girls (28 percent) or even other girls of color (39 percent).[3] As evidence that it was Harris's intersectional identity that made her salient to Black girls, only 25 percent of Black boys paid a lot of attention to her, roughly the same as white boys (27 percent). Furthermore, Black girls were also far more likely to say that Harris was a personal role model for them. On a scale of 0 to 10, where 0 means she is not a role model and 10 means that she is, Black girls gave Kamala Harris an average of 8. By comparison, they rated Joe Biden 6.6 on the same scale. Again, it appears to be the combination of a common race and gender that increases salience. While Black boys gave her a respectable average score of 7—relatively high, but still lower than the rating given by Black girls—for white girls her role model rating was only 4.5, below the midpoint.

The data on Kamala Harris imply that when women of color are candidates, they serve as role models for girls of color, but to date more systematic evidence has been lacking. The reason is straightforward: We have lacked the appropriate data to observe such effects. Because African Americans make up about 14 percent of the population, nationally representative surveys usually do not include sufficient numbers of Black (or other minority) respondents for in-depth analysis. The small number of women candidates of color only adds to the challenge of studying minority women role models. Consider the Family Matters 2 study we discussed in earlier chapters. In a survey of eight hundred teens, roughly one hundred were African American. Of those, half were girls, and only a fraction of those girls lived in communities with African American women candidates. We simply have not had enough data to allow us to draw reasonable conclusions.

In this chapter we are able to get around this problem by turning to a new data source: the Collaborative Multiracial Post-Election Survey (CMPS), a survey that includes "oversamples" of members of minority groups and in 2020 included a sample of teenagers ages sixteen and seventeen. We focus our analysis on the two largest racial minority groups in the United States: African Americans and Latinos.[4] (Unfortunately, data limitations prohibit us from examining other racial and ethnic communities.) Specifically, we ask: What is the impact of women candidates of color on the behavior and attitudes of adolescents, and how do those effects vary by the race and gender of our teens?

Expectations

At pretty much any moment in American history—except perhaps in the last decade or so—an observer could be forgiven for assuming that politics is something white men—and only white men—do. As of January 2023, 12,506 people have served in the US Congress, either House or Senate (US House 2023b). As table 6.1 reveals, a very small number of those members have been people of color. As of 2024, forty-six men have served as president, only one of whom was not white.

Table 6.1. White men rule: Total number of members of Congress and presidents by race and sex, 1789–2024

	All members	Women members	First woman	Presidents
Black	187	58	Shirley Chisholm (1968)	1
Latino	154	31	Ileana Ros-Lehtinen (1988)	0
Asian/Pacific Islander	60	17	Patsy Mink (1964)	0

Source: US House of Representatives

We have argued thus far that the domination of American politics by men sends the message that politics is not for women. Without question, the message that people of color do not belong in politics and political leadership has been strong and clear as well. This dearth of Black and Latino elected leaders throughout American history is not, of course, an accident, but rather the intended consequence of generations of policy and prejudice. Slavery denied African Americans all of the rights of citizenship. The Fifteenth Amendment, ratified in 1870, prohibited racial discrimination in voting rights, but with the exception of the brief Reconstruction period (1863–77), those rights were systematically denied Black citizens by legal and extralegal means until the passage of the 1965 Voting Rights Act (Keyssar 2000). It would be nearly fifty years before Black turnout approached, and in some cases exceeded, white turnout (Fraga 2018). The Supreme Court dismantled key aspects of the Act in 2013's *Shelby County v. Holder* decision. In response, a number of state legislatures have created and implemented restrictive voting rights laws "in places where there is an electoral incentive to exclude minority citizens from the electoral process" (Fraga 2018, 172). The effectiveness of these measures remains an open question, but these restrictions on voter access have generated massive campaigns aimed at mobilizing Black and other racial-minority voters. Not surprisingly, Black members of Congress were extremely rare before the 1970s, and African Americans remain underrepresented (Black and Black 2002). Although the share of the population and that of the US House that is African American are similar (14 percent), Black Americans make up just 3 percent of the US Senate in 2024 (Congressional Research Service 2023).

Both racism and anti-immigration sentiment have circumscribed Latino participation in American politics. In the late nineteenth and early twentieth centuries, the same barriers to voting (poll taxes, literacy tests, and so on) employed to block Black Americans from the polls also impeded Latino voters. English language requirements, directed at a range of immigrant groups, were used to limit Latino turnout as well (Keyssar 2000). Although many, but not all, of those legal barriers fell in the twentieth century, Latino turnout continues to lag behind that of whites (Fraga 2018). The geographic concentration of Latinos in Florida and the southwest has aided political representation, but the number of Latino representatives remains low (US House 2023a). Nearly 20 percent of the US population identifies as Hispanic, but Hispanic representatives made up just 13 percent of the House and 6 percent of the US Senate in 2024 (Congressional Research Service 2023).

As with women, scholars and activists have often hoped and expected that the presence of politicians of color will help shift attitudes about minorities in politics and mobilize racial group members politically. Both Black and Latino Americans experience a history of exclusion, persistent concerns about opportunities for and levels of mass engagement, and a relative lack of descriptive representation, again similar to women and exactly the conditions under which Mansbridge (1999) argues for the importance of role models.

Findings for the impact of Black role models are mixed. A significant body of scholarship finds that Black candidates and officials are positively associated with Black turnout and engagement (Bobo and Gilliam 1990; Clark 2014; Fairdosi and Rogowski 2015; Gilliam and Kaufmann 1998; Griffin and Keane 2006; Hayes et al. 2024; Keele et al. 2017; Lublin and Tate 1995; Rocha et al. 2010; Spence and McClerking 2010; Tate 1991; Vanderleeuw and Liu 2002; Washington 2006; Wolak and Juenke 2021). Others, however, report only null effects (Clark and Block 2019; Fraga 2016; Gay 2001; Keele and White 2019; Marschall and Shah 2007). Mixed findings characterize this relationship among Latinos as well; scholars report that Latino politicians are (Barreto 2007, 2010; Kaufmann 2003; Rocha et al. 2010) and are not (Fraga 2016; Henderson, Sekhon, and Titiunik 2016) associated with higher Latino turnout.

Mixed findings for engagement are not the only way that what we know about minority role models is consistent with what we know about women role models (see chapter 2). Similar to women, members of minority racial groups report more satisfaction with government, more trust, and more efficacy when represented by co-racial members (Bobo and Gilliam 1990; Bowen and Clark 2014; Box-Steffensmeier et al. 2003; Kaufmann 2003; Pantoja and Segura 2003; Sanchez and Morin 2011; Tate 2001; but see Marschall and Shah 2007). We have highlighted Mansbridge's (1999) claim that the presence of underrepresented groups (the "have-nots") in political leadership will convince the haves (here, whites) of their capacity to rule. And indeed, Hajnal (2007) finds that the presence of African American officeholders makes whites more favorable toward African Americans, more supportive of race-related issues, and more likely to vote for Black candidates in the future (see also Chauchard 2014).

Factors such as party, out-group status, and novelty also appear to shape the role model relationship for racial minorities in ways that echo our findings for women, especially in the more extensive literature on Black representation. In terms of novelty, Black mayors spur Black political participation, but as those Black mayors' terms lengthen, the effects diminish (Spence and McClerking 2010). It is among less engaged Black citizens—those with more room to move—that the presence of Black elected officials is associated with greater contact and turnout (Clark 2014). Party and ideology matter: Black Democratic House candidates spur turnout, but Black Republican candidates do not (Fairdosi and Rogowski 2015). More liberal African Americans are more likely to vote when represented by Black members of Congress, but moderate and conservative African Americans actually become less likely to vote (Griffin and Keane 2006). And perhaps similar to the ways in which threat leads to higher turnout among boys when women run, white turnout, as well as Black, increases when Black candidates are on the ballot (Lublin and Tate 1995; Washington 2006).

WOMEN OF COLOR

We have theoretical and (mixed) empirical reasons to expect, then, that the presence of Black or Latino politicians may mobilize their fellow group members (and perhaps others) to greater political participation, encourage trust in government and efficacy, and shape attitudes about the capacity of the marginalized group's capacity to govern. What about women of color specifically? This is a complex question. As first articulated by the legal scholar Kimberlé Crenshaw (1991), the concept of "intersectionality" draws our attention to the ways in which different forms of marginalization are not simply additive but multiplicative and contingent. Women of color experience both racial and gender bias, but those realities intersect in original ways that shape their opportunities and experiences. When it comes to white women, for example, traditional gender stereotypes emphasize dependence, weakness, and purity. For Black men, traditional racial stereotypes focus on strength, laziness, and threat. In our historical context, these combine for Black women into unique stereotypes that deny Black women access to traditional (white) femininity but instead cast them as simultaneously matriarchal, hypersexualized, angry, and independent (Collins 2000).

Spurred on by women scholars of color in particular, political scientists have increasingly adopted an intersectional lens, demonstrating the complexity of cause and consequence when multiple identities interact (see Hancock 2007a, 2007b; Smooth 2006). For example, women of color face unique structural barriers that limit the places where they can plausibly run for office (Phillips 2021), require concerted effort to overcome (Bejarano and Smooth 2022), and shape their decisions to run (Holman and Schneider 2018). As candidates, women of color are evaluated by voters in uniquely race-gendered ways (Brown and Lemi 2021; Gonzalez and Bauer 2022). Once in office, minority women engage in intersectional policymaking that serves the needs of not only women and not only racial minorities but is uniquely targeted at both (Brown 2014; Reingold 2020). In the electorate, women of color vote in ways that differ from the ways both Black men and white women vote (Corder and Wolbrecht 2016; Smooth 2006); in just one example, sexism predicted 2016 Trump support among white women but not among Black women (Frasure-Yokley 2018).

A few pioneering studies have examined intersectional role models directly. Considering both Black and Latino identity, Celeste Montoya and her colleagues (2022) show that people feel best represented by politicians who share both their racial *and* gender identity. Atiya Kai Stokes-Brown and Kathleen Dolan (2010) report that Black women became more likely to proselytize (try to convince others to vote a certain way) and to turn out to vote when an African American woman is on their ballot. Consistent with some of our results, given below, they find that white women also become more engaged when exposed to Black women candidates.

An intersectional lens thus guides our expectations about Black and Latina women as potential political role models. Our theory of political role models leads us to expect that minority-women candidates may shape beliefs about the capacity of women of color for political leadership and perceptions of the quality of democratic representation, as well as encourage political engagement among those who share their identity. But what identity? One possibility is that women candidates of color have a positive effect on nearly everyone—all girls regardless of race due to shared gender, and all adolescents of color regardless of gender due to shared race—leaving white boys, who do not share these candidates' race or gender, as the exception. We might expect these effects to be perfect substitutes for each other—women candidates of color have the same impact on minority girls (with whom they share two identities) as they do on minority boys and white girls, each of which group shares only one identity with women candidates of color.

A clear lesson from previous research, however, is that simple substitution and addition does not capture the complexity of intersectional identities. Should we expect to find that girls respond only to women candidates who share their race or ethnicity—that is, will we observe effects only for white girls exposed to white women candidates and Latina girls who observe Latina candidates? Or will girls respond to all women candidates, regardless of race? And what about boys? Will Black or Latino boys respond to Black or Latina women candidates the same way they respond to Black or Latino men candidates? Do members of marginalized racial groups perceive a shared nonwhite identity? And as a result, do teens of color respond to all women candidates of color, but white girls only to white women candidates? Previous research provides some reason to expect cross-racial identity but is not conclusive (Gonzalez and Bauer 2022; Montoya et al. 2022). On the other hand, to the extent that the role model effect is about counter-stereotypical politicians, women candidates of color challenge both race and gender stereotypes and in so doing may draw attention and admiration that make their presence impactful for all teens, including whites. Indeed, by overcoming multiple forms of bias, we might expect women of color to have particularly substantial impacts on the attitudes and behaviors of adolescents, because they are role models in the extreme.

In this chapter we focus on race rather than party. However, keep in mind that most women candidates are Democrats, and women in the electorate are more likely to vote for Democrats than are men. Among minority communities, this pattern is even more pronounced. The 2020 election boasted a record number (115) of minority-women major-party nominees, including Asian American/Pacific Islander, Black, Latina, Middle Eastern or North African, Native American, and/or multiracial women. Seven out of ten such candidates were Democrats. This is especially the case for Black candidates. More than 75 percent of the sixty-one Black women House nominees were Democrats, and every Black woman who won (a total of twenty-five) was a Democrat. The single Black woman nominee for Senate was also a Democrat (CAWP 2020b, 2021).

Again, as with women, the relationship between race and party is not just about party labels. Since the 1960s Democrats have been the party of civil rights, while Republicans are generally opposed to using government in pursuit of racial equality (Schickler 2016). In the mass electorate, Democrats are far more likely than Republicans to say that more still needs to be done to address racial inequality in the United States (Nadeem 2021). In general, voters believe Black candidates to be more liberal than white candidates, even those with similar policy positions (Jacobsmeier 2015). Teens and adults alike may assume that women of color are Democrats and respond to all women of color similarly, regardless of their actual partisanship.

It's not just candidates of color who are predominantly Democrats; the same is true for the general public, and for young people specifically. A majority of nonwhite voters support Democrats in presidential elections. This is again especially true for Black voters, and Black women in particular, more than 90 percent of whom cast Democratic ballots in most elections (Wolbrecht and Corder 2020). Among the teenage respondents to the CMPS, people of color are also far more likely to identity as Democrats than Republicans. Among both African Americans and Latinos, 61 percent of each group identify as Democrats; only 17 percent of African Americans and 19 percent of Latinos think of themselves as Republicans. The share of Democratic identifiers is slightly higher among Black and Hispanic girls and nonbinary people specifically: 63 percent and 65 percent respectively (Republican identification is 13 percent and 10 percent).

Since a strong majority of both candidates and youth of color are Democrats, our analysis does not differentiate either group by party. There are simply too few Republican candidates or youth for a viable analysis. But rather than omit the Republicans, we include all youth—regardless of party identification—in the models to come. Given that our findings in previous chapters have shown the importance of partisanship, by focusing only on race and not party our analysis here is a conservative test of political role models.

Women of Color as Role Models

By this point the reader is likely as dizzy from the possibilities as the authors are. In the analysis that follows, we seek to make sense of this muddle by teasing out the relationships between race and gender when it comes to women role models of color.

DATA AND MEASUREMENT

The 2020 CMPS featured a sample of 1,457 adolescents (ages sixteen and seventeen), including 661 white, 337 Black, and 282 Latino respondents.[5] Women, and women of color especially, are a small share of all candidates for the House, Senate, and governorship: Roughly 16 percent of our respondents had at least one woman of color run a viable campaign for any of these three offices. That's not a lot, but it is enough for an analysis of how young people respond to their presence on the campaign trail. Table 6.2 has the details of the CMPS.

In addition to the racial oversamples, one advantage of the CMPS is that it asks a more inclusive gender-identity question that permits our

Table 6.2. 2020 Collaborative Multiracial Post-Election Survey (CMPS)

Population	National sample of adolescents (age 16–17)
Mode	Online
Description	Cross-sectional survey
Sample size	1,457
Dates	April–October 2021
Details	Data weighted to match national population parameters for gender, nativity, parent's nativity, and parents' education within each racial category.
	Oversample groups: American Indian, Black Immigrant, Afro-Latino, LGBTQ, MENA-Muslim, Native Hawaiian/Pacific Islander.
	The survey was available in English, Spanish, Chinese (simplified), Chinese (traditional), Korean, Vietnamese, Arabic, Urdu, Farsi, and Haitian Creole.
Firm	Peanut Labs, Inc. (a member of the Dynata group)

respondents to identify as nonbinary. However, the small number of respondents who selected this option (7.5 percent) mean that we cannot analyze this group independently. We do not, however, want to lose them. Because our interest is in people who do not fit the traditional stereotype for political actors, we include nonbinary respondents with female respondents in our analysis. To recognize that this group is not just adolescent girls, but nonbinary people as well, we label these respondents "girls+."

We are able to include the same items gauging political participation, attitudes toward democracy, and beliefs about women as political leaders on the CMPS, as we include on Family Matters 2 (and analyzed in previous chapters). Unfortunately, the CMPS is a single-shot post-election survey, which means that (unlike Family Matters 2) it does not have a panel component; respondents were surveyed in one time period only. As with our earlier analysis, we seek to focus on the effect of exposure to women candidates of color specifically by controlling for a range of district- and state-level characteristics associated with the election of women. In doing so, we increase the likelihood that we are capturing the effect of role models and not some other factors, but it is always possible that other factors we have not included may have played a role. Our analysis here focuses on *presence* only, because the CMPS did not include our *perception* questions.

As in our previous analysis, we focus on the relationship between teens and the candidates for the House, Senate, and governorship in teens' own districts and states, and again only tally those candidates who are viable (they won or came within 10 percentage points of their opponent).[6] The

2020 election also featured a prominent woman of color on the national political stage: California Senator Kamala Harris—a multiracial Black and Asian candidate—sought the Democratic nomination and then was selected by Joe Biden as his vice-presidential running mate. Other prominent women politicians of color included "the Squad": US Representatives Alexandria Ocasio-Cortez (D-NY), Ilhan Omar (D-MN), Ayanna Pressley (D-MA), and Rashida Tlaib (D-MI). These four are Latina, Somali American, African American, and Palestinian American, respectively. All were first elected to the House in 2018 and drew considerable attention in the press and on social media for their accessible style and progressive policy commitments. In terms of our data, this means that all of our respondents were "treated" with exposure to prominent women candidates of color (Harris, the Squad), and so any differences between respondents cannot be attributed to those national figures. However, Harris's historic nomination, along with the media savvy of the Squad, may have meant that local women candidates of color drew particular attention and interest. It is the impact of those district and state candidates that our analysis can identify.

WOMEN OF COLOR MATTER

We begin with our measures of political engagement. Encouraging greater political engagement among historically marginalized communities of color has long been a hope and goal for racial descriptive representation, what Bobo and Gilliam (1990) famously called the "empowerment thesis" (Fraga 2018). Do women candidates of color encourage greater political engagement? In the figures that follow, we show the predicted level of engagement when no women run, when white women run, when women of color who do not share the respondent's racial identity run, and when women with whom the respondent shares a racial identity run. The general women of color category includes not only Black/Hispanic women candidates, but also Asian American, Native American, and Middle Eastern/North African women candidates.

One difference from our earlier analysis of adolescents' political engagement is that the CMPS asks teenage respondents not whether they expect to be politically engaged in the future, but whether they actually participated in each given activity during the course of the 2020 election. Respondents were asked whether they had done any of the following since January 2020:

- Worn a campaign button or posted a campaign sign or sticker
- Attended a meeting to discuss issues facing the community
- Attended a campaign rally, meeting, or event

- Worked or cooperated with others to try and solve a problem affecting your city or neighborhood
- Worked or volunteered for a candidate, political party, ballot issues, or some other campaign organization
- Contributed money to a candidate, political party, ballot issue, or some other campaign organization[7]

For each activity, respondents had a range of potential responses, one of which was the definitive "Yes, I am certain I did that last year." Our Participation Index counts each such response as 1 and anything else as 0, creating an index of the political activity about which our respondents were certain.[8] Lest you think that sixteen- and seventeen-year-olds are politically inert: Fourteen percent had worked with others to solve a neighborhood problem, 12 percent had worn a campaign button or posted a sticker, and 8 percent had contributed money to a political cause or candidate. All in all, almost a third (32 percent) of our teenage respondents engaged in at least one political activity over the course of 2020.

Our general finding is this: Minority girls+ are more politically engaged when women run but tend to be even more engaged when women of their own racial or ethnic group are candidates. We start with Black girls+ and our participation index. As figure 6.1 indicates, Black girls+

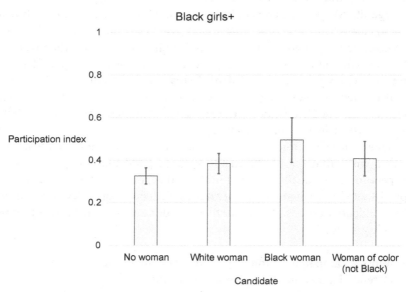

Figure 6.1. Black girls+ are more likely to be engaged when women of color run

Intersectional Role Models

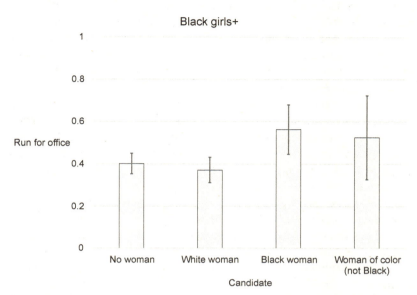

Figure 6.2. Black girls+ are more likely to say they will run for office when women of color run

are more politically engaged when they are exposed to Black women candidates. There is a hint that they are also more engaged when they see either a woman of color who does not share their racial identity or a white woman, but neither of those effects achieve conventional statistical significance.

We see a similar pattern when we look at the interest of Black girls+ in running for office themselves.[9] In figure 6.2, the effects are once again fairly linear, with no effect for exposure to white women candidates, but a marked effect for other women of color (the small numbers of non-Black women candidates of color explain the wide confidence intervals) and the clearest and strongest effect for Black women candidates. Black women candidates are indeed inspiring Black girls+ to greater engagement with politics.

In contrast to African Americans, Latina teens do not evince a role model effect. While there appears to be a slight increase in the participation of Hispanic girls+ when Hispanic women run, the effect is not statistically significant; we also find no effects for any women candidates on their ambition to run for office one day.

Among white girls+ there is a hint of a positive effect on their political participation when women of color run, but it falls short of statistical significance. However, the impact of women candidates of color on the ambition of white girls+ is more striking. Exposure to white women candidates does not move their ambition at all (although, remember, this does not account for co-partisanship), but exposure to women role models of color produces a significant positive effect on whether white girls+ envision themselves as running for office someday.

Our conclusion? Women candidates of color are uniquely mobilizing for teen girls and nonbinary people. For Black and white girls+, in particular, the presence of women candidates of color generates higher interest in campaign engagement and in running for office. For Black girls+, the effect of Black women candidates is especially substantial, but they respond to other women of color as well, and more so than to white women candidates. Like Black girls+, white girls+ respond particularly strongly to women candidates of color, while for Latinas the effect is weaker and limited to Latina candidates. By breaking not one but two barriers—gender and race—women candidates of color appear to make politics more attractive and accessible to teenage girls, leading them to imagine themselves in similar roles—including as candidates!—in their own futures.

Previous research has emphasized that it is racial minorities, and rarely whites, who become more engaged with politics when exposed to candidates of color. How can we explain the fact that white girls respond to women candidates of color, and not to white women candidates? We expect that part of the explanation is that because they are truly exceptional—breaking both gender and racial barriers—women candidates of color attract the admiration of many young women, regardless of race. Moreover, around the 2020 election, a number of high-profile women of color were making waves and perhaps increasing the salience of and drawing attention to other minority women candidates as a result. We see evidence of this in the fact that white girls+ are more likely to report discussing politics when a woman of color is on the ballot in their district or state (Stokes-Brown and Dolan 2010 report similar).[10]

What about boys? As we suggested above, we might expect Black and Latino boys to respond to women candidates who share their racial identity, even if not their gender identity. Alternatively, in our earlier analysis we observed Republican boys becoming *more* politically engaged when exposed to women candidates, an outcome which evidence suggested might be related to a gendered sense of threat. Here we find that political engagement—at least of one type—drops in the presence of women candidates. The strongest effect, and one that is statistically significant, is for Black boys' interest in running for office: They become *less* likely to say that they will be a political candidate one day when exposed to a woman candidate of color, whether African American or another race (see fig. 6.3).

Intersectional Role Models

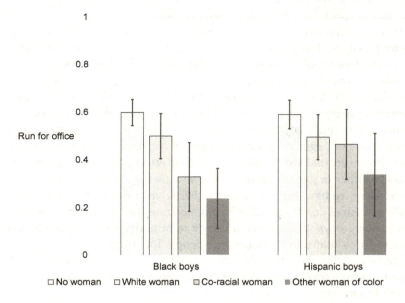

Figure 6.3. Black and Hispanic boys are less likely to say they will run for office when women, especially women of color, run

We see a similar pattern of disengagement among Hispanic boys when women, and especially women of color, run. The effect is again clearest for political ambition, because Hispanic boys are significantly less likely to say that they will run for office when non-Hispanic women of color are candidates (fig. 6.3), with a similar pattern for political participation that is on the cusp of statistical significance ($p = .08$, not shown). The bottom line is that women candidates—and despite a shared racial identity, especially women candidates of color—are not inspiring minority boys to greater political engagement or ambition.

How do we explain minority boys' disengagement with politics when exposed to women candidates overall and especially those who share their racial identity? In models not reported here, we find no significant impact of the presence of minority *men* political candidates on the engagement or ambition of Black or Latino boys. For minority boys, then, shared racial identity with candidates does not seem mobilize them into politics. Our analysis thus adds to the null-effect side of the ledger for studies of racial role models and political engagement. This hardly means that race does not matter! Indeed, in most cases we see that minority boys react *more negatively* to women who share their own racial identity or women of color in general than they do to white women. As an intersectional lens would lead us to expect, race and gender interact here in nuanced ways.

How do white boys react to the presence of woman candidates of color? Do they become less engaged, as we have seen for Black and Hispanic boys? Or does their political involvement increase, as was the case for Republican boys when we looked at the effect of all women candidates (see chapter 5)? The answer is clear: When women of color run for office, white boys become less politically engaged—an effect that is statistically significant. In this analysis, there is no effect when white women run, either positive or negative—only the negative response to women of color. Note, however, that we do not see a similar effect of women candidates of color, either in size or significance, on white boys' intention to run for office. Here we have further evidence that women candidates, and especially women of color, can serve to dampen one type of political engagement among boys. Perhaps the presence of minority women leads white boys to think that politics is not for "people like them." Once more we are reminded that the effects of women candidates can be a double-edged sword, pushing some young people in one direction while pulling others in a different one.

What about the attitudes—toward women as leaders and about democracy—that we have analyzed in our earlier chapters? As we found for women candidates overall (chapter 3), both boys and girls become more positive about women's capacity for leadership when exposed to a woman candidate, but we find little or no "extra" effect for women candidates of color (full model details can be found in the online appendix). Why are our distinctive findings for women candidates of color limited to political engagement, and not attitudes about women leaders? Our theory of role models posits that exposure to women in political roles will challenge traditional stereotypes about women's capacity for political leadership. This effect is not a function of shared (racial) identity but of exposure to counter-stereotypes. A woman of color sends the same message about *women*'s capacity for politics as does a white woman candidate. Recall that our questions about women's capacity for political leadership are about women in general and lack racial specificity. Future research should examine whether women candidates of color change attitudes about the leadership capacity of minority women specifically, in the same way that women candidates in general change attitudes about women in general.

Turning to democratic attitudes, we see a hint of evidence that Black girls+ become more likely to think that the political system is responsive. There is a positive relationship between the presence of a Black woman candidate and whether Black girls+ think "the political system helps people with their genuine needs," but it fails to reach statistical

Table 6.3. The takeaway: Women candidates of color and political engagement

	Woman candidate of the same race		Woman candidate of a different race	
	Political participation	Run for office	Political participation	Run for office
Black girls	↑	↑		
Hispanic girls				
White girls				↑
Black boys				↓
Hispanic boys				↓
White boys			↓	

Note: An upward/downward arrow indicates a positive/negative and statistically significant relationship between the perception of viable women candidates and the attitude in question.

significance.[11] However, among Hispanic girls+ there is nothing close to an effect for a Hispanic woman, or any woman candidate of color, for that matter. These findings are perplexing. Women candidates of color provide evidence of the openness of the system to and the representation of *both* women and marginalized racial communities, so we might expect them to be associated with even more substantial shifts in attitudes about democratic responsiveness. Note, however, that in chapter 4 we find only weak effects on this attitude, and only among Democratic girls. This is not the only way to gauge young people's perception of democratic effectiveness, so we do not consider this the last word on women role models of color and attitudes toward democracy.

Summing Up

On January 21, 2019, Kamala Harris, the second Black women to serve in the US Senate, announced her candidacy for the Democratic presidential nomination. Harris highlighted the historic racial nature of her candidacy by making her announcement on Martin Luther King, Jr. Day. Yet, Harris was not only a Black and Asian candidate, but a woman as well. She emphasized that intersectional identity with campaign materials that evoked the color scheme used by Shirley Chisholm in her presidential bid forty-seven years earlier.[12] In an interview the following month, Harris said of Chisholm, "I stand as so many of us do on her shoulders."[13]

We have seen in this chapter that minority women candidates in general are indeed role models for adolescent girls+. These multiple-barrier-breaking women drew the attention of girls+ to politics and encouraged them to envision themselves as political actors as well. Even in a year in which women of color were highly visible in politics nationally—with Harris's nomination and the media-savvy Squad—living in a district or state where a woman of color ran for a major political office led to increased engagement and ambition for public office among Black and white girls+ alike. Surprisingly, we do not see the same effect for Latina teens. We concede that we do not have an explanation for the lack of an effect among Hispanic girls+ and leave it for future research to further pursue the issue of role models within the Latino community.

Less encouragingly, boys were not inspired by women candidates of color; if anything, they became less engaged when minority women were on the ballot. Why might this be? In chapter 5, Republican boys in particular became *more* engaged when exposed to women candidates, which we suggested might be a response to gendered threat. We suspect a different reaction may be at work here. Scholars have long documented that men tend to leave occupations when women enter them, owing to a perceived devaluing of the field and a resistance to doing "women's work" (Block 2023; Goldin 2014). Perhaps boys disengage from politics for similar reasons when they see women, and especially women of color, on the ballot.

What about other identities? Each of us contains many different personal identities: gender and race, obviously, but also religious, occupational, and national identities, to name a few. Recall, however, that our theory of political role models is fundamentally about groups that have experienced, to use Mansbridge's words, "historical political subordination and low de facto legitimacy" (1999, 628). In other words, it is politicians from traditionally marginalized groups who have the potential to disrupt political-exclusion stereotypes and to inspire greater political trust and engagement.

Race and gender are of course just two axes of marginalization in American politics. Another group where we might also expect to see a role model effect is among sexual minorities. LGBTQ Americans have a long history of exclusion from politics and society (Johnson 2004). In recent years, however, a record number of openly LGBTQ candidates have pursued elected office and won (Flores et al. 2020; Reynolds 2018). Our own former mayor of South Bend, Indiana, Pete Buttigieg, a once (and future?) presidential candidate and the first out member of a presidential cabinet, is often lauded as a role model, especially to gay youth. The then mayor of West Hollywood, Lindsey P. Horvath (a Notre Dame alumna, we hasten to add), lauded Biden's nomination of Buttigieg in 2020: "Representation is vitally important. President-Elect Biden's nomination of Pete Buttigieg to the incoming Administration is especially significant for LGBTQ young people who will be able to see themselves reflected in leadership at the highest levels of government. This is exactly what generations of LGBTQ people and their allies have fought decades for."[14]

We saw in this chapter that studying role models is more challenging with smaller populations and fewer candidates and officeholders. The numbers are growing, however. As of 2024, LGBTQ governors serve in Colorado, Massachusetts, and Oregon. In 2020, the year of our study, nineteen out LGBTQ candidates secured their parties' nominations for the US Congress (eighteen Democrats and one Republican), and nine were elected as members of Congress. Seven were incumbents, but the two new representatives—Ritchie Torres (D-NY) and Mondaire Jones (D-NY)—are the first gay Black members of Congress, and Torres, who identifies as both Black and Latino, is the first openly gay Latino member of Congress as well (Flores et al. 2020; Rubinstein 2020). Intersectionality is everywhere, and potential role models abound. We encourage future scholars to examine the impact of these, and future, barrier-breaking public officials.

In summarizing her own career, Shirley Chisholm wrote, "I hope if I am remembered it will finally be for what I have done, not for what I happen to be. And I hope that my having made it, the hard way, can be some kind of inspiration, particularly to women" (Brown 2020). Chisholm was a historic first, and more than fifty years later, more and more women, and women of color, have followed her into political careers. Only now does the real world provide us with enough candidates of color to systematically trace their impact. Another group is not quite as rare, but nonetheless an uncommon sight: Republican women. In the next chapter we take an experimental approach to evaluating the impact of an alternate universe where Republican women candidates, rather than Democrats, are lauded as barrier breakers.

7 * A World with More Republican Women Candidates

Hey, wait a minute, not every woman is a Democrat.
　　　　　　Republican Stephanie Bice, who defeated incumbent
　　　　　　　　Democratic Rep. Kendra Horn (OK-5) in 2020[1]

To this point, we have relied on observational data, asking questions of teens who are, and are not, exposed to women candidates in their own localities. The advantage of observing people in their natural habitat is that respondents have sustained exposure to real-world political campaigns, complete with news coverage, advertising, campaign outreach, social media, and conversations within their social network. We are describing the world as it is and examining how natural variation in that world is correlated with the attitudes and behaviors we are studying.

In the world as it is, most women candidates are Democrats. In 2020 two out of every three women candidates for the House (69 percent) and for governor (68 percent) were Democrats. The share was slightly smaller in the Senate, but even then, 57 percent of women Senate candidates were Democrats (CAWP 2020a). This was not a new pattern; Democrats have been far overrepresented among women candidates since at least 1992 (Thomsen 2015).

These facts have not escaped the notice of either teenagers or adults. In another 2020 study we conducted (described below), we asked teens whether they thought women candidates in the 2020 election "were mostly Democrats, mostly Republicans, or an even mix of both."[2] Only 7 percent said that women candidates were mostly Republicans, while nearly half (49 percent) said that they were mostly Democrats. Among Democratic girls, 63 percent said that women candidates were predominantly of their party. In contrast, seeing Republican women run for office is novel, even—and perhaps especially—for Republican girls. Just 4 percent of Republican girls thought that women candidates in 2020 were primarily Republicans, and only 15 percent thought they were an even mix of the two parties, leaving 81 percent who thought that they were mostly Democrats. Among adults, 55 percent reported that most women candidates were Democrats, compared to just 7 percent making the claim that most are Republicans. These patterns echo the insights of social role theory about how stereotypes develop from observation of patterns: Observing that most women candidates are Democrats leads people to stereotype women candidates as Democrats (Eagly and Wood 2011).

Why should this matter? The association of women candidates with the Democratic Party may impact how our Democratic and Republican teens respond to the presence of women candidates. Democratic women candidates might be less inspiring to Republican teens, especially boys, who do not identify with either the party or the gender of these candidates. Given contemporary polarization and high levels of affective partisanship, partisan antipathy may trump any gender identification for Republican girls, denying Republican girls the engagement bump that Democratic girls get from observing women politicians. As we emphasized in chapter 2, scholars and activists have long expected that women role models might help close the participation gap between women and men. But we also see a participation gap between Republican and Democratic girls, with Republican girls much less likely to engage in politics (see chapter 5). If Republican girls observed more Republican women candidates, might that gap narrow as well?

Other partisan differences might also shape our results. Republican women candidates may not be as visible as their Democratic counterparts, perhaps because there are fewer opportunities for Republican women to raise funds (Cooperman and Crowder-Meyer 2018). Or perhaps Democratic women candidates draw more attention to gender and diversity—and thus their novelty—while campaigning, while Republican women do not (Bauer and Santia 2022; McDonald, Porter, and Treul 2020; Schneider 2014). For these reasons—or others—the news media may focus more on the gender of Democratic women candidates. The relatively small number of Republican women candidates may simply mean that Republican women have too little statistical power; we cannot detect the impact of Republican women models because there are too few of them to move the needle.

At the same time, Republican women role models may be more novel, and thus more likely to affect the attitudes and behaviors of teens or adults. A Democratic woman running for political office is not unusual; in 2020 nearly half (48 percent) of all Democratic House candidates were women. Women candidates are more exceptional among Republicans; only a quarter (23 percent) of Republican House nominees were women in 2020 (Dittmar 2020). There are certainly prominent Republican women—think Republican presidential candidate Governor Nikki Haley (SC) or Rep. Marjorie

Taylor Greene (GA-14)—but far more prominent Democratic women, such as Vice President Kamala Harris, former Speaker Nancy Pelosi (CA-11), and Rep. Alexandria Ocasio-Cortez (NY-14). As we have seen, women candidates are most likely to affect views on women as leaders or on political engagement when they are novel in some way—when attention is drawn to their historic presence (as in 1984) or when running for an office currently held by a man (as in our observational analysis), to take just two examples. Republican women candidates are certainly more novel than Democratic women candidates.

In other words, there are a number of reasons that we might observe different effects for Democratic versus Republican women. To determine whether there is something different about women candidates from one party over the other in observational data would require the presence of more Republican women running for office. Regrettably, in the real world, this is not something we as researchers are able to do. As much as we would like to think that the national Republican Party would be willing to increase its recruitment of women candidates to further our research, somehow this seems unlikely (but see Karpowitz, Monson, and Preece 2017).

Fortunately, we don't have to rely on a quixotic plan to convince party leaders to recruit women candidates. To determine what would happen in a world with more Republican women candidates, we conducted a survey experiment—that is, an experiment embedded within a nationally representative public opinion survey of American teenagers, known as Time-Sharing Experiments in the Social Sciences (TESS)—and present the details in table 7.1.[3] Because this is an experiment, we can control the information that our teenage respondents see about women candidates. Though we cannot literally create an alternate universe in which there are more Republican women running for office, we can have adolescents read a news story about a Republican wave of women candidates in 2020, which has the added virtue (and ethical requirement) of being true (Dittmar 2020; Dittmar and Hill 2020). We can also control how the Republican wave of women is framed in the story. Specifically, we emphasize the historic nature of so many women running under the GOP banner to draw attention to the novelty of these candidates.

Our primary interest is in what happens when Republican women—something of a novelty—are highlighted. To gauge such an effect, we also need to see how teenagers respond to news about Democratic women running for office. The election year of 2020 serves this purpose as well, for it was also a year in which there was a large number of Democratic women candidates (many defending the seats they won in 2018). A story emphasizing Democratic women candidates is more typical because even in

[154] CHAPTER 7

Table 7.1. Time-Sharing Experiments in the Social Sciences

Population	National sample of adolescents (age 13–17)
Mode	Online
Description	Cross-sectional survey
Sample size	803
Dates	December 2020–March 2021
Details	Data weighted to match national population parameters for age, sex, education, race/ethnicity, housing tenure, telephone status, and Census division. The instrument included multiple survey experiments.
Firm	NORC (AmeriSpeak Panel)

2020, a banner year for Republican women, there were still more women running as Democrats; in this sense, it serves as something of a control case. We include a second control with a case that emphasizes gender without any mention of party. Does this eliminate any partisan differences in how teenagers respond? Or do we find evidence that, without party labels, teens assume women candidates are Democrats and respond in kind? And what about room to move? Absent party information, are teens' responses—particularly whether women possess the necessary skills to be effective political leaders—still shaped by party because Republicans start out with greater skepticism toward women in office?

A survey experiment not only lets us create an alternate universe with more Republican women candidates, but helps address some of the challenges inherent in observational data. In the real world, we do not know whether everyone has been exposed to women candidates—or any candidates, for that matter—in the same way. Some races may have had a high profile, while others may have flown under the radar. In some campaigns the candidates' gender may have been a major issue, in others not. When we look for the role model effect, we do not know whether everyone in a given community has received the same dose of exposure to women candidates. In a survey experiment, we know everyone received the same information and can confirm this with attention checks.

An experimental approach also means that we can make stronger claims about causation, not just correlation. We have gone to great lengths to account for potentially confounding influences on people's political engagement—using panel data, accounting for parents' attitudes, and controlling for the demographics of the individuals and the communities in which they live. Yet, the nature of observational research is that you can never completely rule out threats to causation; as the old saw goes, correlation is not causation.

Why does this matter? Perhaps we have only found a mere correlation—places with more women candidates are also places where young people are more likely to engage in politics—but these two things are not actually related to each other, and one (the presence of women) did not necessarily cause the other (more engagement). This is of course the key claim we seek to evaluate in this book: that the presence of women politicians *causes* adolescents to think or act differently than they would have otherwise. In the experiment, we eliminate all other factors (other aspects of the district or state, variation in exposure to women candidates) and isolate the one variable of interest (exposure to women politicians), which means we can be confident that any observed effects are due to the information we have provided—the treatment—and thus causal.

So far, it might seem that an experiment is a panacea for all of the ambiguity and uncertainty of observational research. However, in research as in life, there is no such thing as a free lunch. An experiment, at least for our purposes, comes with a catch or two. Our understanding of how information circulates in a political campaign—through conversation, media exposure, and campaign outreach—undergirds our theory of political role models. We are less confident that the attitudes and behaviors we examine are subject to short-term manipulation with a one-shot exposure to a single news story about women candidates. Moreover, survey experiments do not fully replicate the real-world phenomenon—women running for political office—that we are trying to understand. In an actual political campaign, adolescents are exposed to women candidates through news stories, campaign ads, lawn signs, and conversations with parents, friends, and teachers—all of the ways that information flows through a community during campaign season. That exposure is repeated across a significant period of time. Conditions mimicking the real word, though, are impossible to recreate in a survey. Our experiment randomly assigns teenagers to read a news story, a far cry from the experience of living through an election campaign. Our teenage respondents then fill out a survey, which includes questions about women as leaders, democracy, and political engagement. One news story, no matter how well crafted, may well not be sufficient to change adolescents' views on these topics. In sum, we have reason to suspect that our experiment will produce no results—not because the role model effect is not real, but because the impact of women as role models requires more than a single dose of exposure to women running for office. Even if we do find effects, we might also question whether attitude change that results from the controlled (and brief) setting of an experiment will persist beyond the context of the survey.

The bottom line is that neither observational nor experimental data are the proverbial silver bullet. Rather, each has complementary strengths and weaknesses. We use an experimental approach to address a shortcoming in the real world—not enough Republican women candidates. Although some of our adolescents were exposed to Republican women candidates during the 2020 campaign, their numbers were sufficiently small to raise questions about our confidence in those results. In highlighting Republican women, we have another angle for gauging the importance of novelty for role model effects. Just as environmental scientists do not limit themselves to a single source of information for evidence of climate change but instead look for common patterns across myriad indicators, so too do we triangulate with multiple sources of data.

The Experiment

The design of our experiment was straightforward. We assigned each of our teen respondents to read one of various versions of a news story about women candidates in the 2020 elections. By comparing their attitudes upon reading versions of the story with different partisan frames about women candidates in 2020, we can see how exposure to one frame versus another affects attitudes toward beliefs about women leaders, democratic attitudes, and political engagement. Randomly assigning people to receive a given story ensures that any effects we observe are causal and not correlational. Respondents did not choose whether to receive a story, thus eliminating the problem of self-selection (some people are more interested in reading about women candidates) and omitted variable bias (something else explains why exposure to women candidates leads to greater engagement). Furthermore, our experiment was with a representative sample of American adolescents, thus giving us confidence that we can generalize our results to the population as a whole.

Our respondents (eight hundred adolescents) were randomly selected to receive one of three variations of a news story about women running in 2020, or—in the control group—no story at all. Since the control group was not exposed to a story about women candidates, their attitudes reflect those held by people "in the wild." After reading the story, our respondents then answered the same series of questions we used in previous chapters to measure attitudes toward women, democracy, and political activity. In presenting our results, we always compare against the control group, thus answering the question of how exposure to news coverage of women candidates does or does not change attitudes. For more details on the survey experiment, see the online appendix.

In brief, the three versions of the story are:

1. Republican Story: The story emphasized the number of Republican

women running for office across the country, and the candidates quoted in the story are both Republicans. With this treatment, we were able to test what happens in an alternate universe where emphasis is placed on Republican women. We stress, however, that everything included in each of the stories is factual. There really was a wave of Republican women running in 2020. There were not as many Republicans in 2020 as there were Democrats in 2018 or 2020, but 2020 was still a record year for the GOP (Dittmar 2020; Dittmar and Hill 2020).
2. Democratic Story: The text was identical to (1), except that the story emphasized the number of Democratic women who ran in 2020. The two candidates quoted in the story were identified as Democrats. Recall that even though Democratic women in 2020 did not receive as much attention as in 2018, it is still accurate to say that there were a large number of Democratic women running. Our story about 2020 is similar to the many stories about women in 2018.
3. Bipartisan Story: The story again described a surge of women candidates but characterized them as both Republicans and Democrats. The party affiliation of the two candidates quoted in the story was not mentioned. In the not-so-distant past, this type of story was common, as emphasis was placed on gender over party. Recall from chapter 5 that in 1992, the original Year of the Woman, media coverage emphasized the number of women, with relatively little mention of the fact that they were predominantly Democrats.

To keep the focus solely on the effect of women qua women, and to ensure that the story was realistic for both parties, the story was devoid of any policy content but instead highlighted the historic nature of the number of women running. The story also spoke of these women candidates as bringing "new voices to politics," with one candidate quoted as saying that she would bring a "fresh perspective to Washington." Likewise, to ensure plausibility for both parties, the story spoke generally of women running for offices at all levels of government. In particular, it did not focus on the presidency, since there were no Republican women in the presidential race in 2020.

As visual reinforcement, the story included three photos of fictional women candidates with the caption: "Three <u>candidates/Democratic candidates/Republican candidates</u> running for seats in Congress, joining a national surge of women candidates across the country." Also, both a headline and pull-out box underscored the theme of a "surge" in women candidates in 2020. The headline of the story was "A Big Year for <u>Both Democratic and Republican Women/Democratic Women/Republican Women</u> in the 2020 Elections." The pull-out box contained a quote from a (fictional) woman candidate: "Women like me will get to work and make a difference for our communities and the rest of the nation," with the candidate identified as "Charlene Washington, newly-elected Democratic/Republican member of Congress." The text of the story included still more quotes, one from a winning woman candidate for the House of Representatives ("Amy Johnson," from Michigan) and another from a scholar ("Maria Gonzalez") commenting on the historic number of women running for office in recent years.[4]

BELIEFS ABOUT WOMEN LEADERS

We start with attitudes about women leaders. Note that we gauged beliefs about women's leadership traits in precisely the same way as in the observational data. Respondents were asked whether men or women (randomized so that half of the time it was phrased "women or men") are better at each aspect of leadership. Their answers were arrayed on a scale of 0 to 10, with 5 representing no difference between women and men. As a reminder, the traits in question were divided into those that are stereotypically feminine—(working out compromises, being honest and ethical) and those that are stereotypically masculine (being a strong leader, working well under pressure). We also asked our respondents whether the country would be better, the same, or worse with more women in political office, again on a scale of 0 to 10. In the observational data (chapter 3), we found the most change among Republican teens, which we suspect is because they have the most room to move. That is, compared to Democrats—especially Democratic girls—Republican-identifying adolescents in the real world are less likely to see women as possessing the traits to be effective in elected office and more likely to change their attitudes when exposed to women candidates.

As we present our results, it is important to keep in mind where we do and do not find results, because the null findings are as informative as where there is an effect. Just as a piece of music is defined as much by silence as sound, so too is social science informed as much by what is not found as what is. In the case of political role models, there is mostly silence when Democratic women run but more sound when Republican women do.

Specifically, we find that in the alternate universe where emphasis is placed on Republican women candidates, boys of both parties are more likely to see women as having stereotypically feminine leadership traits. Similarly, when exposed to the Republican story, Democratic boys also see women as possessing attributes typically thought to be masculine, while Republican boys are more likely to believe the country would be better off with more women in elected office. Compared to the control group (no story), we do not observe role model effects when teens are exposed to the story about a historic number of Democratic women, or Democratic and Republican women.

In our experiment, then, we find the most movement in the perception of women as political leaders when exposed to the more novel Republican women candidates and—once again—among those with the most room to move, specifically boys. In our observational data, we found that Republican boys actually responded more to Democratic women candidates, not Republican; but as we indicated there, this may be attributable to the small number of Republican boys exposed to Republican women candidates in our data. Or perhaps Democratic women emphasize their status as barrier-breaking women more than do Republican candidates; in the survey experiment, we do the work of drawing Republican boys' attention to Republican women's historic status.[5]

We display these results in figure 7.1, the format of which is repeated throughout the chapter. These graphs are similar enough to those in previous chapters that they should look familiar, but, as an experiment, have a few differences from the observational results. In each case, we display the average score for respondents who were in the control group and thus did not read one of the news stories. This bar shows us the attitudes of

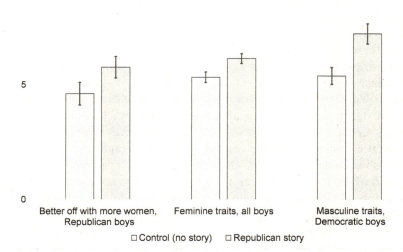

Figure 7.1. Republican women candidates lead boys to see women as political leaders

respondents without any exposure to women candidates. The bar to its right displays the average attitude in question for those respondents who read one of the stories about a wave of women running for office. The difference between the height of the bars is the effect of our experimental treatment. In order to gauge statistical significance, we again display confidence intervals ("margin of error").[6]

In sum, the experiment suggests that novel Republican women candidates can change attitudes toward women as leaders. We find effects most consistently among those whose attitudes have the most room to move—boys.

DEMOCRATIC ATTITUDES

In our observational data, we found that when girls see women run for office, their attitudes toward democracy become more positive; all girls, regardless of party, place a higher value on democracy in communities with women candidates. At the same time, the observational evidence indicates that some young people develop a more negative perspective on the responsiveness of the American democratic system when women run, specifically women of the other party, suggesting that party and gender interact in important ways.

What happens to democratic attitudes in the alternate universe of the experiment, where Republican women are highlighted as barrier breakers? To gauge our respondents' feelings about democracy, we asked two distinct questions that parallel those asked in the observational survey. The first is whether the political system helps people with their genuine needs (democratic responsiveness); the second is whether democracy is the best way to run the country (democratic support).[7] Respondents placed their opinion on a 0–10 sliding scale between "yes" and "no." Because these two questions do not correlate very strongly, we analyze them separately.

We saw in chapter 4 that Democrats' evaluation of democratic responsiveness declined substantially after Hillary Clinton's loss and Donald Trump's election in 2016. Two years later a historically high number of Democratic women candidates ran for office, and Democratic girls' (but not boys') attitudes rebounded. Our experiment lets us consider a parallel world where it is Republicans, not Democrats, who are running in historic numbers. Once again, Republican women candidates have a distinct impact. Compared to the control (no story), we observe a positive effect for every story about women candidates running, regardless of whether it is the bipartisan, Republican, or Democratic version. Yet, while all of the coefficients are positive and of comparable magnitude, not every ef-

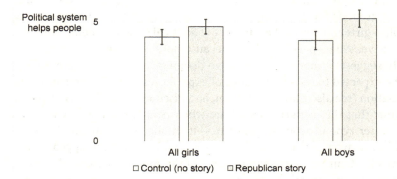

Figure 7.2. Republican women candidates lead boys and girls to see the political system as responsive

fect clears the conventional threshold for statistical significance. Rather, this effect is most powerful for the respondents who were exposed to an alternate reality in which attention is drawn to barrier-breaking Republican women candidates, rather than the more typical story about Democratic women candidates. Moreover, this effect is not limited to one group or the other, but characterizes both girls and boys in our survey. Figure 7.2 displays these results, showing that both boys and girls (regardless of party) come to see the political system as more responsive specifically when Republican women run. Although the difference between the effect on girls and boys is not statistically significant, it is nonetheless consistent with earlier research showing that men weight the presence of women more heavily in evaluating the legitimacy of decision-making processes (Clayton, O'Brien, and Piscopo 2019).

We find less evidence that women candidates, even when Republican women are highlighted, lead to greater support for democracy as a form of governance. In fact, when we look at the effects for all girls and all boys—that is, without differentiating by partisan identity—we see no effects whatsoever. Across the gender-partisan groups, however, there are a few effects, but they do not cohere. For example, Democratic boys are more supportive of democracy when either Democratic or Republican women run. Surprisingly, Democratic girls react to Republican women, but not when they are exposed to women candidates of their own party. Although it is tempting to construct an explanation for these scattershot results, we are more inclined to say that they underscore that the universe—even a controlled, alternate one—is messy. The findings for democratic support seem more noise than signal.

In sum, based on both the observational and experimental results, we see grounds for concluding that women candidates can move young people—girls and boys alike—to see the political system as democratically responsive. We suspect that this is because the sight of women candidates subtly suggests a more representative democracy, where those in power can be expected to reflect the range of experiences and perspectives in the population (see also Clayton, O'Brien, and Piscopo 2019). Our experiment suggests that this is particularly true when people see not just women, but a rarer type of woman candidate—Republicans. When we highlight Republican women candidates, impressionable teenagers appear more optimistic about the representativeness of the American political system.

POLITICAL ENGAGEMENT

Last, we turn to political engagement. Recall that in chapter 5 we saw evidence, both over time and across space, that when women run for office they spur greater political engagement among girls and boys, but for different reasons. Girls, particularly Democratic girls, envision themselves as politically active, becoming more likely to vote and to express an interest in running for office. Our observational findings focus on the impact of Democratic women—Ferraro in 1984, the 1992 and 2018 Years of the Woman, and the Clinton campaigns of 2008 and 2016. In our 2020 data, 36 percent of teens lived in a district with a viable Democratic woman candidate, compared to just 17 percent of our teens exposed to a Republican woman candidate.

What happens when teens are exposed to history-making Republican women candidates? As in the observational data, we again measure young people's intention to participate in politics. Thus, we can interpret a positive effect as meaning that our respondents are more likely to envision themselves as being politically engaged. Our teen respondents saw a note on the screen that read "Even if you've never thought about it, could you see yourself doing any of the following things in the future?" Then, they were instructed to "please rate how likely you are to do any of the following things in the future using a scale of 0 to 10, where 0 is not likely at all and 10 is very likely." The list included:

Vote in a public election
Work in a political campaign
Participate in a lawful demonstration
Write to public officials
Run for political office

We once again find a unique effect for our alternate universe, the Republican women candidates story. Specifically, *Republican* girls become more likely to vote and to engage in other political activity when they see Republican women candidates (see fig. 7.3). We do not find a similar effect, on Republican girls or any other group, when they are exposed to our Democratic or bipartisan stories, suggesting that the role model effect is particularly strong for novel Republican women. That we observe these effects for Republican girls demonstrates the value of creating an alternate universe in which emphasis is placed on a historic wave of Republican women candidates. In the observational data where Democratic women dominate, Democratic girls intended to be more active. When attention is drawn to Republican women in our experiment, Republican girls are inspired to be more politically engaged.

We have further validation that the Republican girls are indeed inspired, as they also become more internally efficacious when Republican women run for office. As in the observational data, we asked respondents whether they feel that they can make a difference in their community. When Republican women run, Republican girls become more likely to see themselves as change makers.

Why aren't Democratic girls inspired and engaged in the same way by women of their own party? We suspect the answer lies in the fact that, for our teen respondents, reading about Democratic women running for office is nothing new. Recall as well that in our experiment the dose of exposure to women candidates is very small: one print news story. As we have noted, the dosage is so low that we might not expect to see any effects whatsoever. The fact that we do see an effect for Republican women candidates underscores that teenagers, and probably Americans in general, are more likely to assume that women running for office are Democrats. When Republican women run, they seem novel, and are thus surprising or attention-grabbing enough to induce a change in anticipated political engagement. Democratic women are ordinary and so are less likely to trigger an effect. Once again, we see evidence suggesting that when women candidates are perceived as unusual, they lead to greater political engagement.

Why is there no similar effect for Republican women candidates in the real world? Our suspicion is that this might reflect the fact that there is

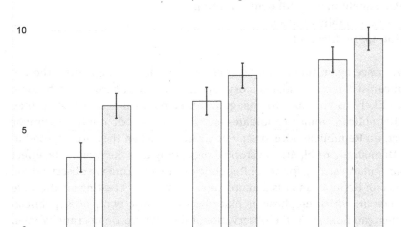

Figure 7.3. Republican girls become more politically engaged when they see Republican women run

generally less public attention drawn to the gender of Republican women. Research indicates that Republican women are less likely to emphasize femininity and gender than Democratic women candidates (Bauer and Santia 2021; McDonald, Porter, and Treul 2020; Schneider 2014). Indeed, recent Republican women candidates often express concern about being associated with "identity politics."[8] The former Republican presidential candidate Nikki Haley, for example, is quick to distance herself from identity politics: "I don't believe in that. And I don't believe in glass ceilings, either."[9]

Or consider the 2022 elections, which featured a record number of women candidates for governor. One of these was Republican Sarah Huckabee Sanders, who was elected the first woman to serve as governor of Arkansas. She took note of her gender in her acceptance speech: "I know it will be the honor of a lifetime to serve as Arkansas's 47th governor and the first female governor the state of Arkansas has had."[10] Maura Healey was another. The newly elected Democratic governor of Massachusetts is both the first woman elected as governor of Massachusetts and the first openly lesbian state chief executive, beating Oregon's Tina Kotek by one day.[11] In addition, Healey's lieutenant governor, Kim Driscoll, is a woman, making Massachusetts the first state to elect women to the top two executive positions. Like Sanders, Healey celebrated the historic nature of her victory in her acceptance speech: "Tonight, I want to say something to every little girl and every LGBTQ person out there. I hope tonight shows you that you can be whatever, whoever, you want to be."[12]

Both candidates acknowledged the historic nature of their election as women. Healey, a Democrat, spoke explicitly of being a role model—echoing language from many other Democrats we have previously cited—while Sanders simply noted that she was the first *female* to serve as governor of Arkansas. Sanders largely left the issue at that, while Healey followed up her speech with multiple tweets emphasizing that she is a role model for young girls, consistent with our expectation that Democratic women are more likely to emphasize their status as barrier breakers and role models.

Of course, we are speaking in generalities; there are certainly examples of Republican women candidates who do emphasize their gender and Democratic women who do not, and of press coverage that describes Republican women as firsts. Moreover, our point is not that the role model effect requires women candidates to speak of themselves as role models, but rather than in the real world, unlike in our experiment, Republican women candidates may be less likely to be recognized for their novelty. When we do draw attention to Republican women as historic firsts, we see an effect.

Although our focus has been on the impact of Republican women candidates, in the experiment, we do see evidence that boys, or at least some of them, become *less* likely to see themselves as politically engaged when women run for office (see fig. 7.4). We do not observe this for all boys or for all versions of the news story (or specifically for the Republican-women story), but there is enough of a pattern to cause us to take notice. For example, boys in general become less likely to vote when they see a story about women in both parties. For the other varieties of political engagement, however, the effects are only among Democratic boys. In most cases, these effects are only marginally significant (generally $p < .10$), but they are worth noting nonetheless.[13]

Why do we see that women candidates lead to disengagement among boys, particularly Democratic boys? Once again, we do not have a conclusive explanation, especially because we do not consistently see this disengagement in the real world (however, recall that we did see less political engagement among boys when women of color run for office). Similar patterns have also been observed in comparative contexts, where men become less interested in politics when exposed to women politicians (Kittilson and Schwindt-Bayer 2012). We also find a hint of an explanation when we again examine what happens to political efficacy in the presence of women candidates. Recall that in the observational data, we found that although Republican boys became more politically engaged when women run, they

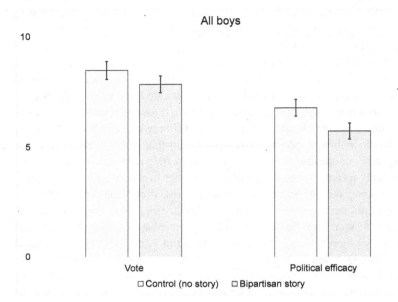

Figure 7.4. Boys become less politically engaged and efficacious when women run

do not become more personally efficacious—measured as making a difference in their community—leading us to infer that the mechanism for their greater engagement is not that they are empowered by women as role models. What happens to boys' efficacy in our controlled experiment? In contrast to the real world, we find an effect only among Democratic boys, and it is in a negative direction. In other words, when Democratic boys are exposed to women candidates in general, they become less likely to see themselves as capable of making a difference in their community.

It is perhaps understandable that boys feel politically disempowered by the presence of women candidates. As they see women run, they may subconsciously question whether politics is for them—the mirror image of the role model effect we observe among girls. Although this one experiment is not enough to conclude that this is a systemic result of women running for office, it calls for more research. Whether confirmed in other studies or not, the fact that we observe disengagement among some boys is yet another reminder that women candidates can potentially have contradictory effects on different groups in the population. Not everyone is inspired by more women in politics.

In terms of running for office—that is, political ambition—we again find evidence of a role model effect for teenage girls; but we cannot conclude that our alternate universe of Republican women creates unique effects. When we look at all girls—which includes Democrats, Republicans, and independents—the effect of exposure to either the Republican or the Democratic story is relatively large and significant, as figure 7.5 shows. The impact appears larger for Democratic women candidates, but the effects of the two treatments cannot be statistically distinguished from each other. Democratic and Republican girls react similarly when they see co-partisan women run for office. For both, the effect size is positive and of comparable size, although in both cases the significance level falls a little short of the standard threshold for significance.[14] Both Democratic and Republican women candidates appear to have the capacity to inspire political ambition among Democratic and Republican girls alike.

Our experiment suggests that Republican women candidates—as Republicans and as novel women candidates—do have a unique effect. Our alternate-universe story about the historic number of Republican women running for office leads boys to become more likely to assign leadership traits to women, girls and boys to become more optimistic about democratic responsiveness, and Republican girls to become more politically engaged. However, remembering that the silence matters as much as the sound, it is also important that when presented with a story that confirms expectations (Democratic women or bipartisan women who are likely assumed to be Democrats), we observe less impact on adolescents' views or actions.[15]

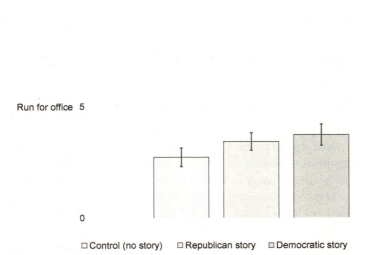

Figure 7.5. Greater political ambition for both Republican and Democratic girls when they see women run

What If More Republican Women Ran?

What have we learned from this strange new world where attention is drawn to Republican (rather than Democratic) women candidates? Table 7.2 demonstrates that, with the few exceptions we have noted above, it is the alternate universe of Republican women candidates that triggers changed attitudes and behaviors among adolescents: Boys become more positive about women as leaders, everyone becomes more positive about democratic responsiveness, and Republican girls in particular become more interested in political engagement, including running for office. The "normal" world of a wave of Democratic women candidates seems to set off a collective yawn among our adolescents: "More of this?" As a result, we see few effects for our story about Democratic women candidates or bipartisan women candidates, who are largely assumed to be Democrats.

How do we reconcile our experimental findings with our observational results showing that women candidates, both Democrats and Republicans, affect these same attitudes and behaviors? One likely explanation is the difference between the experimental treatment and the real world of a woman running for office in your own community. A campaign means ongoing exposure to women who are challenging stereotypes, signaling inclusion, and modeling political engagement. Viability likely means a robust campaign, and novelty means a woman candidate is unusual and pathbreaking. All of these factors contribute to the role model effects we uncovered in earlier chapters.

In the experiment, on the other hand, respondents were exposed to a brief newspaper story that highlighted the historic number of women candidates. For Democrats (and candidates assumed to be Democrats), this was a familiar story by 2020, and that story alone was rarely sufficient to change attitudes or behaviors. The Republican story, on the other hand, was novel, in the sense that a surge in Republican women candidates is in fact out of the ordinary. The novelty spurred role model effects. For example, we are intrigued by the fact that in the real world, it was only girls (both Republican and Democratic) who became more optimistic about democratic responsiveness when women ran. When the experiment highlights Republican women candidates, Republican and Democratic boys join their partisan sisters in their greater optimism. It appears that the possibility of more Republican women in office is sufficiently counterstereotypical to convince girls and boys alike that the system is responsive to a range of interests.

This is not only a story about novelty, however. Party matters. We see this most clearly when it comes to political engagement, running for office, and efficacy. In the real world, where most women candidates are

A World with More Republican Candidates

Table 7.2. The takeaway: The impact of a wave of Republican women candidates

	Beliefs about women leaders	Democratic responsiveness	Democratic support	Vote	Engagement	Efficacy	Run for office
Republican boys	↑	↑					
Republican girls		↑		↑	↑	↑	↑
Democratic boys	↑	↑					
Democratic girls		↑					↑

Note: An upward arrow indicates a positive and statistically significant relationship between exposure to the story about an historic wave of Republican women candidates and the attitude in question.

Democrats, it was Democratic girls who become more engaged, ambitious, and efficacious when exposed to role models. (Recall that Republican boys became more engaged, but not more efficacious, leading us to conclude this is likely a backlash effect.) But in an experimental treatment about Republican women running for office, it was Republican girls who become more engaged and efficacious. Like Democratic girls in the real world, Republican girls in the experiment are inspired to be more politically active when they see women candidates who share their partisanship, and presumably their values and positions as well. The inference is that more Republican women candidates could help close the political participation gap between Democratic and Republican adolescent girls that we observed in chapter 5.

We have presented considerable evidence of the impact of women politicians on the attitudes and behaviors of young people. Our theory of political role models expects younger people's views and actions to be more malleable than those of older folks, but very little previous research has examined that claim directly. In our next-to-last chapter we turn our attention to adults' attitudes and behavior. Are adults less affected by the presence of women political role models? And do the effects we have seen among adolescents shape attitudes and behaviors when those adolescents grow up? Chapter 8 answers both of these questions, demonstrating both that women candidates have more impact on the young than their elders and that the role model effect extends into adulthood.

8 * *Impressionable Years and Enduring Effects*

It makes me smile knowing that, somewhere out there, there are girls who look at me and think that I am a role model and look up to me.
　　　　　　　　　　Nineteen-year-old Cassandra Levesque, member of the
　　　　　　　　　　　　New Hampshire House of Representatives, 2022[1]

As a teenager in 1984, one of your authors (Wolbrecht) vividly remembers her father coming home one evening and excitedly telling her that he had shaken hands with Geraldine Ferraro—the first woman nominated for vice president—at a rally in Wolbrecht's hometown of Portland, Oregon. Political discussion was common in her household, but this memory stands out. Without a causal identification strategy, we cannot definitively prove that this is what led Wolbrecht to be a politically engaged adult, let alone pursue a career as a political scientist, but we cannot rule it out either. Wolbrecht's experience was no doubt repeated across the country, as Ferraro's candidacy sparked many similar conversations between parents and their children, especially daughters, throughout the 1984 campaign. Although most young people are unlikely to grow up to be political science professors, it is plausible to think that trailblazing candidates such as Ferraro—and Harris, Clinton, Palin, and scores of other women running in their local communities—can serve as political role models for young girls.

Wolbrecht's story highlights three fundamental premises that underpin what we referred to in chapter 2 as the folk theory of role models, the widely held expectation that women serve as political role models. First, youth are *impressionable*: Most role model rhetoric highlights how women politicians will affect, even inspire, young people in particular. We see this expectation in the ways in which women politicians often draw attention to young people in their speeches, events, and tweets. Second, often left unsaid but implied nonetheless, is the assumption that women politicians will have far less effect, and perhaps none at all, on the attitudes and behavior of adults. Adults have developed political attitudes and practices from long exposure and experience, and change in either is unlikely. In other words, adults are *immovable*. Third, our suggestion in the Ferraro anecdote recounted above that this is what spurred Wolbrecht's lifelong interest in politics points to the expectation that role models' impact is not fleeting but will affect young people over the course of their lives—that is, that role model effects are *enduring*. This is, of course, the great hope for role models—that young people grow into adults who view women as fit for politics, have faith in democracy, and engage in politics in productive and democracy-sustaining ways.

There is considerable evidence that young people's political attitudes are malleable. From the earliest days of the study of political behavior, party identification in particular has been shown to be a product of childhood socialization (Campbell et al. 1960; Jennings and Niemi 1981). The same is true for attitudes about democracy (Almond and Verba 1963; Easton and Dennis 1969; Hess and Torney 2005), civic participation (Campbell 2006; Jennings, Stoker, and Bowers 2009; Plutzer 2002), political knowledge (Wolak and McDevitt 2011), and—importantly—attitudes about politics and gender (Bos et al. 2022; Diekman and Schneider 2010; Oxley et al. 2020; Pacheco and Kreitzer 2016; Schneider and Bos 2019). To this point, we have presented a great deal of evidence that adolescents' attitudes are pliable, and that their attitudes can be shaped by exposure to women politicians, consistent with the impressionable youth hypothesis. This chapter takes up the other two claims: immovable adults and enduring effects.

While rarely stated explicitly, the focus on role models for youth assumes that older people are not as likely to change their attitudes or behavior, what we call the *immovable adults* hypothesis. The idea that young people are uniquely movable is a foundational assumption in socialization research but has been subjected to little empirical scrutiny. Most studies of socialization focus only on adolescents, without considering the extent to which the attitudes of adults may or may not be shaped by the same environment.

Here we test that assumption and examine whether the role model effects we have observed for adolescents are also found among adults. We hypothesize that there will generally be fewer and less consistent effects on adults because their attitudes and behaviors are more firmly established. Adults certainly change their attitudes and behaviors from time to time in response to their environment, but exposure to one or two women candidates might not be sufficient to shift well-established views and practices. Recall from chapter 2 that the bulk of previous role model research examined adults and often reported no, weak, or incoherent effects. We suggest that one reason is that most research has focused on a population—adults—where we are least likely to see any effects. We shall see whether that is actually the case.

Why would we expect adults to be less likely to change their attitudes than adolescents? One reason is simply that the attitudes we study are potentially of long standing, such as opinions on gender equality, confidence in democracy, and an inclination toward political participation. If adults' attitudes are "sticky," then exposure to a woman politician, even a first such as Ferraro, is unlikely to cause them to change their views. Inertia keeps them from moving. Put another way, the first piece of information one receives will have a big impact on one's views. This is all you know, so the effect is nearly determinative. In comparison, the hundredth or thousandth piece of information—a drop in a sea of experience—is less likely to shift attitudes or behaviors. This does not mean that women politicians never have an effect—past studies have found some evidence for women as role models—but that we should expect such an impact in a small number of situations.

We should not expect that all adult attitudes are equally resistant to influence. Some, such as attitudes toward gender roles, might be considered foundational to someone's worldview and grounded in other key values, like religion and adherence to tradition, and thus more impervious to change (as anyone who has attended Thanksgiving dinner with their cranky uncle can attest). Other attitudes seem more likely to be shaped by one's immediate context, including whether to engage in political activity in a particular year or around a specific election.

At the heart of any claim about the importance of role models is the assumption that their effects endure into adulthood. Why does Elizabeth Warren make pinkie promises with young girls instead of their moms? So that those girls grow up to be politically active women. Their mothers, it is assumed, have long since established their political attitudes and behaviors; it is perhaps too late to set them on a path to the presidency. Inertia cuts two ways. It means that, absent any other force, an object continues to move in the same direction. For adults, this means that their attitudes are hard to change. It also means that the direction set in one's youth puts someone on a trajectory. If a role model inspires them to be politically engaged while young, in the absence of a countervailing force we should expect that level of engagement to endure into adulthood. We call this the *enduring effects* hypothesis.

Previous research on other political behaviors and attitudes (see above) offers support for the general inertia of adolescence. However, to our knowledge, no previous research has demonstrated whether women role models during adolescence have a long-term influence as people age into adulthood. As we will explain further below, testing the enduring effects hypothesis requires data that meet some very specific criteria. Until now, no one has assembled that data. We have, and thus are able to test the enduring effects hypothesis—the linchpin of the notion of women as role models.

Immovable Adults

We have seen in earlier chapters that women role models have the capacity to shape views about women leaders, beliefs about democratic responsiveness, and intentions for political engagement among impressionable youth. If adults are relatively immovable, we should find that in a direct comparison adults are less likely to be affected by women politicians than are adolescents. While that may sound simple enough, the catch is the difficulty in making a comparison that is truly head-to-head. Most data from adults do not have an analogue with those from youth, and vice versa.

We solve this problem by placing the very same questions we asked of teenagers during the 2020 election season on a survey of adults, conducted during the same window of time. Specifically, we added our questions to a module of the Cooperative Election Study (CES), described in table 8.1. The CES has the advantage of being a nationally representative survey, conducted in the fall of the election year, the same time that the Family Matters 2 study was fielded. Its disadvantage is that, with one partial exception, our questions were asked only at one point in time, a post-election survey. Remember that one virtue of Family Matters 2 is that we surveyed the same adolescents before and after the election, allowing us to observe any changes in attitudes and behaviors as a result of exposure to the campaign. We do not have a measure of most of the adult attitudes we examine from *before* the election, which means that we cannot be certain whether the attitudes we observe *after* the election are due to "pre-existing conditions" or exposure to women candidates (with one exception, described below). Once again, we include numerous control variables to isolate the effect of exposure to women, but with cross-sectional data one can never be sure that all threats to causality have been accounted for. For all attitudinal questions, we have asked exactly the same questions in exactly the same way, that is, on a scale of 0 to 10, which means that we can make a direct comparison of effect size on adolescents versus adults.

Our statistical analysis of the CES is similar to that of previous chapters, so we will keep our description short. Those interested in learning more can consult chapter 3 for a general description of the contextual variables we use.[2] In brief, we account for both individual-level and contextual-level variables that may influence both the attitudes we examine and the

Table 8.1. 2020 Cooperative Election Study (Notre Dame module)

Population	National sample of U.S. adult population
Mode	Online
Description	2-wave longitudinal survey
Sample size	Wave 1: 1000 Wave 2: 864
Dates	Wave 1: September–November 2020 Wave 2: November–December 2020
Details	Data weighted to match national population parameters for age, gender, education, and race/ethnicity (based on the American Community Survey)
Firm	YouGov

likelihood of a woman running in a respondent's congressional district. The key variable we focus on is the presence of women candidates for House, Senate, or governor in the 2020 general election. As always, we focus on viable women candidates and, as with many of our previous analyses, also limit the models to novel women: a woman running to replace a man. Given that adult attitudes are hard to move, we are giving women role models their best shot at shifting adult opinion, specifically when women candidates are most salient and when their status as barrier breakers (women running for a job held by a man) is most likely to be highlighted. We are in a sense stacking the deck against our immovable adults hypothesis by focusing on those cases where an adult role model effect is most likely to occur.

BELIEFS ABOUT WOMEN AS LEADERS

As we have noted, the adult data have the disadvantage that they do not include a measure of attitudes from before the election. There is, however, a notable exception. The common content of the CES—questions asked of every respondent—included two of the sexism questions we asked our adolescents in the pre-election survey. We then asked those same questions of the subset of respondents who received our module after the election, meaning that—like the adolescents in the Family Matters 2 study—we can control for their pre-election attitudes and thus have more confidence that we are capturing the impact of exposure to women candidates.[3] In other words, it is truly an apples-to-apples comparison with our adolescent analysis. Because the panel data make this is our most stringent test, we start with the impact of women role models on sexism, measured by agreement with two hostile sexism statements (Glick and Fiske 1996):

Women seek to gain power by getting control over men
Women are too easily offended

Recall that among teenagers, we found that women role models lead Republicans, both girls and boys, to become less sexist. Among adults, however, we find no such effects—not for Republicans or Democrats, men or women. We consider this null effect to be strong evidence in support of the immovable adults hypothesis. Although women candidates change (Republican) adolescents' views about sexism, our most compelling data show no comparable effect on adults. Likewise, women role models do not move adults' views of women's leadership traits, either masculine or feminine, nor for whether they think the country would be better off with more women in office.[4]

DEMOCRATIC ATTITUDES

If attitudes about sexism or women leaders do not move in response to women role models, what about attitudes toward democracy? Our expectations are not clear. On the one hand, perceptions of democracy are often a product of childhood socialization, so perhaps they are not likely to move. On the other hand, we live in a time when liberal democracy is under threat, and many people in democratic nations—the United States included—are questioning democratic norms and democracy as a political system (Levitsky and Ziblatt 2018). Given that we are in a state of democratic flux, it could be that adults' attitudes about democracy are malleable, just as we saw among adolescents. We found in chapter 4 that among teens it is girls who become more positive toward democracy when women run—sometimes Democrats, sometimes Republicans, but only girls.

Among adults, we once again have a question asking respondents to evaluate our democratic system (whether the political system meets people's genuine needs) and a set of questions regarding preference for democracy as a political system. Here we do find one effect: When Democratic women candidates run, Democratic women in the general public become more likely to say that the political system meets people's genuine needs. Signal or noise? Difficult to say, but it is noteworthy that Democratic girls also become more positive about the responsiveness of the political system when women run. Recall, however, that we also found the same for Republican girls, whereas among Republican women there is no comparable effect.

The general conclusion for democratic attitudes is again supportive of the immovable adults hypothesis: With one exception, adults' attitudes about democracy do not budge when they exposed to women candidates.

POLITICAL ENGAGEMENT

Unlike attitudes about women or confidence in democracy, we have more reason to think that adults' political engagement may be affected by the presence of novel women candidates. Although voting is a habit developed in young adulthood (Plutzer 2002), the degree to which any person engages in political activity over their lifetime varies with life stage, the political and social context, and other individual factors. Specific candidates and campaigns may mobilize people to vote, participate in a campaign, protest, or contact government officials. Yet this general expectation that some candidates in some places at some times can mobilize some voters leaves many questions. We saw in chapter 5 that, among adolescents, women candidates of both parties lead to greater engagement, manifested as anticipated political activity in adulthood, among both Democratic girls and Republican boys—but for different reasons. For Democratic girls, it was inspiration; for Republican boys, opposition.

What about adults' political engagement? Recall that in chapter 5 we found that it was the perception of women running, not their presence, that drives the anticipated political participation of adolescents. When we look for the impact of perceived women candidates among adults, we find only one statistically significant result ($p = .05$): Democratic women become more likely to vote when they perceive women candidates.[5] Again we are faced with the question of whether this is a coincidence or a meaningful finding. Although in the absence of further data we cannot say for sure, we do note that as with the result for confidence in the responsiveness of the political system, it is striking that we see a parallel between adults and adolescents—an effect for Democratic women and girls. Keep in mind, however, that neither Democratic women nor girls become more likely to participate in other forms of political activity when they perceive women running.[6] Importantly, we do not see Republican men reacting the way Republican boys do when women run—becoming more engaged because women candidates spark backlash.[7]

Once more, we see that even for political engagement—the outcome most likely to be affected by the political context—the bulk of the evidence favors the immovable adults hypothesis. In the one case where we do see that the perception of women candidates has an effect on political engagement (voting), it is among the same gender and party group, Democratic women, where we find a comparable effect among adolescents.

CHAPTER 8

WHAT ABOUT PARENTS?

We have a second way of evaluating the immovable adults hypothesis. Recall that the Family Matters 2 study includes data collected from both adolescents—our focus—and one parent. In previous chapters we have included the parents' data as control variables to account for influences in the home. However, we can also use these data to see whether parents are reacting in the same way as their children to women candidates. On the one hand, these data are a strict test of adults versus adolescents, as these parents are located in precisely the same communities as the teenaged respondents and are thus subject to the same contextual influences, including the local political environment. Furthermore, the parents were also interviewed twice, once before and once following the 2020 election, enabling the same over-time analysis we have employed for the teenagers. On the other hand, unlike the CES data discussed above, the adults in the Family Matters 2 study are not a representative sample of the whole US population, but rather a sample of parents who have teenage children. Thus, any conclusions drawn from these data cannot be generalized to the adult population as a whole.[8]

Like the CES, results from the parents in the FM2 households support the immovable adults hypothesis. Arguably, they are even more supportive. Across all of the outcomes—gender attitudes, democratic attitudes, political engagement—there is only one significant effect. Democratic men become more likely to endorse democracy[9] when they live in a community where women run. This is in contrast to Democratic boys, whose views about democracy do not budge in the presence of women candidates. Among adolescents it is girls, both Democrats and Republicans, whose views about democracy change when women run.[10] With just one observed effect, there is not much evidence for women as political role models among parents.

As shown in the takeaway for this chapter (table 8.2), overall we find considerable support for the hypothesis that adults' attitudes are relatively immovable. Women candidates are more likely to affect the attitudes and behavior of youth than that of adults, whether it is attitudes about whether women are suited to be political leaders, confidence in democracy, or being politically engaged. As is the case in the role model literature writ large, there are a few effects for adults, some of which are explainable and some of which are puzzling, all of which should be subject to further research. But these effects pale in comparison to the theoretical coherence of role models' impacts on adolescents.

We have thus seen evidence for the first two hypotheses implied by the folk theory of political role models. The impressionable youth hypothesis

Table 8.2. The takeaway: Comparing adults and adolescents

Few effects for adults (summary of results from this chapter)

	Nonsexism	Women's feminine leadership traits	Women's masculine leadership traits	Better off with more women in office	Belief in democracy	Political system helps people	Voting	Participation index
Republican men								
Republican women								
Democratic men						←		
Democratic women							←	

Even fewer effects for parents of the Family Matters 2 teens (summary of results from this chapter)

	Nonsexism	Women's feminine leadership traits	Women's masculine leadership traits	Better off with more women in office	Belief in democracy	Political system helps people	Voting	Participation index	Run for office
Republican men									
Republican women									

(*continues*)

Table 8.2. (*continued*)

Even fewer effects for parents of the Family Matters 2 teens (summary of results from this chapter)

	Nonsexism	Women's feminine leadership traits	Women's masculine leadership traits	Better off with more women in office	Belief in democracy	Political system helps people	Voting	Participation index
Democratic men					↑			
Democratic women								

Many more effects for adolescents (summary of results from chaps. 3–5)

	Nonsexism	Women's feminine leadership traits	Women's masculine leadership traits	Better off with more women in office	Belief in democracy	Political system helps people	Voting	Participation index	Run for office
Republican boys						↑	↑		↑
Republican girls	↑	↑	↑	↑ ↑					
Democratic boys	↑				↑	↑	↑		
Democratic girls					↑				↑

Note: An upward/downward arrow indicates a positive/negative and statistically significant relationship between the presence or perception of viable, novel women candidates and the attitude or behavior in question for adults.

is supported by everything we have presented in previous chapters. The immovable adults hypothesis is supported by everything covered thus far in this chapter. This still leaves the third hypothesis, which lies at the heart of any claim that someone serves as a role model: Do the effects among youth endure into adulthood?

Enduring Effects

In principle, testing to see whether role model effects are fleeting or enduring is straightforward. One simply needs to observe whether young people live in a community with women candidates, just as we have done throughout this book. But instead of contemporaneous outcome measures, we need to know about people's attitudes and behavior years after their adolescent exposure (or not) to women role models. Does a person's experience of women candidates in adolescence have a long-term effect into adulthood?

What sounds simple in principle is actually very difficult in practice. Longitudinal studies—those that involve interviewing the same people at different points in time—are difficult and expensive. Getting people to fill out a survey once, much less twice, is a considerable challenge. In the Family Matters 2 study discussed in earlier chapters, the same people were interviewed about six months apart, and that was hard enough. Now we want to survey people as adolescents, then find them many years later as adults and convince them to complete another survey. Keep in mind that early adulthood is one of the most unstable periods of any person's life, as education, relationships, and work often result in multiple changes in address and situation.

Fortunately, however, we have been able to draw on a study that manages to overcome these challenges, the Educational Longitudinal Study (ELS). Conducted by the US Department of Education, this study meets all of the criteria for testing the enduring effects hypothesis. First, the ELS surveys were administered to a nationally representative sample of roughly fifteen thousand adolescents who were in tenth grade in 2002. Second, the same teenagers, now adults, completed follow-up surveys in 2004, 2006, and 2012. Third, the follow-up survey in 2012 asked whether they had voted in presidential and other elections, because by that time all of the respondents had both reached the age of majority and lived through a presidential election. Fourth, we were able to obtain the geographic location of the respondents when they were first surveyed in 2002, which means that we were able to measure whether, in that year, they experienced women candidates running for governor, Senate, or the US House of Representatives.[11] See table 8.3 for more on the ELS.

Table 8.3. Educational Longitudinal Study

Population	National sample of adolescents in 10th grade and one parent (sampling frame comprised of public and private schools)
Mode	Wave 1: paper and pencil Wave 4: online, phone, in person
Description	4-wave panel survey
Sample size	Wave 1 (2002): 15,370 Wave 4 (2012): 12,615
Dates	Wave 1: Spring 2002 Wave 4: July 2012–February 2013
Details	Data weighted to account for school nonresponse and student nonresponse within schools, stratified by Hispanic, Asian, Black, and Other race/ethnicity. Geographic data provided with a restricted data license from the National Center for Education Statistics.
Firm	RTI International (contracted by US Department of Education, National Center for Education Statistics)

In other words, we can test whether exposure to women candidates in adolescence has an enduring effect on the most fundamental political act: voting. We are not aware of any other study that has directly tested whether role model effects are enduring with such a rigorous test, let alone using data of such high quality as this. The idea that exposure to role models as a child shapes future behavior is often assumed but up until now has not been demonstrated.

As informative as these data are, however, they do have limitations. For starters, we can only test for a role model effect on voting, not on other forms of political participation, such as working on campaigns, contacting elected officials, and so on. Similarly, we have no attitudinal measures of women's leadership traits, antisexism, or feelings about democracy. Our attention here is on behavior, and voter turnout specifically.

Also, the survey does not include any questions about party affiliation or vote choice, either of the adolescents or of their parents. Up to this point we have considered both party identification and gender to see whether any observed role model effects are limited to youth who identify with one party rather than the other, or to co-partisan candidates only. For this analysis, we can test for role model effects by gender, that is, whether women candidates have a different impact on girls and boys. But we cannot test for effects by party. Keep in mind that this makes our analysis a conservative test of the enduring effects hypothesis, especially given that our cross-sectional models find partisan effects: In 2020, it was Democratic girls and Republican boys who became more politically engaged where women ran for office.

The political context for women candidates in 2002, the year of the first wave of the ELS, was different from that in 2020, the year on which we have focused most of our analysis thus far. In 2002 there were far fewer women candidates: 122 for the House, 11 for the Senate, 10 for governor. In 2020 nearly two and a half times more women were major-party candidates for the House (298) and nearly twice as many for the Senate (21). (Interestingly, 2002 was a big year for women gubernatorial candidates; only three women ran for governor in 2020.) And the numbers are even smaller still when we consider women who were viable candidates, either winners or within ten percentage points of winning: seventy (House), five (Senate), and seven (governor). Because there were relatively few incumbent women in office in 2002, the majority of the candidates were novel. In 2002 as in 2020, most (66 percent) women candidates were Democrats. Among viable women that figure is 65 percent, and when looking only at novel women, 61 percent.

To summarize the gender context in 2002, there were fewer viable women candidates than in 2020, but, of those who ran, more were novel. Of those novel candidates, the majority were Democrats.

As for the general political context, gender issues were not very salient in the 2002 election. Because it was the first national election since the September 11, 2001, terrorist attacks, foreign policy dominated the campaigns and news coverage. The United States and its allies had invaded Afghanistan, and the war in Iraq was imminent. It was ten years after the Year of the Woman, two years after Hillary Clinton won a Senate seat in New York, and six years before Clinton first ran for the Democratic presidential nomination and Sarah Palin ran for vice president. Contrary to the norm, the president's party gained seats in this midterm election, largely attributable to the post-9/11 rally around the flag for President George W. Bush.

The fact that gender was not a dominant theme in 2002 is one more reason ours is a conservative test of the enduring effect of women role models. Women candidates, as women, were not highly salient in 2002—no *Time* magazine covers or talk of a Year of the Woman. To the extent that women were salient, it was in their own states and districts, without the context of a national wave of women candidates or particularly high-profile women running for office to generate attention.

The analysis should again look familiar. We have merged data on viable, novel women candidates into the ELS, which means that we know whether any given respondent lived in a community with women candidates for the House, Senate, and/or governor as a tenth grader. Does the presence of women candidates predict their likelihood of voting years later?[12] We once again control for potentially confounding variables, including the predictors of where women candidates are most likely to run. We account for influences in the home, including parental education and income, measured when our respondents were adolescents. Though we obviously cannot control for our respondents' likelihood of voting in 2002, because they were only in tenth grade, we can control for their level of political interest with a question that asks how frequently they discuss current affairs with their parents. In addition, we also account for their exposure to the social norm of voting by controlling for voter turnout in their county in the 2000 presidential election.[13] Our controls also include a set of demographic variables that are likely to affect political participation, measured contemporaneously with voter turnout in the 2012 survey: educational attainment, income, marital status, having children, homeownership, full- or part-time employment, and being a student. In other words, we have thrown the proverbial kitchen sink at this question to ensure that exposure to women candidates is not confounded with anything else that might affect voter turnout. See the online appendix for the full models.

We present results for adolescent girls and boys separately. Our theory of political role models has the strongest expectations for girls, because both changing gender stereotypes and increased interest and attention should encourage more engagement among girls. Remember that we have seen empirical evidence that girls, or at least Democratic girls, are more likely to expect to vote and run for office when women run.

As for boys, our theory of political role models does not expect that boys, compared to girls, are as likely to be inspired to political engagement by women candidates. As has been noted above, in 2020 boys—Republican boys specifically—became more likely to intend to vote when women run, which evidence suggests is a product of backlash. We view the 2002 context as less conducive to backlash, however; far fewer women were running, and little attention was paid to women's advances. The 2020 election, on the other hand, came in the wake of the 2018 midterms, when women candidates were strongly associated with opposition to Republicans in general and Donald Trump in particular. The heightened gender politics of the time (from #MeToo to abortion) likely contributed to the threat response we observed among adolescent boys in 2020. Still, it is an empirical question whether exposure to women candidates in 2002 will affect girls, boys, or both as they become potential voters as adults.

In our previous chapters, we displayed results for respondents' exposure to 0, 1, and 2 women candidates. There were so few women candidates in 2002 that we will instead report 0 or 1 candidate only.[14] Because our outcome

Impressionable Years and Enduring Effects

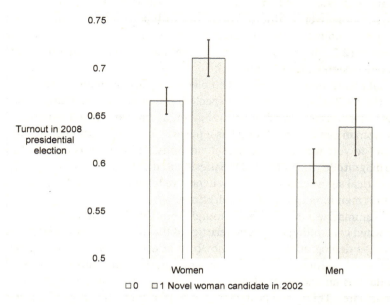

Figure 8.1. When adolescent girls experience a viable, novel woman candidate, they are more likely to vote six years later

is binary—the respondent voted or not—we employ logistic regression but have converted the coefficients into a predicted probability of voting.

The results are clear: The role model effect endures. Figure 8.1 shows the effect of living in a community with one viable, novel woman as an adolescent in 2002 on voter turnout in the 2008 presidential election, which for many of these respondents was the first presidential contest in which they were eligible to vote.[15] Girls who were exposed to *a single woman running for a visible office in 2002* were more likely to vote in 2008 than those who did not experience any women running—an effect that meets the standard for statistical significance ($p < .05$). Among men, the difference between those exposed and those not exposed to women role models as adolescents is not statistically significant, although the impact is positive.

The effect of one woman candidate is roughly a 4.5 percentage point boost in the likelihood of voting. This is statistically significant—but is it a substantively meaningful increase? Consider how it compares to other well-established predictors of voting: county-level voter turnout, frequency of political discussion in the home (measured when they were in high school), and parental education (the highest level of education attained by either parent). Living in a community with a viable, novel woman candidate leads to a larger increase in turnout among women than going from the twenty-fifth to the seventy-fifth percentile in county voter turnout (2.4 points), "sometimes to always" in the frequency of political discussion (2.7 points), and a parent who has a high school diploma to an associate's degree (3.1 points).

What about turnout in less salient elections, such as in nonpresidential years (in 2009–11)? As would be expected, respondents report turning out in such elections at a much lower rate. Yet, again, we see that experiencing a woman candidate in 2002 has a positive impact on whether women turn out to vote for these less salient elections. Although it is roughly the same magnitude (3.6 points) as the presidential vote, it is only on the cusp of statistical significance ($p < .10$). Exposure to women candidates has no effect on men in nonpresidential elections.

To summarize what we have found from this longitudinal analysis: Even when controlling for characteristics of the district, county, and state, as well as demographic factors known to affect turnout—including the adolescents' political engagement in tenth grade—exposure to a woman candidate as an adolescent leads to higher voter turnout among women six years later. This is powerful evidence for the enduring effect of women as role models. Whether it is politicians, pundits, or members of the public talking about role models, this is what they mean: When girls see women running for office, it will lead them to have a lifetime of political engagement.

While our data only extend to a few years after high school, there is good reason to think that the role model effect endures longer. Voting is habitual (Coppock and Green 2016; Gerber, Green, and Shachar 2003; Plutzer 2002). If people have voted once, they are much more likely to vote again. Furthermore, voting in early adulthood sets citizens on a lifetime trajectory of voting regularly (Franklin 2004). If young people do vote when they are first able, they are very likely to be habitual voters for the rest of their lives. It is also plausible that young people who vote

Table 8.4. The takeaway: Enduring effects hypothesis

	Vote in 2008 presidential election	Vote in nonpresidential elections
Men		
Women	↑	↑*

Note: An upward arrow indicates a positive and statistically significant relationship between the presence of viable, novel women candidates in adolescence (2002) and voting in adulthood.

*$p < .10$

are also likely to engage in other forms of political participation—voting being the "gateway drug" to other political activity, including running for office.

Role models today lead to voting tomorrow. And perhaps even running for office some days after that.

Summing Up

Whether they realize it or not, when people speak of role models for young people, in politics or any other domain, they are actually making three interrelated but separate claims at once: Youth are impressionable, adults are immovable, and effects are enduring. Among social scientists, these three claims—better described as hypotheses—have rarely, if ever, been examined together. A small body of scholarship on political socialization has examined the political attitudes of young people, establishing that their opinions can be shaped by home, school, community, and culture. Very little of that research, however, has specifically examined whether women politicians are role models for young people. In fact, having read this far in this book, you have now seen most of it. Even though the fundamental assumption underpinning most socialization research is that young people are more impressionable than their elders, very few studies make direct comparisons between young and old. We have made such a comparison, and our results show that, with only a few intriguing exceptions, adults are relatively immovable.

The missing link in most socialization research—and, previously, all studies of political role models—is the important assumption that experiences in one's youth endure into adulthood. Whether in career planning, athletics, or politics, to say that someone is a role model to young people is to expect that they have a long-term effect. Yet, up until now, evidence for this all-important hypothesis has been lacking. If women politicians do not have a long-term effect on young people's political engagement, the impact of role models is diminished. It is, after all, adults who can cast ballots and engage in other forms of political activity that shape the outcome of elections and the trajectory of public policy. We look to role models because we expect them to shape the adults that young people become. The stakes are high when it comes to showing whether effects on young people endure. According to the best available data, they do.

Evidence for enduring effects is thus critical to the very concept of political role models. This is true in the narrow sense of providing evidence for a hypothesis but also, more broadly, for the fundamental idea that when democratic actors reflect the diversity of the people they hope to represent, those people are more likely to take an interest in their democracy. Put another way, when politicians do not fully reflect the public, those who look around at the political landscape and do not see people like them often conclude that politics is not for them. The stakes for enduring effects are high not only for the sake of a theory, but for upholding the ideals of American democracy.

9 * A Democracy for Everyone

Democracy without women is no democracy.

International feminist slogan

In 1977 Kathy Whitmire made history: In Houston's municipal election she beat four male opponents to win the office of city controller, making her the first woman elected to the city's government. Nationwide, her election was also unusual. Across the United States, women were just 13 percent of city council members and a mere 6 percent of mayors. An academic study conducted after Whitmire's first term in office found that about a third of Houstonians said that, because of Whitmire, they were more positive about women serving in city government. Nor was this idle talk. In the next municipal election two women were elected to Houston's city council. Writing about the effect of Houston's first woman in city government, MacManus (1981, 98) concluded that Whitmire "legitimized these candidates in the eyes of the general public."

This book is about what happens when many Kathy Whitmires run, for many different offices, in many different communities across the nation. Our central conclusion is that women role models matter, although how and for whom they matter depends on the outcome in question. Specifically, we find that women role models matter most for young people, and young women most of all. Compared to their wizened elders, young people's minds are most likely to be shaped by seeing political role models, because they are in their impressionable years. We suspect that previous research on the impact of women politicians has found inconsistent results in part because most authors have looked for effects among adults, the population whose minds are least likely to change. Our evidence shows that adults are far less likely to react to women role models than adolescents. It is indeed difficult to teach old dogs new tricks.

Although we have presented many different findings from a wide array of data sources, a few broad conclusions stand out.

- Women political role models change young people's minds about *women* as political leaders. Specifically, they change the minds of those whose minds most need changing—both Republican boys and girls. They also make adolescent boys of either party less sexist.
- Women political role models change girls' minds about *democracy*, leading them to have more faith in the nation's political system.
- Women political role models change girls' minds about *politics*, mobilizing them to be more politically engaged. Girls become more politically active when they see women run viable, visible campaigns for office, especially when those candidates are their co-partisans.
- *Women political role models of color* motivate girls of color *and* white girls to be more politically active.
- Women political role models can cause *backlash*. For example, although Republican boys are more politically engaged when women run, it is not because they are made to feel efficacious, but rather out of opposition or perhaps even a sense of threat. In other cases, women politicians can lead some boys to become less interested in politics.
- Women political role models affect adults in less consistent ways than they do adolescents, who are in their *impressionable years*.
- The role model effect *endures* from adolescence into adulthood. Exposure to women political role models can lead to political participation years later.

We summarize our conclusions in table 9.1. This table is a simplification of the many findings across the preceding chapters, since it focuses on all girls and all boys, without differentiating by party or race or by the different measures we use within this book. Put simply, there is something to the folk theory of political role models after all. More precisely, we have found evidence for our theory of political role models: Women politicians change stereotypes about women's capacity for political leadership for both girls and boys, make girls more confident in the representativeness of the political system, and, for different reasons, lead girls and boys to be more politically engaged, especially as voters and candidates. Moreover, role mode effects persist, at least when it comes to voting.

A seemingly ironic conclusion is woven throughout our analysis. The women candidates who matter most are those who are novel. Our whole research agenda began with the observation that teenage girls' political interest spiked in 1984, when Geraldine Ferraro was the first woman on a major-party presidential ticket, and in 1992, when there was considerable public attention to a wave of women candidates during the Year of the Woman. We have likewise seen the effects of women congressional candidates in 2018, another record year for women running for Congress

Table 9.1 The meta-takeaway: Summary of evidence for women as political role models

	Women as leaders	Support for democracy	Political engagement: all women candidates	Political engagement: women candidates of the same race	Enduring effect (adolescence to adulthood)
Girls	↑	↑	↑	↑	↑
Boys	↑		↑	↑	

Note: An upward/downward arrow indicates at least one positive/negative and statistically significant relationship between the presence of viable (and in some cases, novel) women candidates and that outcome.

(chap. 4). The significance of novelty shows up in many other ways as well. For example, in our analysis of how women candidates affect attitudes toward women (chap. 3), recall that the biggest effects are for women running to replace men—races in which the unusual nature of a woman candidate is most likely to be salient. Similarly, our examination of political engagement (chap. 5) demonstrates that it is not enough for women candidates to be present. Young people do not become more politically active unless they are consciously aware that women are running. In the experiments we describe in chapter 7, Republican girls respond when exposed to fellow Republican women candidates (chap. 7). We suspect part of the reason is that those Republican women are unusual, since in the real world most women candidates for office are Democrats. Likewise, why do teenage girls, of all backgrounds, become more politically engaged when women of color compete for office (chap. 6)? We suspect that it is because there are relatively few women from underrepresented groups in government. They stand out because they are extraordinary.

For all the gains that women have made in American politics, the fact remains that they are still unusual enough to generate news stories about their gender. News coverage of elections is replete with headlines like "Oklahoma Has Record Number of Female Candidates for Statewide Office" (*The Oklahoman*, 2022) and "Historic Number of Women Running for Office in Alabama" (*Montgomery Advertiser*, 2018). Imagine how strange it would seem if there were headlines such as "Historic Number of Men Running for Office." It sounds odd because we *expect* to see men in politics. Therein lies the irony. Women garner attention because they remain unusual in politics. Journalists love stories about firsts and records— "man [or woman] bites dog" is news, "dog bites man [woman]" is not. When attention is drawn to how women are challenging and overcoming the stereotype that politics is a man's game, those stereotypes weaken, perceptions of representation improve, and girls are inspired to political action themselves.

Testing Novelty

Many clues point toward novelty as the driver of role model effects, but we were curious to directly test whether the effect of women as role models depends on their being unusual. To find out, we conducted one final study in the spring of 2022, designed to isolate the impact of an "historic" woman candidate versus a woman who is not described as breaking new ground. As in chapter 7, we employed an experiment embedded in a survey. Like our previous experiments, this type of study enables us to control the information respondents received.

The study zeroes in on novelty. There are three treatments, all identical stories featuring interviews with newly elected House members "in our district." The stories vary only in the description of the subject: a woman candidate who is a historic first, a woman candidate, and a candidate who is a man. The party affiliation of the candidate was matched to that of the respondent, (e.g., Democratic [and Democratic-leaning] respondents were shown a story about a Democratic candidate) to make it more likely that respondents would heed the story and not dismiss it because it featured a candidate of the "other party."[1]

The candidate was either Jane or Jim Miller, names chosen because they are common. The interview questions are anodyne, including "What are your priorities in Congress?" and "How have you prepared yourself to serve in Congress?" The candidate gives nonpartisan responses, employing phrases such as "Let me assure the people of our community that I do not take this responsibility lightly" and "I will bring common sense to Washington." To describe Jane Miller as historic, the story included both a headline and text describing her as the district's first woman elected to Congress, while throughout the story she specifically notes her gender—for example, "As a woman, I will bring common sense to Washington."[2] Respondents were randomly assigned to read either a single news story or, if selected for the control group, no story at all. Following the story, respondents then answered a series of questions that will look familiar, as they are identical to the measures we have employed in our previous studies, both experimental and observational. The survey thus asked about their attitudes toward women as leaders, democracy, and political engagement.[3] Further details about this experiment can be found in the online appendix.

The respondents in this study were 878 young adults aged from eighteen to twenty, a cohort that roughly matches the teens in Family Matters 2, who had been interviewed two years prior. They were all enrolled in college, because we recruited participants by asking other professors around the country to distribute the survey to their students. Though not a nationally representative sample, it does enable us to test the impact of novelty on a population that is likely already politically engaged. Most of the professors we know are fellow political scientists, which means that they were most likely to distribute the survey in political science classes. In some cases these were general introductory classes that enroll a wide range of students, not necessarily those with a political bent. In others, the classes were more specialized, and were made up of students who are probably more politically engaged than the typical undergraduate. Either way, because students were randomly assigned to a news story, we can be confident that any effects we observe are owing to the news story they read. The fact that many of the study participants had the "preexisting condition" of political interest and are slightly older—and thus less impressionable—than the respondents in our adolescent studies means that our study is a conservative test of whether framing a woman candidate as novel and historic affects young people's attitudes.

A nonnegligible number of respondents (34 of 878 respondents, or 4 percent) self-describe with a gender identity other than male or female, including nonbinary, trans, genderqueer, two-spirit, or similar terms, with nonbinary being the most common self-description. Thirty-four cases with four treatment conditions (an average of only about eight each) are far too few to produce statistically valid results as a separate group. As in chapter 6, we have opted to group those respondents who do not identify as either male or female with our female-identifying respondents, because they represent a group that, like women, have not been fully represented in American politics—indeed, even more than women, as there are very few nonbinary or transgender politicians (Magni and Reynolds 2021). Following our practice from chapter 6, we employ the label "young women+," with + reflecting the multiple gender identities found within this group. Since these respondents are eighteen or older, we have opted to describe them as "young" rather than as "girls" or "boys."

When compared to the control group (no news story), and similar to our findings in chapter 7, exposing young men to women candidates makes them more likely to agree that the nation would be better off with more women in office, although the effect falls just short of conventional statistical significance. Novelty, however, does not matter, because the effect is the same whether the woman candidate is described as a first or not. As expected, reading about a man elected to Congress registers no effect. Once again, then, we see a (weak) effect on beliefs about women leaders among those Mansbridge (1999) described as the "haves"—boys

CHAPTER 9

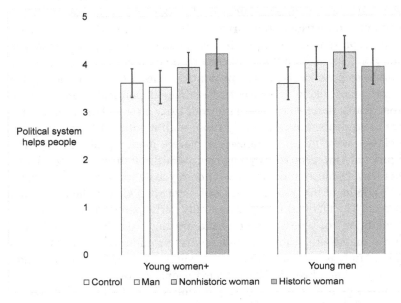

Figure 9.1. A historic woman fosters stronger faith in democracy for young women+

who fit the traditional stereotype of a political leader and whose attitudes have the most room to move, regardless of whether women politicians are described as novel or not. There are no effects on girls regardless of the treatment.

To gauge attitudes toward American democracy, we once again asked respondents whether they feel that the political system "helps people with their genuine needs." As seen in figure 9.1, when compared to the baseline (no news story), young women+ respondents are most likely to view the political system as responsive when they read about a historic woman's being elected to Congress. Importantly, this effect is only significant for a candidate who is both a woman and a pathbreaker. Reading about a man or a nonhistoric woman elicits no change in the perceived responsiveness of the system.[4] Furthermore, as we observed in the "real world" (see chapter 4), a woman politician has no effect on young men's perception of the political system.

Finally, what about *politics*? The results for an index of political activity (campaigning, writing to elected officials, attending a rally) merely suggest that novel women spur greater political engagement among both young men and women—positive but not statistically significant.

When we turn to ambition, however, we see the most compelling evidence for the importance of novelty. A pathbreaking woman inspires

A Democracy for Everyone

young women and nonbinary people to envision themselves running for office one day—a statistically significant effect that is the largest in the whole study. As we see in figure 9.2, there is no comparable effect on political ambition for a woman who is not described as novel nor for a man; neither one causes an increase in respondents' interest in running for office. Nor do we see a statistically significant effect among young men.

Of course, we do not mean to suggest that this small study will lead many of these youth to actually run for office. Instead, this question about political ambition gauges how respondents feel about their place in the political system. Can they imagine themselves ever throwing their hat in the ring, or is the prospect of running for office too alien even to contemplate? In other words, does running for office seem like something people like them could do? Although not everyone who says that they will run for office follows through, we suspect that virtually everyone who does run for office at some point imagined themselves doing so.

In short, here is further evidence for the key argument of this whole book. When women run, they serve as role models for young women+— inspiring direct emulation by causing these young people to think of themselves as running for office one day. And it is not just any woman politician who serves as a role model, but a woman who has made history by being a first. Novelty matters.

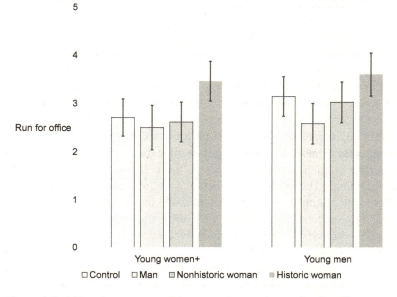

Figure 9.2. A historic woman candidate spurs interest in running for office

CHAPTER 9

The Ironies of Novelty

One might argue that the significance of novelty for explaining the role model effect is counterintuitive, perhaps even troubling. Women only have an impact when they are portrayed as out of place, unusual, or even weird. That is, only when young people are reminded that women are underrepresented in politics do women politicians produce positive effects on attitudes about women leaders, faith in democracy, and political engagement. Why? We posit that exposure to women politicians, in a context that highlights how pathbreaking they are, works to emphasize their counter-stereotypical power: Women *can* do politics! Our political system *is* more representative! And for girls: I also can do that thing—politics—that girls do! Barrier breakers challenge stereotypes and inspire others.

The importance of novelty to role model effects also suggests that as more women enter the political arena, they will cease to be role models. We would frame this irony a different way. Yes, in the world as we know it now, women candidates are more likely to change minds when they stand out as unusual. Yet this hardly means that as women politicians become more common—less novel—they are not serving as role models. Instead, women's greater presence would mean that their role modeling is pervasive—women in politics are *normal*—and thus less likely to register when a particular woman runs for office. Why don't we observe a spike in boys' political engagement when they see men running for office? Because they live in a political culture saturated with male role models—they simply aren't novel. Generations of men in political life have reinforced that politics is "what boys do." Someday generations of women politicians may do the same for girls.

We have already seen hints of what happens when women politicians have a greater presence. Democratic girls are more likely to see themselves as politically active than Republican girls, even in places where there are no Democratic women running for office. This is not just a partisan difference: Republican boys are just as likely as Democratic boys to be politically engaged—in fact, a little more so. Rather, we suggest that the reason for Democratic girls' engagement is that they are used to seeing Democratic women politicians, both on the national stage (e.g., Hillary Clinton, Kamala Harris, Nancy Pelosi) and at the state and congressional district levels. Republican girls are less likely to say that they will be involved in politics, including running for office themselves, in part because they have witnessed so few Republican women role models.

In other words, as women candidates become more common, the less likely we are to observe the role model effect in any given place at any given time. Eventually, we expect that the role model effect as we have defined it here—women candidates sparking a change in attitudes and engagement—will not be detectable at all. This is not because role models will have ceased to matter, but because they matter so much that they have become the norm. Women politicians demonstrate that politics is "what girls do."

The Possibility of Backlash

We would be remiss not to acknowledge the potential dark side of women's greater participation in the political arena. Throughout our analysis we have identified instances of possible backlash among adolescent boys, where we suspect women politicians have spurred their engagement out of antagonism or dampened their interest in political participation. Although this is not always the case, there are enough examples to give us pause. Our findings add to the growing literature documenting the ways in which women's inclusion in the traditionally male domain of politics, combined with other economic and social disruptions, spurs negative responses from men in particular (Cassese and Holman 2019; Cassino and Besen-Cassino 2021). Suffice it to say, we do not recommend that women exit politics so as to avoid these outcomes. Social change is always disruptive and contentious, but history tells us that in the long run, more equitable societies thrive and advance.

Our data also support that expectation. While we did see evidence of boys recoiling from politics when women politicians are salient, we also saw that women politicians can change boys' (and girls') minds about women as a group. Recall from chapter 3 that seeing women candidates run leads Republican boys to become less sexist and more likely to view women as capable of political leadership. While there may be backlash in the short run, in the long run we would expect that women candidates contribute to broader shifts in gender attitudes and expectations.

Democratic Legitimacy

Why should anyone care whether there is gender equality in terms of who participates in politics and ultimately in who governs? The answer goes to the heart of a representative democracy. Democracy—whether in the United States or anywhere else—is stronger and closer to its ideals when the public square fully reflects the entire population. This includes not just equality for gender, but also for any group whose voices have not been fully heard in the public arena, or whose members have not been fully represented in the corridors of power.

We stress that our emphasis on equal representation for women is not partisan in nature. It is a myth that women hold uniform political views or monolithically support one party over the other. While in the contemporary political environment women are more likely to cast Democratic ballots than men, plenty of women support Republicans. Among white women, a majority identify with the GOP (Wolbrecht and Corder 2020). Those who call for more women in politics need to be prepared for women candidates with whom they disagree. After all, the Congress elected in 2022 includes both Alexandria Ocasio-Cortez and Marjorie Taylor Greene. In fact, because the Democratic Party has long led the way with a larger number of women candidates, more women in office will require increasing the number of Republican women running for office.

A political system with greater representation of women, whatever their party, would look different from the status quo. Women often have distinct life experiences, prioritize different interests, and prefer different policies. For many reasons, including a sense of responsibility to represent women's interests, women in office legislate differently, with more emphasis on women's issues and the issues with which women are often associated, such as education and health care (Dittmar, Sanbonmatsu, and Carroll 2018; Griffin, Newman, and Wolbrecht 2012; Reingold 2008; Swers 2013, 2020). At this moment in history, when issues that affect women in particular (such as abortion rights, in vitro fertilization, birth control, child care, and sexual violence) and in general (including free speech, immigration, and health care) are all on the national agenda, women's voices are essential. Women will not necessarily agree on which policies best address these and many other matters, but they have a perspective that no man can claim.

Women's impact is felt beyond public policy. Women also legislate better and more effectively (Anzia and Berry 2011; Pearson and Dancey 2011; Thomsen and Sanders 2020; Volden, Wiseman, and Wittmer 2013). When women are underrepresented in politics, representation is diminished, and women's collective skills and talents go untapped. In a democratic republic, it seems bizarre not to draw on the insights and abilities of the entire population. We are much better off with all hands on deck.

If appeals to improving American democracy and creating better public policy are not persuasive for increasing women's representation, there are also strategic reasons for it. Republicans in particular would be wise to follow Democrats' lead and recruit more women candidates, lest there be few role models for the next generation. In the Family Matters 2 study, 63 percent of adolescent girls identified as Democrats, and Democratic girls were substantially more likely to express interest in political engagement than any other group. We have good reason to expect that those Democratic girls will grow up to be politically active women. If Republican girls grow up to be women who remain reluctant to enter politics, the Republican

Party will lose out on key potential supporters and further confirm their reputation as a party that serves the interests of men and not women (Winter 2010). The GOP's weakness among the most politically active young women is not a promising sign for the party's future. Furthermore, given that women candidates of color are far likely to be Democrats, absent more women of color running as Republicans, the GOP risks perpetuating their image as the party of white men—which, in a diversifying nation, does not bode well for future electoral success.

Activists from Russia to India and beyond have long proclaimed, "Democracy without women is no democracy!" (NEZHDI and Edmondson 1991; Piscopo and Shames 2020; Waters and Posadskaya 1995). A democratic society's foundation is the claim that legitimate government is representative. If members of an ostensibly democratic society do not believe that their voices will be heard, they risk a democratic death spiral. If people do not see the point in participating, it only further diminishes the legitimacy of the system, which only leads more people to lose faith and withdraw, and so on. Just as the value of currency rests on the confidence of consumers, so too does a democracy rest on the faith of the people.

This is not a mere abstraction. We live in times when democracy cannot be taken for granted, especially among young people. As we saw in chapter 4, the loss of Hillary Clinton to Donald Trump led many adolescent girls (Democrats especially) to become disillusioned with American democracy. Though their faith in democracy was partly restored when and where women ran for office in 2018, we are reminded that young people are in the most politically formative stage of their lives. What they learn about the political world will guide their beliefs and behaviors throughout their lives.

Greater representation of women can help create a virtuous cycle, for it leads people to rethink old prejudices about women as leaders. As we have stressed throughout, it is not only the attitudes of have-nots, in this case girls and women, that are our concern. Mansbridge (1999) reminds us that the attitudes of the haves—those already in power—are distinctly important. As more women run for, and serve in, positions of power, more boys—and, eventually, men—will see that women are equally capable of governing. This in turn should lead to still more women in politics, which will change more minds—a self-reinforcing feedback loop that keeps contributing to ever greater gender equality, and thus faith in democracy.

Even total gender equality, however, would not mean a fully inclusive democracy, for there are many other underrepresented groups. We have examined how women role models of color can inspire greater participation among girls, regardless of race, but there is more to be learned about the ways that seeing candidates who look like them can motivate young people's political engagement and their attitudes about democracy. Likewise, we expect that role models for other marginalized groups, such as the LGBTQ community or religious minorities, will also motivate greater participation in politics among those who are currently left out.

Which brings us back to Houston and the election of Kathy Whitmire to city government in 1977. In recognition of her place in history, a local Houston television station caught up with Whitmire—who went on to serve five terms as the city's mayor—in 2021, over four decades after her first electoral victory. When asked about her political legacy, she replied, "To me, having that opportunity to break that glass ceiling was very important not only for Houston, not only for me, but for women and for other glass ceilings that needed to be broken."[5] How times have changed! In 2020 Houstonians elected their first majority-female city council. Yet women role models are not merely a relic of the past. As one member of that female city council majority remarked, "Just to have so many women on council to be role models to show young women they can do it too is really a great thing."[6]

The more women run for office, the more young people will see that "politics is for girls." And the more all politicians fully reflect the diversity of the nation, the more all people—no matter their gender, race, or sexuality—can believe that America's democracy is truly for them.

ACKNOWLEDGMENTS

We are often asked how long we have been working on this book. That is a hard question to answer. Although we wrote the words above over a relatively short period of time, we have been working together on the topic of women politicians as role models for twenty years. But we can go back even farther. We both had been thinking about the representation of women before we even met, let alone collaborated.

For Dave, the beginning came when, as a graduate student, he worked as a research assistant for Nancy Burns, Kay Schlozman, and the late Sidney Verba. It was during that work that he first examined gender differences in adolescents' political engagement, using a dataset that is mostly unknown in political science, the Monitoring the Future study. He found that teenage girls' engagement spiked after Geraldine Ferraro's historic candidacy for the vice presidency in 1984 and the first Year of the Woman in 1992. That initial discovery got him thinking about how women politicians can affect adolescents' political attitudes.

For Christina, the origins were much earlier. She was raised to believe she could do anything, but almost every adult in her life worked for a church that did not permit women's leadership. Role models, where art thou? Women's studies courses in college helped Christina understand that the limits she was bumping up against were social, political, and, importantly, collective, not individual. Her first semester in graduate school coincided with the original Year of the Woman, prompting an interest in women and representation that has characterized nearly every aspect of Christina's professional career. She has benefited from too many women role models in her profession to list here but is grateful nonetheless.

When we became colleagues at Notre Dame, our collaboration began, and we brought complementary areas of expertise to the study of role models. Given our formative experiences as research assistants, it is appropriate that we too have benefited from the work of both undergraduate and graduate students. When we worked on our first paper together, we were grateful for the assistance of Ericka Benavides, David Fleming, Beth

McLeod, and Philip Wells. When, years later, we needed to update the work of that first team of research assistants, we were fortunate to employ Maggie Clark, Bridget Harrington, and Alice McCullough. We also express our gratitude to Emma Schroeder, who brought to the project both her considerable talents and her passion for the subject. Likewise, we were aided by Carey Stapleton, who, as a postdoctoral fellow at Notre Dame, provided critical assistance with our data collection and analysis. Matthew Sisk did excellent work with all things geographic—creating maps, geocoding respondents, and assembling tallies of women candidates.

Over the many years of our collaboration, our colleagues at Notre Dame have endured numerous presentations of our research. We are especially thankful for the regular participants in the research seminar of the Rooney Center for the Study of American Democracy. Their questions, comments, and suggestions forced us to think hard about the implications of our theory, particularly regarding the intersection of gender and race. It was through the generosity of our colleague Ricardo Ramirez that we were able to employ the Collaborative Multiracial Post-Election Study for, to our knowledge, the first-ever test of the role model effect among adolescents of color when women of different minority groups run for office.

As we neared the completion of the first draft of this book, we asked three scholars whose work has informed ours for their feedback: Kay Schlozman, Monica Schneider, and Jennifer Wolack. We are deeply grateful for the incredible amount of time each spent reviewing and critiquing the manuscript. The book is much improved because of their guidance. We also thank Sara Doskow, senior editor at the University of Chicago Press and a repeat editor for both of us. Sara has been enthusiastic about this project since we first broached it with her, and her thoughtful suggestions helped us refine the manuscript. And while we do not know their identities, thanks also to our anonymous reviewers. Their constructive criticism was a refreshing example of how peer review ought to work. Notwithstanding the suggestions we have received from others, we of course remain responsible for any errors.

We each are grateful to our families as well.

Dave writes: I am grateful to my wife, Kirsten, who has been both my sharpest critic and my biggest supporter. She has heard more than any human should about testing theories, wrangling data, and responding to reviews. Just as important, her insights have been a constant reminder that politics is not merely a subject to study but has real-world consequences.

Christina writes: As always, my husband Matt's support and humor make all things possible. As our daughters, Ella and Jane, move toward adulthood, the question of role models has taken on a new urgency.

Everything about both of them gives me hope for the future. Being their mom is the best role I've ever had.

Christina also welcomes suggestions for how her next book can have the name "Ella" in the title.

Finally, we thank all those women who have run—and are yet to run—for political office. May you continue to be role models for all of us.

NOTES

Chapter 1

1. @HillaryClinton, "To every little girl who dreams big: Yes, you can be anything you want—even president. Tonight is for you.—H." Twitter, June 7, 2016.
2. Barbie Celebrates Role Models (website), https://shop.mattel.com/pages/barbie-role-models, accessed March 13, 2024.
3. The other three are Kirsten Gillibrand, Tulsi Gabbard, and Marianne Williamson.
4. Statistics are from the Center for American Women and Politics. See https://womenrun.rutgers.edu/2022-report/, accessed June 14, 2023.
5. For international comparisons, see https://www.ipu.org/resources/publications/infographics/2023-03/women-in-politics-2023, accessed June 9, 2024. For data on gender quotas, see https://www.idea.int/data-tools/data/gender-quotas-database, accessed June 9, 2024.
6. UN Women, "Facts and Figures: Women's Leadership and Political Participation," September 15, 2023, https://www.unwomen.org/en/what-we-do/leadership-and-political-participation/facts-and-figures, accessed June 10, 2024. Note that heads of state do not include monarchies.

Chapter 2

1. Clinton Foundation (@ClintonFdn), "Women being in politics matters." @JuliaGillard on lessons learned throughout her career and work with @GIWLkings #WomensVoices,| http://clintonfoundation.org/womensvoices; https://twitter.com/ClintonFdn/status/1598818928305836033, accessed January 2, 2023.
2. Pew Research Center, *Pew Research Center: American Trends Panel Wave 36*, Question 77, 31115369.00081, Roper Center for Public Opinion Research, June 19, 2018 (Ithaca, NY: Cornell University), http://doi:10.25940/ROPER-31115369.
3. "Read the Transcript of Kamala Harris's Victory Speech in Wilmington, Del," *The Washington Post*, November 7, 2020, https://www.washingtonpost.com/politics/2020/11/07/kamala-harris-victory-speech-transcript/, accessed June 14, 2023.
4. Senator Patty Murray (@PattyMurray), "I'm honored to officially become the President Pro Tempore of the Senate today. It's not lost on me the significance of what it means to be the first woman to serve in this role. This is another sign that slowly but surely, Congress is looking more like America." Twitter, January 3, 2023,

https://twitter.com/PattyMurray/status/1610345553451421696?s=20&t=w43td EJJ3ZranTg9rC-LgA, accessed January 20, 2023.

5. Internal efficacy—the idea that one is capable of engaging in politics—is a more common measure in this literature. We group internal efficacy with other engagement measures because it is a more direct antecedent to political engagement: When one feels they can negotiate politics, they are more likely to do so.

6. See Wells 2024.

7. Collin Gallant, "Clark Becomes Hat's First Female Mayor in Landslide Win," *Medicine Hat (Alberta, Canada) News*, October 18, 2021, https://medicinehatnews.com/news/local-news/2021/10/18/clark-becomes-hats-first-female-mayor-in-land slide-win/, accessed November 18, 2021.

8. Lucille Leimert, "Rep. Clare Booth Luce Sees Women Taking Leading Role in Postwar Politics," *Los Angeles Times*, January 9, 1944, B1.

Chapter 3

1. @ewarren, "Whenever I meet a little girl, I tell them 'I'm running for president, because that's what girls do.' Then we pinky promise that they'll remember. I want every girl to know that when they fight from the heart, they can win. #WomensEqualityDay." Twitter, August 26, 2019.

2. All names are pseudonyms.

3. Specifically, there are high Cronbach alpha scores for each additive index separately: feminine traits (0.70) and masculine traits (0.80).

4. As with leadership traits, these questions about sexism all hang together and so are combined into a single index. The instrument also included a question to tap into benevolent sexism (women should be cherished and protected by men), but it does not load well with the other sexism items. Hostile sexism is more consistently related to political phenomena than is benevolent sexism (Schaffner 2021).

5. For the 2020 statistics, see https://cawp.rutgers.edu/2020-summary-women-candidates. For 2018, see https://cawp.rutgers.edu/2018-summary-women-candidates-0. For 2022, see https://womenrun.rutgers.edu/2022-report/congress/.

6. We are grateful to Matt Sisk for his excellent work creating the maps used in this chapter.

7. See chap. 5 for a more detailed discussion of how we measured the perception of women candidates.

8. So named because it was preceded by Family Matters 1, which will be introduced in chap. 4.

9. More precisely, we include a lagged dependent variable in each of our models. See Finkel (1995) for a discussion of what can and cannot be inferred from panel data.

10. While we include these contextual control variables to ensure that our results are not due to spurious statistical relationships, the reader might nonetheless wonder if they are somehow affecting our findings. It turns out, however, that they have little to no effect on our substantive results. For details, including an example of results with and without the contextual controls, please consult the online appendix at https://christinawolbrecht.com/see-jane-run.

11. "Clustering" simply means that our statistical models employ robust standard errors, which adjusts them to account for respondents who live in the same

congressional district and thus are not completely independent of one another. Practically speaking, this means that it is slightly more difficult to find statistical significance. We do not have many respondents who live in the same district, so the clustering makes little difference for our results. Nonetheless, we employ this method to err on the side of caution.

12. Our results are conservative in another sense as well. Because many of our outcomes (dependent variables) are scales that include more than one item but are measured using the same format, range, directionality, etc., we run the risk of introducing measurement error, as the scales are likely to be correlated with one another simply because of commonalities across questions. Owing to this potential error—which introduces noise into the measures—we are less likely to detect a signal. In other words, it is more difficult to detect a relationship between the presence of women candidates and the outcomes we are measuring, again underscoring any relationships we do find. We are grateful to the anonymous reviewer who pointed this out.

13. Another exception is Democratic girls, who puzzlingly become less nonsexist (that is, more sexist) when women run. Note, however, that even with this decline, they are still less sexist than boys of either party, and about the same as Republican girls. We have no explanation for this unexpected finding, and since it is inconsistent with every other finding, we suspect it is noise, not signal.

Chapter 4

1. Jamie Margolin, "Advice To Teens, From a Teen: What to Do If You're Unhappy with the 2016 Election Results," *HuffPost*, December 4, 2016, https://www.huffpost.com/entry/advice-to-teens-from-a-teen-what-to-do-if-youre_b_5844c6b4e4b0cf3f64558b2a, accessed May 25, 2022.

2. See https://www.cnn.com/2016/07/28/politics/hillary-clinton-speech-prepared-remarks-transcript, accessed October 15, 2024.

3. See https://www.cnn.com/2016/11/09/politics/hillary-clinton-concession-speech, accessed October 15, 2024.

4. "Transcript: Donald Trump's Taped Comments About Women," *The New York Times*, October 8, 2016, https://www.nytimes.com/2016/10/08/us/donald-trump-tape-transcript.html, accessed August 31, 2022.

5. We acknowledge that there is a debate about whether young people are becoming disillusioned with democracy as a form of governance globally. We do not claim to make a contribution to the debate about trends across nations, over time, or between generations, as our analysis simply examines whether women candidates affect American teenagers' attitudes toward democracy in 2018 and 2020. For more on the debate, see Foa and Mounk 2016, 2017; Mounk 2018; and an exchange with critics at https://www.journalofdemocracy.org/online-exchange-democratic-deconsolidation/, accessed October 15, 2024.

6. These numbers combine responses for "usually all" and "nearly always all."

7. See, for example, Christina Cauterucci, Celeste Katz, Latifa Lyles, and Hanna Rosin, "Female Candidates Finally Feel OK About Being Female Candidates," *Slate*, October 25, 2018, https://slate.com/human-interest/2018/10/2018-midterms-women-candidates-campaign-trail.html, accessed August 31, 2022; and Annika Neklason, "Moms Running for Office Are Finally Advertising Their Motherhood," *The*

Atlantic, July 23, 2018, https://www.theatlantic.com/family/archive/2018/07/midterms-2018-mothers/565703/, accessed February 15, 2023.

8. There was less of an increase in races for governor in 1992, but there were jumps in 1994 and 1998, especially for Democratic women candidates.

9. As in the previous chapters, these models control for the parent's attitude in the baseline year, as well as all of the other control variables discussed previously (see chap. 3 for a full explanation). Also, the standard errors have been clustered by congressional district.

10. Given these results for Republican girls, the reader may wonder why, in the aggregate, Republican girls did not become more positive about the political system between 2017 and 2018. The answer is that, compared to Democratic girls, Republican-identifying teens were far less likely to live in a community with a viable co-partisan woman candidate. In the Family Matters 1 data, 60 percent of Democratic girls lived in a place with at least one viable Democratic woman candidate, compared to only 27 percent of Republican girls who were exposed to a viable Republican woman.

11. Everything else in the model is the same, including a control for the parent's opinion, the questions being asked identically, the control variables being identical, and the standard errors being clustered by congressional district.

12. Importance of democracy and democracy is the best form of government correlate at 0.76, and a Cronbach's alpha of 0.86. The item about democracy helping people with their genuine needs only correlates with these questions at 0.11 and 0.09 respectively.

13. The *p* value of "All viable women candidates" for Democratic boys is 0.20.

Chapter 5

1. See Feller 2021. We thank Emma Schroeder for her stellar research assistance for this chapter.

2. While our attention to young people was new, we were fortunate to benefit from the work of others who had examined the possibility of role model effects. Indeed, Campbell's initial discovery came while assisting Nancy Burns, Kay Schlozman, and the late Sidney Verba as they wrote *The Private Roots of Public Action: Gender, Equality, and Political Participation* (2001), a groundbreaking book that, among many other conclusions, found a correspondence between women's salience in politics—in their case, serving in elected office—and greater engagement of women in the electorate.

3. Richard Berke, "The Year of the Woman," *The New York Times*, April 30, 1992. While Yeakel did not win her race against the incumbent, Arlen Spector, history nonetheless remembered that the Clarence Thomas confirmation was her personal turning point: the first paragraph of her *New York Times* obituary in 2022 described how the hearings ignited her desire to run for office (Seelye 2022).

4. There had only ever been two women serving in the Senate at the same time. From September to December of 1992, North Dakota was represented by Jocelyn Burdick, who had been appointed to her office, bringing the total number of women in the Senate briefly to three. For details on 1992, see https://cawp.rutgers.edu/facts/levels-office/congress/history-women-us-congress.

5. Timothy Egan, "Another Victory by a Woman, This One 'Mom': She Tops Field in Senate Race in Washington," *The New York Times*, September 17, 1992.

NOTES TO CHAPTER 6

6. Jill Abramson and Alex Kotlowitz, "Surprising Illinois Vote Lifts Women's Hopes, Worries Incumbents: Carol Moseley Braun Taps Grass-Roots Anger Aimed at Men Running Congress," *The Wall Street Journal*, March 20, 1992.

7. For more details on Monitoring the Future, see https://monitoringthefuture.org/, accessed October 15, 2024.

8. We are grateful to the University of Notre Dame students Maggie Clark, Bridget Harrington, and Alice McCullough for their excellent research assistance in 2021, and to the Notre Dame students Ericka Benavides, David Fleming, Beth McLeod, and Philip Wells for their equally valuable research assistance in 2003.

9. Print stories were cataloged using the *New York Times Index*, which ceased publication in 2017. Television news stories were compiled using the TV News Archive at Vanderbilt University.

10. Leslie Bennetts, "Record Number of Women to Hold Seats in Congress," *The New York Times*, November 6, 1980, A30.

11. Diane Sawyer, "113th Congress/Female Senators (Part I)," CBS Evening News, January 3, 2013.

12. "'Dean' of Women in Congress Is Retiring," *The New York Times*, March 10, 1976, 47.

13. Elizabeth Vargas, "Women and Politics," NBC Evening News, August 26, 1995.

14. Charles Gibson and Terry Moran, "A Closer Look (Madame Speaker)," ABC Evening News, November 8, 2006.

15. These figures display the annual count of news stories from June 1 to May 31. This range is used under the assumption that attitudes can only be affected by news coverage prior to the survey. While we do not know the exact date on which each Monitoring the Future respondent took the survey, MTF is always administered in the spring, concluding by the end of May. The June–May time frame ensures that the data do not include any news stories that occurred after the survey was administered.

16. Regression models confirm the relationship. For TV news coverage, regressing the female-male difference on the number of stories about gender produces a highly significant, positive coefficient ($p < 0.001$) and an R-squared of 0.27. For *New York Times* stories, the effect is also positive but not as strong: $p = 0.12$, with an R-squared of 0.06.

17. As of this writing, Monitoring the Future data for 2021, the year after Kamala Harris was elected as the first woman vice president, are not yet available.

18. We are indebted to Mack Mariani, Bryan Marshall, and A. Lanethea Mathews-Schultz, who in a 2015 article documented the increasing importance of polarization in the role model effect: see Mariani, Marshall, and Mathews-Schultz 2015.

19. We have found that on occasion the presence of women candidates has an effect (sometimes positive, sometimes negative) on engagement. With so many models, we would expect to find sporadic significant results through sheer chance alone. However, as we will do throughout this book, we focus on results that are consistently observed across multiple statistical models—the signal, not the noise.

Chapter 6

1. See Feller 2021. This chapter was written with Ricardo Ramirez. We are grateful to him for his generous assistance with the Collaborative Multiracial Post-Election Survey.

NOTES TO CHAPTER 6

2. Alexandria Ocasio-Cortez (@AOC), "Shirley Chisholm broke barriers so the rest of us could too." Twitter, February 26, 2018, https://twitter.com/AOC/status/968129138774233089?s=20.

3. Kamala Harris is both African American and Indian American, but our data do not allow us to look at the views of adolescent girls of Indian descent specifically. They are included among other girls of color, but given Harris's background, they were likely also paying particular attention to her.

4. We use the terms Black and African American, and Latino/Latina and Hispanic, interchangeably throughout the chapter (see Fraga 2018).

5. The remainder include other groups, such as Native Americans and Asian American/Pacific Islanders, but there are too few respondents and candidates in these groups for a viable statistical analysis. We welcome future research that focuses on these underrepresented groups.

6. Respondents were matched to their congressional districts on the basis of their zip code. Specifically, districts were tied to US Census Zip Code Tabulation Areas (ZCTA) by performing a spatial union between the two layers. For ZCTAs that did not fully fall within a single congressional district, population data at the census tract level was used to calculate the likelihood of an individual from that ZCTA residing in each congressional district of overlap. We are grateful to Matt Sisk for performing this match.

7. Exploratory factor analysis confirms that these activities are closely related to one another, as they form a single factor with an eigenvalue of 2.04.

8. The other options were:

I think I did that, I can't remember for sure
No, I did not do this, and I am unlikely to do this
No, I did not do this, but I might do this in the future
No, I did not do this, but I will definitely do this in the future

As the 2020 campaign was conducted in the midst of the COVID-19 pandemic, the items about working on a campaign and attending meetings or events included a follow-up about whether this was done remotely or in-person. We counted either one.

9. This question is worded differently than in our previous analysis:

If offered the opportunity, would you consider running for office to further the issues that you care about most?

Yes, would do this
No, would not do this
Unsure

The variable is coded as a scale, ranging from "No" to "Unsure" to "Yes."

10. The question is worded: "Since January 2020, have you discussed politics with family and friends," with the same response options as for the items in the Participation Index. We have coded "Yes, I am certain" as 1, every other response as 0.

11. The p value is 0.285 (two-tailed).

12. Caitlin O'Kane, "Kamala Harris' Campaign Launch Pays Tribute to Shirley Chisholm's 1972 Run," CBSNews.com, January 21, 2019, https://www.cbsnews.com/news/kamala-harris-2020-presidential-campaign-logo-pays-tribute-to-shirley-chisholm/, accessed January 27, 2023.

NOTES TO CHAPTER 7

13. April Ryan, "Remembering the Historical [sic] Presidential Run of Shirley Chisholm 50 Years Later," *The Grio*, January 24, 2022, https://thegrio.com/2022/01/24/historic-presidential-campaign-shirley-chisholm-50-years/, accessed June 24, 2023.

14. City of West Hollywood, "City Applauds President-Elect Biden's Nomination of Pete Buttigieg for Secretary of Transportation," press release, December 15, 2020, https://www.weho.org/Home/Components/News/News/9580/, accessed May 10, 2021.

Chapter 7

1. Caroline Kitchener, "More Women Are Running for House Seats than Ever. Even 2018," *The Lily*, May 13, 2020, https://www.thelily.com/more-women-are-running-for-house-seats-than-ever-even-2018/, accessed June 16, 2023. The article explicitly notes that Democratic women candidates have more role models to look to than do Republican women candidates.

2. This question was only asked of the teens in our survey who received the control condition, which was no story about women candidates.

3. We are grateful to the principal investigators of TESS, Jamie Druckman and Jeremy Freese; the reviewers of our proposals; the National Science Foundation for funding the TESS project; and the staff of the National Opinion Research Center for their excellent work on our project.

4. Immediately after the treatment, subjects assigned to one of the three experimental treatments were given an attention check:

Based on the story you just read, which party had a surge of women candidates for political office in 2020?

1. Democrats
2. Republicans
3. Both Democrats and Republicans

Seventy-eight percent answered correctly. In light of this relatively high accuracy rate, results include all subjects.

5. We also tested the effect of these treatments on nonsexist attitudes. The results are mixed. On the one hand, all the boys—regardless of their partisan identity—became less sexist when they read the story about a historic wave of Republican women candidates. This suggests that counter-stereotypical women do drive attitudes in a less sexist direction for those adolescents with the most room to move. On the other hand, girls (both Democrats and Republicans) *also* become less sexist when they read the version of the story that highlights women candidates of both parties. And while we see the effect among girls in general, it is greatest among Democratic girls. In this case, women candidates push the group that is already the least likely to hold sexist attitudes in an even more nonsexist direction.

6. As in the previous chapters, the confidence interval is 85 percent, rounded up from 83.5 percent, which is the correct interval to determine statistical significance between two point estimates.

7. In the observational data discussed in chap. 4, this question was combined with a similar one that asked whether they felt it was important to live in a democracy, which was not asked in the experiment.

8. Sarah Fitzpatrick, Kristen Welker, and Kenzi Abou-Sabe, "More Republican Women than Ever Are Planning to Run for Office," NBCNews.com, August 26, 2019, https://www.nbcnews.com/politics/politics-news/more-republican-women-ever-are-planning-run-office-n1022376, accessed June 16, 2023.

9. Katie Glueck and Lisa Lerer, "Haley Walks Treacherous Road for G.O.P. Women," *The New York Times*, February 19, 2023, https://www.nytimes.com/2023/02/19/us/politics/haley-campaign-gop-women.html, accessed June 16, 2023.

10. For her election night speech, see https://www.nbcnews.com/now/video/sarah-huckabee-sanders-gives-victory-speech-in-arkansas-as-first-female-governor-152971845649, accessed November 15, 2022.

11. However, Healey is not the first woman to serve as governor: Jane Swift was elevated from lieutenant governor to governor when Governor Paul Cellucci resigned to become ambassador to Canada in 2001. Kotek is not the first governor who is a member of the LGBTQ community: Oregon's previous governor, Kate Brown, is openly bisexual.

12. See https://www.wbur.org/news/2022/11/08/maura-healey-governor-wins-election-victory, accessed November 15, 2022.

13. The exception is when Democratic boys are exposed to Republican women candidates, as the negative effect is statistically significant at $p = .02$. While this is only a tentative conclusion, we find it interesting that the strongest effect is for counter-stereotypical women candidates, suggesting that just as they can lead teens to see the political system as responsive, they can lead boys (or at least some of them) to be less likely to engage in politics. They may see the system as more responsive, but responsive to people unlike themselves.

14. When they read about the historic wave of Democratic women candidates, the p value for political ambition for Democratic girls is .07. For Republican girls who read about Republican women, it is .21.

15. In light of the next chapter, in which we test the hypothesis that adolescents' attitudes are more movable than those of adults, the reader may wonder how adults respond to the alternate universe of our experiment. To find out, we conducted precisely the same study with a representative sample of adults. The detailed results are reported in the online appendix (https://christinawolbrecht.com/see-jane-run), but the summary is that the results for adults are both less common and consistent than for adolescents. Where we do find experimental effects, they often parallel the findings among adolescents.

Chapter 8

1. Casey McDermott, "Speak Out for Change," *New Hampshire Magazine*, October 16, 2022, https://www.nhmagazine.com/speak-out-for-change/, accessed March 12, 2024.

2. Note that we employ robust standard errors, clustered by congressional district.

3. For readers unfamiliar with it, the Cooperative Election Study is a large collaborative study that includes scholars from many different institutions. All respondents—roughly sixty thousand people—answer the same set of questions, known as the common content. Each partner institution then asks a unique set of questions of a subset of respondents, typically a sample of one thousand people.

4. As a reminder, this is measured with the question:

NOTES TO CHAPTER 8

If we had more women in elected office, America would be

Worse———Better (sliding scale)

5. We have a high degree of confidence in the voting rate reported in the CES because it does not rely simply on respondents' self-reports about whether they voted, which we know are likely to be inflated. Instead, it validates whether the respondent has voted by cross-referencing the voter file. Note that respondents without a match in the voter file are coded as missing.

6. To make this an apples-to-apples comparison, the presence of women candidates is limited to those who are viable. Likewise, the political participation index matches the one for adolescents: work on a campaign; give money to a candidate or party; contact an elected official; and/or participate in a march, protest, or demonstration. The difference, however, is that the adolescents were asked about their *anticipated* participation—whether they envision themselves ever doing these things—whereas the adults were asked whether, in the past year, they had actually *done* any of them.

7. We find that Republican men and women are less likely to engage in political activity where women run (presence of women candidates). However, we hesitate to make much of this finding, as it only appears with a control for the perception of women candidates running. In other words, the presence of women only correlates with lower participation among Republicans who are unaware that there are any women running, which suggests that this should be interpreted as demonstrating merely that Republicans with low political attention are less likely to participate in politics.

8. There are 820 households in the Family Matters 2 study. Of the parents who participated, 59 percent (481) were mothers.

9. Specifically, this is the same democracy index used with the adolescents, combining a question about the importance of living in a democracy with one about whether democracy is the best form of government.

10. There is also a negative effect for the presence of women candidates on the likelihood of voting among both Republican and Democratic men. However, as with the similar negative effects for political participation in the CES among Republican men and women, this effect appears only when controlling for the perception of women candidates, again suggesting that it actually means that men with low awareness of their political context are less likely to vote.

11. We were only able to conduct this analysis with a restricted data license from the National Center for Educational Statistics, which enabled us to learn the geographic location of the ELS respondents. We appreciate the help of the Data Security Office of the Institute for Education Sciences and those at Notre Dame who assisted us in obtaining the license: Nathan Krakowski, Greg Luttrell, and Matt Sisk.

12. The ELS did not ask about the perception of women candidates, and so we can only measure their presence—another reason this is a conservative test of women as role models.

13. As before, standard errors are clustered by congressional district.

14. Only 2.5 percent of our respondents had two novel, viable women candidates.

15. The survey asked about turnout in 2008 because it was conducted in the spring of 2012 and thus prior to the 2012 presidential election.

Chapter 9

1. The 8 percent of our participants who are "pure" independents were randomly assigned to either a Democratic or Republican candidate.

2. Full details about the experiment are found in the online appendix: see https://christinawolbrecht.com/see-jane-run.

3. Because virtually every respondent passed the attention check (95 percent), we present results for everyone.

4. Note that this result differs from what we found in chap. 4, where the impact of women candidates on democratic attitudes did not depend on the candidates' novelty.

5. Michelle Choi, "Here's Where Kathy Whitmire, Houston's First Woman Mayor, Has Been Living for the Last 20 Years," KHOU.com, March 20, 2021, https://www.khou.com/article/life/people/kathy-whitmire-houstons-first-woman-mayor-reflects-and-past-and-looks-to-future/285-42d32fde-1e04-4009-92c0-ac383b20fe02, accessed February 15, 2022.

6. Damali Keith, "Houston City Council Making History with 9 Women Elected," Fox26 Houston, January 8, 2020, https://www.fox26houston.com/news/houston-city-council-making-history-with-9-women-elected, accessed February 15, 2022.

REFERENCES

Abramowitz, Alan I., and Steven W. Webster. 2018. "Negative Partisanship: Why Americans Dislike Parties but Behave like Rabid Partisans." *Political Psychology* 39: 119–35.

Achen, Christopher H. 2002. "Parental Socialization and Rational Party Identification." *Political Behavior* 24(2): 151–70.

Alexander, Amy C. 2012. "Change in Women's Descriptive Representation and the Belief in Women's Ability to Govern: A Virtuous Cycle." *Politics & Gender* 8(04): 437–64.

Alexander, Deborah, and Kristi Anderson. 1993. "Gender as a Factor in the Attribution of Leadership Traits." *Political Research Quarterly* 46(3): 527–45.

Alford, John R., Carolyn L. Funk, and John R. Hibbing. 2005. "Are Political Orientations Genetically Transmitted?" *The American Political Science Review* 99(2): 153–67.

Allen, Peter, and David Cutts. 2018. "How Do Gender Quotas Affect Public Support for Women as Political Leaders?" *West European Politics* 41(1): 147–68.

Almond, Gabriel A., and Sidney Verba. 1963. *The Civic Culture: Political Attitudes and Democracy in Five Nations*. Princeton, NJ: Princeton University Press.

Alter, Charlotte. 2018. "A Year Ago, They Marched. Now a Record Number of Women Are Running for Office." *Time*, January 18. https://time.com/5107499/record-number-of-women-are-running-for-office/ (accessed March 26, 2022).

Anzia, Sarah F., and Christopher R. Berry. 2011. "The Jackie (and Jill) Robinson Effect: Why Do Congresswomen Outperform Congressmen?" *American Journal of Political Science* 55(3): 478–93.

Asgari, Shaki, Nilanjana Dasgupta, and Nicole Gilbert Cote. 2010. "When Does Contact with Successful Ingroup Members Change Self-Stereotypes? A Longitudinal Study Comparing the Effect of Quantity vs. Quality of Contact with Successful Individuals." *Social Psychology* 41(3): 203–11.

Asgari, Shaki, Nilanjana Dasgupta, and Jane G. Stout. 2012. "When Do Counter-stereotypic Ingroup Members Inspire Versus Deflate? The Effect of Successful Professional Women on Young Women's Leadership Self-Concept." *Personality and Social Psychology Bulletin* 38(3): 370–83.

Atkeson, Lonna Rae. 2003. "Not All Cues Are Created Equal: The Conditional Impact of Female Candidates on Political Engagement." *The Journal of Politics* 65(4): 1040–61.

REFERENCES

Atkeson, Lonna Rae, and Nancy Carrillo. 2007. "More Is Better: The Influence of Collective Female Descriptive Representation on External Efficacy." *Politics & Gender* 3(1): 79–101.

Atkeson, Lonna Rae, and Ronald B. Rapoport. 2003. "The More Things Change the More They Stay the Same." *Public Opinion Quarterly* 67(4): 495–521.

Badas, Alex, and Katelyn E. Stauffer. 2018. "Someone like Me: Descriptive Representation and Support for Supreme Court Nominees." *Political Research Quarterly* 71(1): 127–42.

Bade, Rachael. 2020. "GOP Women's Record-Breaking Success Reflects Party's Major Shift on Recruiting and Supporting Female Candidates." *The Washington Post*, December 7. https://www.washingtonpost.com/politics/house-republicans-women-election/2020/12/07/0563e418-367c-11eb-8d38-6aea1adb3839_story.html (accessed September 1, 2022).

Banda, Kevin K., and Erin C. Cassese. 2022. "Hostile Sexism, Racial Resentment, and Political Mobilization." *Political Behavior* 44(3): 1317–35.

Bandura, Albert. 1977. *Social Learning Theory*. Englewood Cliffs, NJ: Prentice Hall.

Barnes, Samuel H., and Max Kaase. 1979. *Political Action: Mass Participation in Five Western Democracies*. Beverly Hills, CA: Sage.

Barnes, Tiffany D., and Emily Beaulieu. 2014. "Gender Stereotypes and Corruption: How Candidates Affect Perceptions of Election Fraud." *Politics & Gender* 10(3): 365–91.

———. 2019. "Women Politicians, Institutions, and Perceptions of Corruption." *Comparative Political Studies* 52(1): 134–67.

Barnes, Tiffany D., and Stephanie M. Burchard. 2013. "'Engendering' Politics: The Impact of Descriptive Representation on Women's Political Engagement in Sub-Saharan Africa." *Comparative Political Studies* 46(7): 767–90.

Barreto, Matt. 2007. "¡Sí Se Puede! Latino Candidates and the Mobilization of Latino Voters." *American Political Science Review* 101(3): 425–42.

———. 2010. *Ethnic Cues: The Role of Shared Ethnicity in Latino Political Participation*. Ann Arbor: University of Michigan Press.

Bauer, Nichole M. 2020. "A Feminine Advantage? Delineating the Effects of Feminine Trait and Feminine Issue Messages on Evaluations of Female Candidates." *Politics & Gender* 16(3): 660–80.

Bauer, Nichole M., and Colleen Carpinella. 2018. "Visual Information and Candidate Evaluations: The Influence of Feminine and Masculine Images on Support for Female Candidates." *Political Research Quarterly* 71(2): 395–407.

Bauer, Nichole M., and Martina Santia. 2022. "Going Feminine: Identifying How and When Female Candidates Emphasize Feminine and Masculine Traits on the Campaign Trail." *Political Research Quarterly* 75(3): 691–705.

Bauer, Nicole, Yanna Krupnikov, and Sara Yeganeh. 2019. "Can Good Intentions Fail? How Focusing on Political Exclusion Affects Women's and Men's Willingness to Run for Office." Working paper.

Baxter, Sandra, and Marjorie Lansing. 1983. *Women and Politics: The Visible Majority*. University of Michigan Press.

Beaman, Lori, Raghabendra Chattopadhyay, Esther Duflo, Rohini Pande, and Petia Topalova. 2009. "Powerful Women: Does Exposure Reduce Bias?" *The Quarterly Journal of Economics* 124(4): 1497–1540.

REFERENCES

Beaman, Lori, Esther Duflo, Rohini Pande, and Petia Topalova. 2012. "Female Leadership Raises Aspirations and Educational Attainment for Girls: A Policy Experiment in India." *Science* 335(6068): 582–86.

Beck, Paul Allen, and M. Kent Jennings. 1982. "Pathways to Participation." *American Political Science Review* 76(1): 94–108.

Bejarano, Christina, and Wendy Smooth. 2022. "Women of Color Mobilizing: Sistahs Are Doing It for Themselves from GOTV to Running Candidates for Political Office." *Journal of Women, Politics & Policy* 43(1): 8–24.

Bennett, Linda M., and Stephen Earl Bennett. 1989. "Enduring Gender Differences in Political Interest: The Impact of Socialization and Political Dispositions." *American Politics Quarterly* 17(1): 105–22.

Betz, Diana E., and Denise Sekaquaptewa. 2012. "My Fair Physicist? Feminine Math and Science Role Models Demotivate Young Girls." *Social Psychological and Personality Science* 3(6): 738–46.

Biernat, Monica, Christian S. Crandall, Lissa V. Young, Diane Kobrynowicz, and Stanley M. Halpin. 1998. "All That You Can Be: Stereotyping of Self and Others in a Military Context." *Journal of Personality and Social Psychology* 75(2): 301–17.

Black, Earl, and Merle Black. 2002. *The Rise of Southern Republicans*. Cambridge, MA: Belknap Press of Harvard University Press.

Blinder, Scott, and Meredith Rolfe. 2018. "Rethinking Compassion: Toward a Political Account of the Partisan Gender Gap in the United States." *Political Psychology* 39(4): 889–906.

Block, Per. 2023. "Understanding the Self-Organization of Occupational Sex Segregation with Mobility Networks." *Social Networks* 73 (May): 42–50.

Bobo, Lawrence, and Franklin Gilliam. 1990. "Race, Sociopolitical Participation, And Black Empowerment." *American Political Science Review* 84(2): 377–93.

Bonneau, Chris W., and Kristin Kanthak. 2018. "Stronger Together: Political Ambition and the Presentation of Women Running for Office." *Politics, Groups, and Identities* 8(3): 576–94.

Bos, Angela L., Jill Greenlee, Mirya R. Holman, Zoe M. Oxley, and J. Celeste Lay. 2022. "This One's for the Boys: How Gendered Political Socialization Limits Girls' Political Ambition and Interest." *American Political Science Review* 116(2): 484–501.

Bos, Angela L., Monica C. Schneider, and Brian L. Utz. 2017. "Navigating the Political Labyrinth: Gender Stereotypes and Prejudice in US Elections." In *APA Handbook of the Psychology of Women*, 367–84. Washington, DC: American Psychological Association.

Bowen, Daniel, and Christopher Clark. 2014. "Revisiting Descriptive Representation in Congress: Assessing the Effect of Race on the Constituent-Legislator Relationship." *Political Research Quarterly* 67(3): 695–707.

Box-Steffensmeier, Janet, David Kimball, Scott Meinke, and Katherine Tate. 2003. "The Effects of Political Representation on the Electoral Advantages of House Incumbents." *Political Research Quarterly* 56(3): 259–70.

Broockman, David E. 2014. "Do Female Politicians Empower Women to Vote or Run for Office? A Regression Discontinuity Approach." *Electoral Studies* 34 (June): 190–204.

REFERENCES

Brown, DeNeen L. 2020. "Shirley Chisholm Blazed the Way for Kamala Harris to Be Biden's VP Pick." *The Washington Post*, August 11. https://www.washingtonpost.com/history/2020/08/01/shirley-chisholm-black-women-biden-vp/ (accessed January 27, 2023).

Brown, Nadia. 2014. *Sisters in the Statehouse: Black Women and Legislative Decision Making*. Oxford and New York: Oxford University Press.

Brown, Nadia E., and Danielle Casarez Lemi. 2021. *Sister Style: The Politics of Appearance for Black Women Political Elites*. New York: Oxford University Press.

Burden, Barry C., and Yoshikuni Ono. 2020. "Ignorance Is Bliss? Age, Misinformation, and Support for Women's Representation." *Public Opinion Quarterly* 84(4): 838–59.

Burden, Barry C., Yoshikuni Ono, and Masahiro Yamada. 2017. "Reassessing Public Support for a Female President." *The Journal of Politics* 79(3): 1073–78.

Burnet, Jennie E. 2011. "Women Have Found Respect: Gender Quotas, Symbolic Representation, and Female Empowerment in Rwanda." *Politics & Gender* 7(03): 303–34.

Burns, Nancy, Kay Lehman Schlozman, and Sidney Verba. 2001. *The Private Roots of Public Action: Gender, Equality, and Political Participation*. Cambridge, MA: Harvard University Press.

Burns, Nancy, Kay Lehman Schlozman, Ashley Jardina, Shauna Shames, and Sidney Verba. 2018. "What's Happened to the Gender Gap in Political Participation? How Might We Explain It?" In *100 Years of the Nineteenth Amendment: An Appraisal of Women's Political Activism*, edited by Holly J. McCammon and Lee Ann Banaszak. New York: Oxford University Press.

Campbell, Angus, Philip E. Converse, Warren E. Miller, and Donald E. Stokes. 1960. *The American Voter*. New York: Wiley.

Campbell, David E. 2006. *Why We Vote: How Schools and Communities Shape Our Civic Life*. Princeton, NJ: Princeton University Press.

Campbell, David E., and Christina Wolbrecht. 2006. "See Jane Run: Women Politicians as Role Models for Adolescents." *The Journal of Politics* 68(2): 233–47.

———. 2019. "The Resistance as Role Model: Disillusionment and Protest Among American Adolescents After 2016." *Political Behavior* 42: 1143–68.

Carian, Emily K., and Tagart Cain Sobotka. 2018. "Playing the Trump Card: Masculinity Threat and the U.S. 2016 Presidential Election." *Socius* 4. https://doi.org/10.1177/2378023117740699.

Carreras, Miguel. 2017. "High-Profile Female Executive Candidates and the Political Engagement of Women: A Multilevel Analysis." *Political Research Quarterly* 70(1): 172–83.

Cassese, Erin C., and Tiffany D. Barnes. 2019. "Reconciling Sexism and Women's Support for Republican Candidates: A Look at Gender, Class, and Whiteness in the 2012 and 2016 Presidential Races." *Political Behavior* 41(3): 677–700.

Cassese, Erin C., and Mirya R. Holman. 2019. "Playing the Woman Card: Ambivalent Sexism in the 2016 US Presidential Race." *Political Psychology* 40(1): 55–74.

Cassino, Dan, and Yasemin Besen-Cassino. 2021. *Gender Threat: American Masculinity in the Face of Change*. Stanford, CA: Stanford University Press.

REFERENCES

Castorena, Oscar. 2022. "Female Officeholders and Women's Political Engagement: The Role of Parties." *Political Behavior* 45:1609–35.

CAWP—Center for American Women and Politics. 2020a. "2020 Summary of Women Candidates." https://cawp.rutgers.edu/2020-summary-women-candidates (accessed March 24, 2023).

———. 2020b. "The 2020 Primaries Are Over. Here's What You Need to Know about the Record Numbers of Women Nominees," September 18. https://cawp.rutgers.edu/blog/2020-primaries-are-over-heres-what-you-need-know-about-record-numbers-women-nominees (accessed May 21, 2023).

———. 2021. "By the Numbers: Black Women in the 117th Congress." https://cawp.rutgers.edu/sites/default/files/resources/higher_heights_black_women_in_congress_fact_sheet_12.30.pdf (accessed March 21, 2023).

———. 2023a. "Women in Elective Office 2023." https://cawp.rutgers.edu/facts/current-numbers/women-elective-office-2023 (accessed June 20, 2023).

———. 2023b. "Women in State Legislatures 2023." https://cawp.rutgers.edu/facts/levels-office/state-legislature/women-state-legislatures-2023 (accessed February 12, 2023).

———. 2023c. "Women Presidential and Vice Presidential Candidates: A Selected List." https://cawp.rutgers.edu/facts/levels-office/federal-executive/women-presidential-and-vice-presidential-candidates-selected (accessed February 10, 2023).

———. 2023d. "History of Women in the U.S. Congress." https://cawp.rutgers.edu/facts/levels-office/congress/history-women-us-congress (accessed October 15, 2023).

———. 2024. "Women in Elective Office 2024." https://cawp.rutgers.edu/facts/current-numbers/women-elective-office-2024 (accessed March 1, 2024).

Chaney, Carole, and Barbara Sinclair. 1994. "Women and the 1992 House Elections." In *The Year of the Woman: Myths and Realities*, edited by Elizabeth Adell Cook, Sue Thomas, and Clyde Wilcox, 123–40. Boulder, CO: Westview Press.

Chauchard, Simon. 2014. "Can Descriptive Representation Change Beliefs about a Stigmatized Group? Evidence from Rural India." *American Political Science Review* 108(2): 403–22.

Chenoweth, Erica, and Marie Berry. 2018. "Who Made the Women's March?" In *The Resistance: The Dawn of the Anti-Trump Opposition Movement*, edited by David S. Meyer and Sidney Tarrow, 75–89. Oxford and New York: Oxford University Press.

Cheryan, Sapna, Benjamin J. Drury, and Marissa Vichayapai. 2013. "Enduring Influence of Stereotypical Computer Science Role Models on Women's Academic Aspirations." *Psychology of Women Quarterly* 37(1): 72–79.

Clark, Christopher. 2014. "Collective Descriptive Representation and Black Voter Mobilization in 2008." *Political Behavior* 36(2): 315–33. https://doi.org/10.1007/s11109-013-9237-1.

Clark, Christopher J., and Ray Block. 2019. "Descriptive Representation and Black Political Involvement." In Christopher J. Clark, *Gaining Voice: The Causes and Consequences of Black Representation in the American States*, 97–122. New York: Oxford University Press.

Clark, Richard, Roza Khoban, and Noah Zucker. 2023. "Breadwinner Backlash: The Gendered Effects of Industrial Design." Working paper.

REFERENCES

Clayton, Amanda. 2015. "Women's Political Engagement Under Quota-Mandated Female Representation: Evidence From a Randomized Policy Experiment." *Comparative Political Studies* 48(3): 333–69.

Clayton, Amanda, Diana Z. O'Brien, and Jennifer M. Piscopo. 2019. "All Male Panels? Representation and Democratic Legitimacy." *American Journal of Political Science* 63(1): 113–29.

———. 2023. "Women Grab Back: Exclusion, Policy Threat, and Women's Political Ambition." *American Political Science Review* 117(4): 1465–85.

Coffé, Hilde, and Marion Reiser. 2021. "How Perceptions and Information about Women's Descriptive Representation Affect Support for Positive Action Measures." *International Political Science Review* 44(2): 139–56.

Collins, Patricia Hill. 2000. *Black Feminist Thought: Knowledge, Consciousness, and the Politics of Empowerment*. Rev. 10th anniversary ed. New York: Routledge.

Conroy, Meredith, Danielle Joesten Martin, and Kim L. Nalder. 2020. "Gender, Sex, and the Role of Stereotypes in Evaluations of Hillary Clinton and the 2016 Presidential Candidates." *Journal of Women, Politics & Policy* 41(2): 194–218.

Conway, Margaret. 1985. *Political Participation in the United States*. Washington, DC: Congressional Quarterly Press.

Cooperman, Rosalyn, and Melody Crowder-Meyer. 2018. "A Run for Their Money: Republican Women's Hard Road to Campaign Funding." In *The Right Women: Republican Party Activists, Candidates, and Legislators*, edited by Malliga Och and Shauna L. Shames, 107–30. Santa Barbara, CA: ABC-CLIO.

Coppock, Alexander, and Donald P. Green. 2016. "Is Voting Habit Forming? New Evidence from Experiments and Regression Discontinuities." *American Journal of Political Science* 60(4): 1044–62.

Corder, J. Kevin, and Christina Wolbrecht. 2016. *Counting Women's Ballots: Female Voters from Suffrage Through the New Deal*. New York: Cambridge University Press.

Costa, Mia, and Isabel Wallace. 2021. "More Women Candidates: The Effects of Increased Women's Presence on Political Ambition, Efficacy, and Vote Choice." *American Politics Research* 49(4): 358–80.

Cott, Nancy F. 1990. "Across the Great Divide: Women in Politics Before and After 1920." In *Women, Politics, and Change*, edited by Louise A. Tilly and Patricia Gurin, 153–76. New York: Russell Sage Foundation.

Crenshaw, Kimberlé. 1991. "Mapping the Margins: Intersectionality, Identity Politics, and Violence Against Women of Color." *Stanford Law Review* 43(6): 1241–99.

Croson, Rachel, and Uri Gneezy. 2009. "Gender Differences in Preferences." *Journal of Economic Literature* 47(2): 448–74.

Congressional Research Service. 2023. "Membership of the 118th Congress: A Profile." https://crsreports.congress.gov/product/pdf/R/R47470 (accessed May 23, 2023).

Dabelko, Kirsten la Cour, and Paul S. Herrnson. 1997. "Women's and Men's Campaigns for the U.S. House of Representatives." *Political Research Quarterly* 50(1): 121–35.

Dasgupta, Nilanjana, and Shaki Asgari. 2004. "Seeing Is Believing: Exposure to Counterstereotypic Women Leaders and Its Effect on the Malleability of Automatic Gender Stereotyping." *Journal of Experimental Social Psychology* 40(5): 642–58.

REFERENCES

Deckman, Melissa, and Erin Cassese. 2021. "Gendered Nationalism and the 2016 US Presidential Election: How Party, Class, and Beliefs About Masculinity Shaped Voting Behavior." *Politics & Gender* 17(2): 277–300.

Deckman, Melissa, and Jared McDonald. 2022. "Uninspired by Old White Guys: The Mobilizing Factor of Younger, More Diverse Candidates for Gen Z Women." *Politics & Gender* 19(1): 195–219.

Delli Carpini, Michael X., and Scott Keeter. 1996. *What Americans Know About Politics and Why It Matters.* New Haven, CT: Yale University Press.

DeMora, Stephanie L., Christian Lindke, Sean Long, Jennifer L. Merolla, and Maricruz A. Osorio. 2023. "The Effect of the Political Environment on White Women's Political Ambition." *Political Research Quarterly* 76(4): 1987–2003.

DeSilver, Drew. 2016. "Near-Record Number of House Members Not Seeking Re-Election in 2018." *Pew Research Center: Short Reads*, April 11. https://www.pewresearch.org/fact-tank/2018/04/11/near-record-number-of-house-members-not-seeking-re-election-in-2018/ (accessed February 15, 2023).

Diekman, Amanda B., Elizabeth R. Brown, Amanda M. Johnston, and Emily K. Clark. 2010. "Seeking Congruity Between Goals and Roles: A New Look at Why Women Opt Out of Science, Technology, Engineering, and Mathematics Careers." *Psychological Science* 21(8): 1051–57.

Diekman, Amanda B., and Alice H. Eagly. 2000. "Stereotypes as Dynamic Constructs: Women and Men of the Past, Present, and Future." *Personality & Social Psychology Bulletin* 26(10): 1171–88.

Diekman, Amanda B., Mansi P. Joshi, Andrew D. White, and Heidi A. Vuletich. 2021. "Roots, Barriers, and Scaffolds: Integrating Developmental and Structural Insights to Understand Gender Disparities in Political Leadership." *Psychological Inquiry* 32(2): 77–82.

Diekman, Amanda B., and Monica C. Schneider. 2010. "A Social Role Theory Perspective on Gender Gaps in Political Attitudes." *Psychology of Women Quarterly* 34(4): 486–97.

Diekman, Amanda B., and Mia Steinberg. 2013. "Navigating Social Roles in Pursuit of Important Goals: A Communal Goal Congruity Account of STEM Pursuits." *Social and Personality Psychology Compass* 7(7): 487–501.

Diekman, Amanda B., Mia Steinberg, and Emily K. Clark. 2017. "A Goal Congruity Model of Role Entry, Engagement, and Exit: Understanding Communal Goal Processes in STEM Gender Gaps." *Personality and Social Psychology Review* 21(2): 142–75.

DiMuccio, Sarah H., and Eric D. Knowles. 2020. "The Political Significance of Fragile Masculinity." *Current Opinion in Behavioral Sciences* 34 (August): 25–28.

———. 2021. "Precarious Manhood Predicts Support for Aggressive Policies and Politicians." *Personality and Social Psychology Bulletin* 47(7): 1169–87.

Dittmar, Kelly. 2020. "The 2020 Primaries Are Over. Here's What You Need to Know About the Record Numbers of Women Nominees." *Center for American Women and Politics.* https://cawp.rutgers.edu/blog/2020-primaries-are-over-heres-what-you-need-know-about-record-numbers-women-nominees (accessed February 3, 2022).

———. 2022. *Women in Election 2022: Marking Midterm Progress.* Report, Center for American Women and Politics, Eagleton Institute of Politics, Rutgers University,

New Brunswick, NJ. https://womenrun.rutgers.edu/2022-report/ (accessed June 14, 2023).
Dittmar, Kelly, and Chelsea Hill. 2020. "What You Need to Know About the Record Number of Women State Legislative Nominees in 2020." *Center for American Women and Politics.* https://cawp.rutgers.edu/blog/what-you-need-know-about-record-number-women-state-legislative-nominees-2020 (accessed February 3, 2022).
Dittmar, Kelly, Kira Sanbonmatsu, and Susan J. Carroll. 2018. *A Seat at the Table: Congresswomen's Perspectives on Why Their Presence Matters.* Oxford and New York: Oxford University Press.
Doherty, Leanne. 2011. "Filling the Female Political Pipeline: Assessing a Mentor-Based Internship Program." *Journal of Political Science Education* 7(1): 34–47.
Dolan, Kathleen. 2005. "Do Women Candidates Play to Gender Stereotypes? Do Men Candidates Play to Women? Candidate Sex and Issues Priorities on Campaign Websites." *Political Research Quarterly* 58(1): 31–44.
———. 2006. "Symbolic Mobilization? The Impact of Candidate Sex in American Elections." *American Politics Research* 34(6): 687–704.
———. 2008. "Is There a 'Gender Affinity Effect' in American Politics? Information, Affect, and Candidate Sex in U.S House Elections." *Political Research Quarterly* 61(1): 79–89. http://www.jstor.org/stable/20299712 (accessed September 30, 2015).
———. 2011. "Do Women and Men Know Different Things? Measuring Gender Differences in Political Knowledge." *The Journal of Politics* 73(1): 97–107.
———. 2014. *When Does Gender Matter? Women Candidates and Gender Stereotypes in American Elections.* Oxford and New York: Oxford University Press.
Dovi, Suzanne, and Christina Wolbrecht. 2023. "Reevaluating the Contingent 'Yes': Essays on 'Should Blacks Represent Blacks and Women Represent Women?'" *Politics & Gender* 19(4): 1231–33.
Drury, Benjamin J., John Oliver Siy, and Sapna Cheryan. 2011. "When Do Female Role Models Benefit Women? The Importance of Differentiating Recruitment from Retention in STEM." *Psychological Inquiry* 22(4): 265–69.
Eagly, Alice H., Christa Nater, David I. Miller, Michèle Kaufmann, and Sabine Sczesny. 2020. "Gender Stereotypes Have Changed: A Cross-Temporal Meta-Analysis of U.S. Public Opinion Polls from 1946 to 2018." *American Psychologist* 75(3): 301–15.
Eagly, Alice H., and Maureen Crowley. 1986. "Gender and Helping Behavior: A Meta-Analytic Review of the Social Psychological Literature." *Psychological Bulletin* 100(3): 283–308.
Eagly, Alice H., and Steven J. Karau. 2002. "Role Congruity Theory of Prejudice Toward Female Leaders." *Psychological Review* 109(3): 573–98.
Eagly, Alice H., and Anne M. Koenig. 2021. "The Vicious Cycle Linking Stereotypes and Social Roles." *Current Directions in Psychological Science* 30(4): 343–50.
Eagly, Alice H., and Wendy Wood. 2011. "Social Role Theory." In *Handbook of Theories of Social Psychology*, edited by Paul A. M. Van Lang, Arie W. Kruglanski, and E. Tory Higgins, 458–76. Thousand Oaks, CA: Sage,.
Easton, David, and Jack Dennis. 1969. *Children in the Political System: Origins of Political Legitimacy.* 1st ed. New York: McGraw Hill.

REFERENCES

Erikson, Robert S., Michael MacKuen, and James A. Stimson. 2002. *The Macro Polity*. Cambridge and New York: Cambridge University Press.

Evans, Alice. 2016. "'For the Elections, We Want Women!' Closing the Gender Gap in Zambian Politics." *Development and Change* 47(2): 388–411.

Fairdosi, Amir, and Jon Rogowski. 2015. "Candidate Race, Partisanship, and Political Participation: When Do Black Candidates Increase Black Turnout?" *Political Research Quarterly* 68(2): 337–49.

Feller, Madison. "7 Young Women of Color Explain What the New Congress Means to Them." *Elle*, November 29, 2021. https://www.elle.com/culture/career-politics/a25702461/women-of-color-on-new-congress/ (accessed May 25, 2022).

Ferreira, Fernando, and Joseph Gyourko. 2014. "Does Gender Matter for Political Leadership? The Case of U.S. Mayors." *Journal of Public Economics* 112(C): 24–39.

Finkel, Steven E. 1995. *Causal Analysis with Panel Data*. Thousand Oaks, CA: Sage.

Fiorina, Morris P. 1981. *Retrospective Voting in American National Elections*. New Haven, CT: Yale University Press.

Fitzpatrick, Ellen F. 2016. *The Highest Glass Ceiling: Women's Quest for the American Presidency*. Cambridge, MA: Harvard University Press.

Flores, Andrew, Charles Gossett, Gabriele Magni, and Andrew Reynolds. 2020. "11 Openly LGBTQ Lawmakers Will Take Their Seats in the next Congress. That's a Record in Both Numbers and Diversity." *The Washington Post*, November 30. https://www.washingtonpost.com/politics/2020/11/30/11-lgbtq-legislators-will-take-their-seats-next-congress-largest-most-diverse-group-ever/ (accessed May 22, 2023).

Foa, Roberto, and Yascha Mounk. 2016. "The Danger of Deconsolidation: The Democratic Disconnect." *Journal of Democracy* 27(3): 5–17.

———. 2017. "The Signs of Deconsolidation." *Journal of Democracy* 28(1): 5–16.

Foos, Florian, and Fabrizio Gilardi. 2020. "Does Exposure to Gender Role Models Increase Women's Political Ambition? A Field Experiment with Politicians." *Journal of Experimental Political Science* 7(3): 157–66.

Fraga, Bernard. 2016. "Candidates or Districts? Reevaluating the Role of Race in Voter Turnout." *American Journal of Political Science* 60(1): 97–122.

Fraga, Bernard L. 2018. *The Turnout Gap: Race, Ethnicity, and Political Inequality in a Diversifying America*. Cambridge and New York: Cambridge University Press.

Fraile, Marta, and Raul Gomez. 2017. "Why Does Alejandro Know More About Politics than Catalina? Explaining the Latin American Gender Gap in Political Knowledge." *British Journal of Political Science* 47(1): 91–112.

Franklin, Mark N. 2004. *Voter Turnout and the Dynamics of Electoral Competition in Established Democracies Since 1945*. Cambridge: Cambridge University Press.

Frasure-Yokley, Lorrie. 2018. "Choosing the Velvet Glove: Women Voters, Ambivalent Sexism, and Vote Choice in 2016." *Journal of Race, Ethnicity, and Politics* 3(1): 3–25.

Fridkin, Kim L., and Patrick J. Kenney. 2014. "How the Gender of U.S. Senators Influences People's Understanding and Engagement in Politics." *The Journal of Politics* 76(4): 1017–31.

REFERENCES

Fuesting, Melissa A., and Amanda B. Diekman. 2017. "Not by Success Alone: Role Models Provide Pathways to Communal Opportunities in STEM." *Personality & Social Psychology Bulletin* 43(2): 163–76.

Gadarian, Shana Kushner, Sara Wallace Goodman, and Thomas B. Pepinsky. 2022. *Pandemic Politics: The Deadly Toll of Polarization in the Age of COVID*. Princeton, NJ: Princeton University Press.

Gay, Claudine. 2001. "The Effect of Black Congressional Representation on Political Participation." *American Political Science Review* 95(3): 589–602.

Gerber, Alan S., Donald P. Green, and Ron Shachar. 2003. "Voting May Be Habit-Forming: Evidence from a Randomized Field Experiment." *American Journal of Political Science* 47(3): 540–50.

Gerring, John. 1998. *Party Ideologies in America, 1828–1996*. Cambridge and New York: Cambridge University Press.

Gidengil, Elisabeth, and Dietlind Stolle. 2021. "Beyond the Gender Gap: The Role of Gender Identity." *The Journal of Politics* 83(4): 1818–22.

Gilardi, Fabrizio. 2015. "The Temporary Importance of Role Models for Women's Political Representation." *American Journal of Political Science* 59(4): 957–70.

Gilberstadt, Hannah, Hannah Hartig, Bradley Jones, Amina Dunn, Carroll Doherty, Jocelyn Kiley, Andrew Daniller, Ted Van Green, and Vianney Gomez. 2020. "Election 2020: Voters Are Highly Engaged, but Nearly Half Expect To Have Difficulties Voting." *Pew Research Center: Report*, August 13. https://www.pewresearch.org/politics/2020/08/13/election-2020-voters-are-highly-engaged-but-nearly-half-expect-to-have-difficulties-voting/ (accessed March 1, 2024).

Gilliam, Franklin, and Karen Kaufmann. 1998. "Is There an Empowerment Life Cycle? Long-Term Black Empowerment and Its Influence on Voter Participation." *Urban Affairs Review* 33(6): 741–66.

Glick, Peter, and Susan T. Fiske. 1996. "The Ambivalent Sexism Inventory: Differentiating Hostile and Benevolent Sexism." *Journal of Personality and Social Psychology* 70(3): 491–512.

———. 1997. "Hostile and Benevolent Sexism: Measuring Ambivalent Sexist Attitudes Toward Women." *Psychology of Women Quarterly* 21(1): 119–35.

———. 2001. "An Ambivalent Alliance: Hostile and Benevolent Sexism as Complementary Justifications for Gender Inequality." *The American Psychologist* 56(2): 109–18.

Goldin, Claudia. 2014. "A Pollution Theory of Discrimination: Male and Female Differences in Occupations and Earnings." In *Human Capital in History: The American Record*, 313–48. Chicago: University of Chicago Press.

Gonzalez, Sylvia, and Nichole Bauer. 2022. "Strong and Caring? The Stereotypic Traits of Women of Color in Politics." *Politics, Groups, and Identities* 12(1): 124–41.

Gothreau, Claire, Kevin Arceneaux, and Amanda Friesen. 2022. "Hostile, Benevolent, Implicit: How Different Shades of Sexism Impact Gendered Policy Attitudes." *Frontiers in Political Science* 4 (July). https://doi.org/10.3389/pos.2022.817309.

Green, Donald P., Bradley Palmquist, and Eric Schickler. 2002. *Partisan Hearts and Minds: Political Parties and the Social Identities of Voters*. New Haven, CT: Yale University Press.

Greenlee, Jill S., Mirya R. Holman, and Rachel VanSickle-Ward. 2014. "Making It Personal: Assessing the Impact of In-Class Exercises on Closing the Gender Gap in Political Ambition." *Journal of Political Science Education* 10(1): 48–61.

REFERENCES

Greenstein, Fred I. 1961. "Sex-Related Political Differences in Childhood." *The Journal of Politics* 23(2): 353–71.

———. 1974. *Children and Politics*. Rev. ed. New Haven, CT: Yale University Press.

Griffin, John, and Michael Keane. 2006. "Descriptive Representation and the Composition of African American Turnout." *American Journal of Political Science* 50(4): 998–1012.

Griffin, John D., Brian Newman, and Christina Wolbrecht. 2012. "A Gender Gap in Policy Representation in the U.S. Congress?" *Legislative Studies Quarterly* 37 (1): 35–66.

Gutierrez, Angela, Angela X. Ocampo, Matt A. Barreto, and Gary Segura. 2019. "Somos Más: How Racial Threat and Anger Mobilized Latino Voters in the Trump Era." *Political Research Quarterly* 72(4): 960–75.

Hajnal, Zoltan. 2007. *Changing White Attitudes Toward Black Political Leadership*. Cambridge and New York: Cambridge University Press.

Hancock, Ange-Marie. 2007a. "Intersectionality as a Normative and Empirical Paradigm." *Politics & Gender* 3(2): 248–54.

———. 2007b. "When Multiplication Doesn't Equal Quick Addition: Examining Intersectionality as a Research Paradigm." *Perspectives on Politics* 5(1): 63–79.

Hanmer, Michael J., and Kerem Ozan Kalkan. 2013. "Behind the Curve: Clarifying the Best Approach to Calculating Predicted Probabilities and Marginal Effect from Limited Dependent Variable Models." *American Journal of Political Science* 57(1): 263–77.

Hansen, Susan B. 1997. "Talking About Politics: Gender and Contextual Effects on Political Proselytizing." *The Journal of Politics* 59(1): 73–103.

Harris, Kamala. 2018. "Forward." In *The Chisholm Effect: Black Women in American Politics 2018*, Center for American Women and Politics. http://cawp.rutgers.edu/sites/default/files/resources/chisholm_effect_black_women_in_politics.pdf (accessed May 22, 2023).

Hatemi, Peter K., John R. Alford, and Lindon J. Eaves. 2009. "Is There a 'Party' in Your Genes?" *Political Research Quarterly* 62(3): 584–600.

Hatemi, Peter K., and Christopher Ojeda. 2021. "The Role of Child Perception and Motivation in Political Socialization." *British Journal of Political Science* 51(3): 1097–1118.

Hayes, Matthew, Cara Wong, Andrew Bloeser, Mark Fredrickson, and Chera laForge. 2024. "Elected Officials, Empowered Voters: The Impact of Descriptive Representation on Voter Turnout." *Political Behavior* 46(1): 185–207.

Heilman, Madeline E. 1980. "The Impact of Situational Factors on Personnel Decisions Concerning Women: Varying the Sex Composition of the Applicant Pool." *Organizational Behavior and Human Performance* 26(3): 386–95.

Henderson, John, Jasjeet Sekhon, and Rocío Titiunik. 2016. "Cause or Effect? Turnout in Hispanic Majority-Minority Districts." *Political Analysis* 24(3): 404–12.

Herrmann, Sarah D., Robert Mark Adelman, Jessica E. Bodford, Oliver Graudejus, Morris A. Okun, and Virginia S. Y. Kwan. 2016. "The Effects of a Female Role Model on Academic Performance and Persistence of Women in STEM Courses." *Basic and Applied Social Psychology* 38(5): 258–68.

Herrnson, Paul S., J. Celeste Lay, and Atiya Kai Stokes. 2003. "Women Running 'as Women': Candidate Gender, Campaign Issues, and Voter-Targeting Strategies." *The Journal of Politics* 65(1): 244–55.

Hess, Robert D., and Judith V. Torney. 2005. *The Development of Political Attitudes in Children*. New Brunswick, NJ: Aldine Transaction.

High-Pippert, Angela, and John Comer. 1998. "Female Empowerment." *Women & Politics* 19(4): 53–66.

Hinojosa, Magda, and Miki Caul Kittilson. 2020. *Seeing Women, Strengthening Democracy: How Women in Politics Foster Connected Citizens*. Oxford and New York: Oxford University Press.

Holman, Mirya R., Jennifer L. Merolla, and Elizabeth J. Zechmeister. 2011. "Sex, Stereotypes, and Security: A Study of the Effects of Terrorist Threat on Assessments of Female Leadership." *Journal of Women, Politics & Policy* 32(3): 173–92.

Holman, Mirya R., and Monica C. Schneider. 2018. "Gender, Race, and Political Ambition: How Intersectionality and Frames Influence Interest in Political Office." *Politics, Groups, and Identities* 6(2): 264–80.

Horowitz, Juliana Menasce, Ruth Igielnik, and Kim Parker. 2018. "Women and Leadership 2018." *Pew Research Center: Report*, September 20. https://www.pewresearch.org/social-trends/2018/09/20/women-and-leadership-2018/ (accessed June 7, 2022).

Hoyt, Crystal L., Jeni L. Burnette, and Audrey N. Innella. 2012. "I Can Do That: The Impact of Implicit Theories on Leadership Role Model Effectiveness." *Personality and Social Psychology Bulletin* 38(2): 257–68.

Hoyt, Crystal L., and Stefanie Simon. 2011. "Female Leaders: Injurious or Inspiring Role Models for Women?" *Psychology of Women Quarterly* 35(1): 143–57.

Huddy, Leonie, and Alexa Bankert. 2017. "Political Partisanship as a Social Identity." *Oxford Research Encyclopedia of Politics*, May 24.

Huddy, Leonie, Lilliana Mason, and Lene Aarøe. 2015. "Expressive Partisanship: Campaign Involvement, Political Emotion, and Partisan Identity." *American Political Science Review* 109(1): 1–17.

Hutchings, Vincent L. 2001. "Political Context, Issue Salience, and Selective Attentiveness: Constituent Knowledge of the Clarence Thomas Confirmation Vote." *The Journal of Politics* 63(3): 846–68.

Jacobsmeier, Matthew L. 2015. "From Black and White to Left and Right: Race, Perceptions of Candidates' Ideologies, and Voting Behavior in U.S. House Elections." *Political Behavior* 37(3): 595–621.

Jennings, M. Kent, and Gregory B. Markus. 1984. "Partisan Orientations over the Long Haul: Results from the Three-Wave Political Socialization Panel Study." *American Political Science Review* 78(4): 1000–1018.

Jennings, M. Kent, and Richard G. Niemi. 1968. "The Transmission of Political Values from Parent to Child." *American Political Science Review* 62(1): 169–84.

———. 1981. *Generations and Politics: A Panel Study of Young Adults and Their Parents*. Princeton, NJ: Princeton University Press.

Jennings, M. Kent, Laura Stoker, and Jake Bowers. 2009. "Politics Across Generations: Family Transmission Reexamined." *The Journal of Politics* 71(3): 782–99.

Johnson, David K. 2004. *The Lavender Scare: The Cold War Persecution of Gays and Lesbians in the Federal Government*. Chicago: University of Chicago Press.

REFERENCES

Jones, Philip Edward. 2014. "Does the Descriptive Representation of Gender Influence Accountability for Substantive Representation?" *Politics & Gender* 10(2): 175–99.

Kahn, Kim Fridkin. 1993. "Gender Differences in Campaign Messages: The Political Advertisements of Men and Women Candidates for U.S. Senate." *Political Research Quarterly* 46(3): 481–502.

Karp, Jeffrey A., and Susan A. Banducci. 2008. "When Politics Is Not Just a Man's Game: Women's Representation and Political Engagement." *Electoral Studies* 27(1): 105–15.

Karpowitz, Christopher F., J. Quin Monson, and Jessica Robinson Preece. 2017. "How to Elect More Women: Gender and Candidate Success in a Field Experiment." *American Journal of Political Science* 61(4): 927–43.

Kaufmann, Karen. 2003. "Black and Latino Voters in Denver: Responses to Each Other's Political Leadership." *Political Science Quarterly* 118(1): 107–25.

Keele, Luke, Paru Shah, Ismail White, and Kristine Kay. 2017. "Black Candidates and Black Turnout: A Study of Viability in Louisiana Mayoral Elections." *The Journal of Politics* 79(3): 780–91.

Keele, Luke, and Ismail White. 2019. "African American Turnout and African American Candidates." *Political Science Research and Methods* 7(3): 431–49.

Kerber, Linda K. 1976. "The Republican Mother: Women and the Enlightenment—An American Perspective." *American Quarterly* 28(2): 187–205.

———. 1988. "Separate Spheres, Female Worlds, Woman's Place: The Rhetoric of Women's History." *The Journal of American History* 75(1): 9–39.

Kerber, Linda K., Nancy F. Cott, Robert Gross, Lynn Hunt, Carroll Smith-Rosenberg, and Christine M. Stansell. 1989. "Beyond Roles, Beyond Spheres: Thinking About Gender in the Early Republic." *The William and Mary Quarterly* 46(3): 565–85.

Keyssar, Alexander. 2000. *The Right to Vote: The Contested History of Democracy in the United States*. New York: Basic Books.

Kim, Jessica, and Kathleen M. Fallon. 2023. "Making Women Visible: How Gender Quotas Shape Global Attitudes Toward Women in Politics." *Politics & Gender* 19(4): 981–1006.

Kittilson, Miki Caul, and Leslie Schwindt-Bayer. 2012. *The Gendered Effects of Electoral Institutions: Political Engagement and Participation*. Oxford and New York: Oxford University Press.

Koch, Jeffrey. 1997. "Candidate Gender and Women's Psychological Engagement in Politics." *American Politics Quarterly* 25(1): 118–33.

Koenig, Anne M., and Alice H. Eagly. 2014. "Evidence for the Social Role Theory of Stereotype Content: Observations of Groups' Roles Shape Stereotypes." *Journal of Personality and Social Psychology* 107(3): 371–92.

Koenig, Anne M., Alice H. Eagly, Abigail A. Mitchell, and Tiina Ristikari. 2011. "Are Leader Stereotypes Masculine? A Meta-Analysis of Three Research Paradigms." *Psychological Bulletin* 137(4): 616–42.

Kroh, Martin, and Peter Selb. 2009. "Inheritance and the Dynamics of Party Identification." *Political Behavior* 31(4): 559–74.

Krosnick, Jon A., Penny S. Visser, and Joshua Harder. 2010. "The Psychological Underpinnings of Political Behavior." In *Handbook of Social Psychology*, edited by Susan T. Fiske, Daniel T. Gilbert, and Gardner Lindzey, 1288–1342. Hoboken, NJ: John Wiley & Sons.

Ladam, Christina, Jeffrey J. Harden, and Jason H. Windett. 2018. "Prominent Role Models: High-Profile Female Politicians and the Emergence of Women as Candidates for Public Office:" *American Journal of Political Science* 62(2): 369–81.

Lawless, Jennifer L. 2004. "Politics of Presence? Congresswomen and Symbolic Representation." *Political Research Quarterly* 57(1): 81–99.

Lawless, Jennifer L., and Richard L. Fox. 2010. *It Still Takes a Candidate: Why Women Don't Run for Office*. Rev. ed. Cambridge: Cambridge University Press.

———. 2017. *Running from Office: Why Young Americans Are Turned Off to Politics*. Oxford and New York: Oxford University Press.

Levitsky, Steven, and Daniel Ziblatt. 2018. *How Democracies Die*. 1st ed. New York: Crown.

Lippa, Richard. 1998. "Gender-Related Individual Differences and the Structure of Vocational Interests: The Importance of the People-Things Dimension." *Journal of Personality and Social Psychology* 74(4): 996–1009.

Lips, Hilary M. 1989. "Gender-Role Socialization: Lessons in Femininity." In *Women: A Feminist Perspective*, edited by Jo Freeman, 128–48. Mountain View, CA: Mayfield.

Liu, Shan-Jan Sarah. 2018. "Are Female Political Leaders Role Models? Lessons from Asia." *Political Research Quarterly* 71(2): 255–69.

Liu, Shan-Jan Sarah, and Lee Ann Banaszak. 2017. "Do Government Positions Held by Women Matter? A Cross-National Examination of Female Ministers' Impacts on Women's Political Participation." *Politics & Gender* 13(1): 132–62.

Lizotte, Mary-Kate, and Andrew H. Sidman. 2009. "Explaining the Gender Gap in Political Knowledge." *Politics & Gender* 5(2): 127–51.

Lockwood, Penelope. 2006. " 'Someone like Me Can Be Successful': Do College Students Need Same-Gender Role Models?" *Psychology of Women Quarterly* 30(1): 36–46.

Lockwood, Penelope, and Ziva Kunda. 1997. "Superstars and Me: Predicting the Impact of Role Models on the Self." *Journal of Personality and Social Psychology* 73(1): 91–103.

Lublin, David Ian, and Katherine Tate. 1995. "Racial Group Competition in Urban Elections." In *Classifying by Race*, edited by Paul E. Peterson, 245–61. Princeton, NJ: Princeton University Press.

MacManus, Susan A. 1981. "A City's First Female Officeholder: 'Coattails' for Future Female Officeseekers?" *The Western Political Quarterly* 34(1): 88–99.

Maghsoodloo, Saeed, and Ching-Ying Huang. 2010. "Comparing the Overlapping of Two Independent Confidence Intervals with a Single Confidence Interval for Two Normal Population Parameters." *Journal of Statistical Planning and Inference* 140(11): 3295–3305.

Magni, Gabrielle and Andrew Reynolds. 2021. "Voter Preferences and the Political Underrepresentation of Minority Groups: Lesbian, Gay, and Transgender Candidates in Advanced Democracies." *The Journal of Politics* 83(4): 1199–1883.

Major, Brenda, Alison Blodorn, and Gregory Major Blascovich. 2018. "The Threat of Increasing Diversity: Why Many White Americans Support Trump in the 2016 Presidential Election." *Group Processes & Intergroup Relations* 21(6): 931–40.

REFERENCES

Manento, Cory, and Marie Schenk. 2021. "Role Models or Partisan Models? The Effect of Prominent Women Officeholders." *State Politics & Policy Quarterly* 21(3): 221–42. https://doi.org/10.1017/spq.2020.3.

Mansbridge, Jane. 1999. "Should Blacks Represent Blacks and Women Represent Women? A Contingent 'Yes.'" *The Journal of Politics* 61(3): 628–57.

Mariani, Mack, Bryan W. Marshall, and A. Lanethea Mathews-Schultz. 2015. "See Hillary Clinton, Nancy Pelosi, and Sarah Palin Run? Party, Ideology, and the Influence of Female Role Models on Young Women." *Political Research Quarterly* 68(4): 716–31.

Marschall, Melissa, and Paru Shah. 2007. "The Attitudinal Effects of Minority Incorporation: Examining the Racial Dimensions of Trust in Urban America." *Urban Affairs Review* 42(5): 629–58.

Marx, David M., and Jasmin S. Roman. 2002. "Female Role Models: Protecting Women's Math Test Performance." *Personality and Social Psychology Bulletin* 28(9): 1183–93.

Marx, David M., Diederik A. Stapel, and Dominique Muller. 2005. "We Can Do It: The Interplay of Construal Orientation and Social Comparisons Under Threat." *Journal of Personality and Social Psychology* 88(3): 432–46.

Mason, Lilliana. 2015. "'I Disrespectfully Agree': The Differential Effects of Partisan Sorting on Social and Issue Polarization." *American Journal of Political Science* 59(1): 128–45.

———. 2018. *Uncivil Agreement: How Politics Became Our Identity*. Chicago: University of Chicago Press.

Mason, Lilliana, and Julie Wronski. 2018. "One Tribe to Bind Them All: How Our Social Group Attachments Strengthen Partisanship." *Political Psychology* 39(S1): 257–77.

Matland, Richard E. 1994. "Putting Scandinavian Equality to the Test: An Experimental Evaluation of Gender Stereotyping of Political Candidates in a Sample of Norwegian Voters." *British Journal of Political Science* 24(2): 273–92.

Mayhew, David R. 1974. *Congress: The Electoral Connection*. New Haven, CT: Yale University Press.

McCaskill, Noland D. 2016. "Trump: Clinton Walked in Front of Me and 'I Wasn't Impressed.'" *Politico*, October 14. https://www.politico.com/story/2016/10/trump-clinton-debate-walk-not-impressed-229810 (accessed June 14, 2023).

McDermott, Monika L. 2016. *Masculinity, Femininity, and American Political Behavior*. Oxford and New York: Oxford University Press.

McDonald, Maura, Rachel Porter, and Sarah A. Treul. 2020. "Running as a Woman? Candidate Presentation in the 2018 Midterms." *Political Research Quarterly* 73(4)

McIntyre, Rusty B., René M. Paulson, and Charles G. Lord. 2003. "Alleviating Women's Mathematics Stereotype Threat Through Salience of Group Achievements." *Journal of Experimental Social Psychology* 39(1): 83–90.

Meyer, David S., and Sidney Tarrow, eds. 2018. *The Resistance: The Dawn of the Anti-Trump Opposition Movement*. Oxford and New York: Oxford University Press.

Midgley, Claire, Gabriela DeBues-Stafford, Penelope Lockwood, and Sabrina Thai. 2021. "She Needs to See It to Be It: The Importance of Same-Gender Athletic Role Models." *Sex Roles* 85(3): 142–60.

REFERENCES

Milbrath, Lester W., and M. L. Goel. 1977. *Political Participation: How and Why Do People Get Involved in Politics?* 2nd ed. Chicago: Rand McNally.

Miller, Joanne M., and Jon A. Krosnick. 2004. "Threat as a Motivator of Political Activism: A Field Experiment." *Political Psychology* 25(4): 507–23.

Miller, Melissa K. 2019. "Who Knows More About Politics? A Dual Explanation for the Gender Gap." *American Politics Research* 47(1): 174–88.

Mitchell, Alison. 2016. "To Understand Clinton's Moment, Consider That It Came 32 Years After Ferraro's." *The New York Times*, June 11. https://www.nytimes.com/2016/06/12/us/politics/women-white-house-clinton-geraldine-ferraro.html (accessed August 31, 2022).

Mondak, Jeffery J., and Mary R. Anderson. 2004. "The Knowledge Gap: A Reexamination of Gender-Based Differences in Political Knowledge." *The Journal of Politics* 66(2): 492–512.

Montoya, Celeste M., Christina Bejarano, Nadia E. Brown, and Sarah Allen Gershon. 2022. "The Intersectional Dynamics of Descriptive Representation." *Politics & Gender* 18(2): 483–512.

Morgan, Jana, and Melissa Buice. 2013. "Latin American Attitudes Toward Women in Politics: The Influence of Elite Cues, Female Advancement, and Individual Characteristics." *American Political Science Review* 107(4): 644–62.

Morgenroth, Thekla, Michelle K. Ryan, and Kim Peters. 2015. "The Motivational Theory of Role Modeling: How Role Models Influence Role Aspirants' Goals." *Review of General Psychology* 19(4): 465–83.

Mounk, Yascha. 2018. *The People vs. Democracy: Why Our Freedom Is in Danger and How to Save It.* Cambridge, MA: Harvard University Press.

Nadeem, Reem. 2021. "Deep Divisions in Americans' Views of Nation's Racial History—and How to Address It." *Pew Research Center: Report*, August 12. https://www.pewresearch.org/politics/2021/08/12/deep-divisions-in-americans-views-of-nations-racial-history-and-how-to-address-it/ (accessed May 21, 2023).

NEZHDI (Independent Women's Democratic Initiative) and Linda Edmondson. 1991. "Feminist Manifesto: 'Democracy Without Women Is No Democracy!'" *Feminist Review* 39 (Autumn): 127–32.

North, Anna. 2017. "'We've Never Seen Anything Like This': How Trump Inspired Women to Run for Office." *Vox*, November 8. https://www.vox.com/identities/2017/11/6/16571570/female-candidates-trump-clinton-2016-election (accessed August 31, 2022).

Ojeda, Christopher, and Peter K. Hatemi. 2015. "Accounting for the Child in the Transmission of Party Identification." *American Sociological Review* 80(6): 1150–74.

Ondercin, Heather L. 2022. "Location, Location, Location: How Electoral Opportunities Shape Women's Emergence as Candidates." *British Journal of Political Science* 52(4): 1523–43.

Oser, Jennifer, Fernando Feitosa, and Ruth Dassonneville. 2023. "Who Feels They Can Understand and Have an Impact on Political Processes? Socio-Demographic Correlates of Political Efficacy in 46 Countries, 1996–2016." *International Journal of Public Opinion Research* 35(2): edad013.

Oxley, Zoe M., Mirya R. Holman, Jill S. Greenlee, Angela L. Bos, and J. Celeste Lay. 2020. "Children's Views of the American Presidency." *Public Opinion Quarterly* 84(1): 141–57.

Pacheco, Julianna, and Rebecca Kreitzer. 2016. "Adolescent Determinants of Abortion Attitudes: Evidence from the Children of the National Longitudinal Survey of Youth." *Public Opinion Quarterly* 80(1): 66–89.

Palley, Marian Lief. 1993. "Elections 1992 and the Thomas Appointment." *PS: Political Science and Politics* 26(1): 28–31.

Palmer, Barbara, and Dennis Michael Simon. 2008. *Breaking the Political Glass Ceiling: Women and Congressional Elections*. 2nd ed. New York: Routledge.

Pantoja, Adrian, and Gary Segura. 2003. "Does Ethnicity Matter? Descriptive Representation in Legislatures and Political Alienation Among Latinos." *Social Science Quarterly* 84(2): 441–60.

Pateman, Carole. 1980. "Women, Nature, and the Suffrage." *Ethics* 90(4): 564–75.

———. 1994. "Three Questions about Womanhood Suffrage." In *Suffrage and Beyond: International Feminist Perspectives*, 331–48. New York: New York University Press.

Paxton, Pamela Marie, Melanie M. Hughes, and Tiffany Barnes. 2020. *Women, Politics, and Power: A Global Perspective*. 4th ed. Lanham, MD: Rowman & Littlefield.

Pearson, Kathryn, and Logan Dancey. 2011. "Speaking for the Underrepresented in the House of Representatives: Voicing Women's Interests in a Partisan Era." *Politics & Gender* 7(4): 493–519.

Pereira, Frederico Batista. 2019. "Gendered Political Contexts: The Gender Gap in Political Knowledge." *The Journal of Politics* 81(4): 1480–93.

Pérez, Efrén O. 2015. "Xenophobic Rhetoric and Its Political Effects on Immigrants and Their Co-Ethnics." *American Journal of Political Science* 59(3): 549–64.

Peters, Kim, Niklas K. Steffens, and Thekla Morgenroth. 2018. "Superstars Are Not Necessarily Role Models: Morality Perceptions Moderate the Impact of Competence Perceptions on Supervisor Role Modeling." *European Journal of Social Psychology* 48(6): 725–46.

Peterson, Bill. 1984. "Ferraro Joins '84 Ticket by Acclamation." *The Washington Post*, July 19, A1. https://www.washingtonpost.com/archive/politics/1984/07/20/ferraro-joins-84-ticket-by-acclamation/cfb071a7-0080-4c57-9b65-4eb07a1a6daa/ (accessed May 19, 2022).

Phillips, Anne. 1998. *The Politics of Presence*. Oxford and New York: Oxford University Press.

Phillips, Christian Dyogi. 2021. *Nowhere to Run: Race, Gender, and Immigration in American Elections*. Oxford and New York: Oxford University Press.

Piscopo, Jennifer M., and Shauna L. Shames. 2020. "Without Women There Is No Democracy." *Boston Review*, May 20, 2020. https://www.bostonreview.net/articles/jennifer-m-piscopo-shauna-l-shames-without-women-there-no-democracy/ (accessed June 10, 2024).

Pitkin, Hanna Fenichel. 1967. *The Concept of Representation*. Berkeley and Los Angeles: University of California Press.

Plaks, Jason E., Steven J. Stroessner, Carol S. Dweck, and Jeffrey W. Sherman. 2001. "Person Theories and Attention Allocation: Preferences for Stereotypic Versus Counterstereotypic Information." *Journal of Personality and Social Psychology* 80(6): 876–93.

Plutzer, Eric. 2002. "Becoming a Habitual Voter: Inertia, Resources, and Growth in Young Adulthood." *American Political Science Review* 96(1): 41–56.

Putnam, Robert D. 2001. *Bowling Alone: The Collapse and Revival of American Community*. New York: Simon & Schuster.

Putnam, Robert D., and David E. Campbell. 2012. *American Grace: How Religion Divides and Unites Us*. With new epilogue. New York: Simon & Schuster.

Radean, Marius. 2023. "The Significance of Differences Interval: Assessing the Statistical and Substantive Difference Between Two Quantities of Interest." *The Journal of Politics* 85(3): 969–83.

Rakove, Jack, and Michael W. McConnell. 2016. "Should We Abolish the Electoral College?" *Stanford Magazine* (September–October). https://stanfordmag.org/contents/should-we-abolish-the-electoral-college (accessed February 15, 2023).

Reingold, Beth. 2008. "Women as Officeholders: Linking Descriptive and Substantive Representation." In *Political Women and American Democracy*, edited by Christina Wolbrecht, Karen Beckwith, and Lisa Baldez, 128–47. New York: Cambridge University Press.

———. 2020. *Race, Gender, and Political Representation: Toward a More Intersectional Approach*. Oxford and New York: Oxford University Press.

Reingold, Beth, and Jessica Harrell. 2010. "The Impact of Descriptive Representation on Women's Political Engagement: Does Party Matter?" *Political Research Quarterly* 63(2): 280–94.

Reynolds, Andrew. 2018. *The Children of Harvey Milk: How LGBTQ Politicians Changed the World*. Oxford and New York: Oxford University Press.

Rios, Desdamona, Abigail J. Stewart, and David G. Winter. 2010. "'Thinking She Could Be the Next President': Why Identifying with the Curriculum Matters." *Psychology of Women Quarterly* 34(3): 328–38.

Rocha, Rene R., Caroline J. Tolbert, Daniel C. Bowen, and Christopher J. Clark. 2010. "Race and Turnout: Does Descriptive Representation in State Legislatures Increase Minority Voting?" *Political Research Quarterly* 63(4): 890–907.

Rossi, Alice S., ed. 1973. *The Feminist Papers: From Adams to de Beauvoir*. New York: Bantam Books.

Rouse, Stella, and Ashley Ross. 2018. *The Politics of Millennials: Political Beliefs and Policy Preferences of America's Most Diverse Generation*. Ann Arbor: University of Michigan Press.

Rubinstein, Dana. 2020. "Torres and Jones Win and Will Become 1st Gay Black Members of Congress." *The New York Times*, November 4. https://www.nytimes.com/2020/11/04/nyregion/ny-house-torres-jones.html (accessed May 22, 2023).

Rucker, Philip. 2015. "Trump Says Fox's Megyn Kelly Had 'Blood Coming Out of Her Wherever.'" *The Washington Post*, August 8. https://www.washingtonpost.com/news/post-politics/wp/2015/08/07/trump-says-foxs-megyn-kelly-had-blood-coming-out-of-her-wherever/ (accessed August 31, 2022).

Safarpour, Alauna C., SoRelle Wyckoff Gaynor, Stella M. Rouse, and Michele L. Swers. 2022. "When Women Run, Voters Will Follow (Sometimes): Examining the Mobilizing Effect of Female Candidates in the 2014 and 2018 Midterm Elections." *Political Behavior* 44(4): 365–88.

REFERENCES

Sanbonmatsu, Kira. 2002. "Gender Stereotypes and Vote Choice." *American Journal of Political Science* 46(1): 20–34.

———. 2008. "Representation by Gender and Parties." In *Political Women and American Democracy*, edited by Christina Wolbrecht, Karen Beckwith, and Lisa Baldez, 96–109. Cambridge and New York: Cambridge University Press.

Sanchez, Gabriel, and Jason Morin. 2011. "The Effect of Descriptive Representation on Latinos' Views of Government and of Themselves." *Social Science Quarterly* 92(2): 483–508.

Sapiro, Virginia. 1981. "Research Frontier Essay: When Are Interests Interesting? The Problem of Political Representation of Women." *American Political Science Review* 75(3): 701–16.

Sapiro, Virginia, and Pamela Johnston Conover. 1997. "The Variable Gender Basis of Electoral Politics: Gender and Context in the 1992 US Election." *British Journal of Political Science* 27(4): 497–523.

Schaffner, Brian F. 2021. "Optimizing the Measurement of Sexism in Political Surveys." *Political Analysis* 30(3): 364–80.

Schickler, Eric. 2016. *Racial Realignment: The Transformation of American Liberalism, 1932–1965*. Princeton, NJ: Princeton University Press.

Schlozman, Kay Lehman, Henry E. Brady, and Sidney Verba. 2018. *Unequal and Unrepresented: Political Inequality and the People's Voice in the New Gilded Age*. Princeton, NJ: Princeton University Press.

Schneider, Monica C. 2014. "Gender-Based Strategies on Candidate Websites." *Journal of Political Marketing* 13(4): 264–90.

Schneider, Monica C., and Angela L. Bos. 2014. "Measuring Stereotypes of Female Politicians." *Political Psychology* 35(2): 245–66.

———. 2019. "The Application of Social Role Theory to the Study of Gender in Politics." *Political Psychology* 40(S1): 173–213.

Schneider, Monica C., and Mirya Holman. 2020. "Can Role Models Help Increase Women's Desire to Run? Evidence from Political Psychology." In *Politicking While Female: The Political Life of Women*, 34–52. Baton Rouge: Louisiana State University Press.

Schneider, Monica C., Mirya R. Holman, Amanda B. Diekman, and Thomas McAndrew. 2016. "Power, Conflict, and Community: How Gendered Views of Political Power Influence Women's Political Ambition: Power, Conflict, and Community." *Political Psychology* 37(4): 515–31.

Schneider, Monica C., Jennie Sweet-Cushman, and Taylor Gordon. 2023. "Role Model Do No HARM: Modeling Achievable Success Inspires Social Belonging and Women's Candidate Emergence." *Journal of Women, Politics & Policy* 44(1): 105–20.

Schwartz, Shalom H., and Tammy Rubel. 2005. "Sex Differences in Value Priorities: Cross-Cultural and Multimethod Studies." *Journal of Personality and Social Psychology* 89(6): 1010–28.

Schwarz, Susanne, and Alexander Coppock. 2022. "What Have We Learned About Gender from Candidate Choice Experiments? A Meta-Analysis of Sixty-seven Factorial Survey Experiments." *The Journal of Politics* 84(2): 655–68.

Schwindt-Bayer, Leslie A., and William Mishler. 2005. "An Integrated Model of Women's Representation." *The Journal of Politics* 67(2): 407–28.

Schwindt-Bayer, Leslie A., and Catherine Reyes-Housholder. 2017. "Citizen Responses to Female Executives: Is It Sex, Novelty or Both?" *Politics, Groups, and Identities* 5(3): 373–98.

Sears, David O., and Nicholas A. Valentino. 1997. "Politics Matters: Political Events as Catalysts for Preadult Socialization." *American Political Science Review* 91(1): 45–65.

Seelye, Katharine Q. 2022. "Lynn Yeakel, Spurred into Politics by Anita Hill, Dies at 80." *The New York Times*, March 17. https://www.nytimes.com/2022/03/17/us/politics/lynn-yeakel-dead.html (accessed July 13, 2022).

Shames, Shauna. 2017. *Out of the Running: Why Millennials Reject Political Careers and Why It Matters*. New York: New York University Press.

Shivaram, Deepa. 2022. "Vermont Ends Streak as the Last State to Send a Woman to Congress." NPR, November 8. https://www.npr.org/2022/11/08/1134352130/vermont-balint-election-day-results-2022 (accessed February 13, 2023).

Shortell, Christopher, and Melody E. Valdini. 2022. "The Politics of Women's Presence on High Courts: Bias and the Conditional Nature of Cultivating Legitimacy." *Politics & Gender* 18(3): 858–77.

Simon, Mallory, and Kynug Lah. 2017. "Trump Opened the Floodgates. Now Democratic Women Are Running for Office in Record Numbers." CNN Politics, November 3. https://www.cnn.com/2017/11/03/politics/women-candidates-ballot/index.html (accessed August 31, 2022).

Skocpol, Theda, and Caroline Tervo, eds. 2020. *Upending American Politics: Polarizing Parties, Ideological Elites, and Citizen Activists from the Tea Party to the Anti-Trump Resistance*. Oxford and New York: Oxford University Press.

Smooth, Wendy. 2006. "Intersectionality in Electoral Politics: A Mess Worth Making." *Politics & Gender* 2(3): 400–414.

Solotaroff, Paul. 2015. "Trump Seriously: On the Trail with the GOP's Tough Guy." *Rolling Stone*, September 9. https://www.rollingstone.com/politics/politics-news/trump-seriously-on-the-trail-with-the-gops-tough-guy-41447/ (accessed August 31, 2022).

Spence, Lester, and Harwood McClerking. 2010. "Context, Black Empowerment, and African American Political Participation." *American Politics Research* 38(5): 909–30.

Stacks, John. 1984. "An Interview with Ferraro." *Time*, July 23, 34. https://content.time.com/time/subscriber/article/0,33009,952431,00.html (accessed May 19, 2022).

Stauffer, Katelyn E. 2021. "Public Perceptions of Women's Inclusion and Feelings of Political Efficacy." *American Political Science Review* 115(4): 1226–41.

Steele, Claude M. 1997. "A Threat in the Air: How Stereotypes Shape Intellectual Identity and Performance." *American Psychologist* 52(6): 613–29.

Steinberg, Blema S. 2008. *Women in Power: The Personalities and Leadership Styles of Indira Gandhi, Golda Meir, and Margaret Thatcher*. 1st ed. Montreal: McGill–Queen's University Press.

REFERENCES

Stewart, Sheridan, and Robb Willer. 2022. "The Effects of Racial Status Threat on White Americans' Support for Donald Trump: Results of Five Experimental Tests." *Group Processes & Intergroup Relations* 25(3): 791–810.

Stockman, Farah. 2015. "In Debate, Hillary Clinton's Clarion Call for Women Thrills Many." *The New York Times*, October 20. https://www.nytimes.com/2016/10/21/us/politics/hillary-clinton-women.html (accessed June 14, 2023).

Stokes-Brown, Atiya Kai, and Kathleen Dolan. 2010. "Race, Gender, and Symbolic Representation: African American Female Candidates as Mobilizing Agents." *Journal of Elections, Public Opinion and Parties* 20(4): 473–94.

Stokes-Brown, Atiya Kai, and Melissa Olivia Neal. 2008. "Give 'Em Something to Talk About: The Influence of Female Candidates' Campaign Issues on Political Proselytizing." *Politics & Policy* 36(1): 32–59.

Stolle, Dietlind, and Elisabeth Gidengil. 2010. "What Do Women Really Know? A Gendered Analysis of Varieties of Political Knowledge." *Perspectives on Politics* 8(1): 93–109.

Stout, Jane G., Nilanjana Dasgupta, Matthew Hunsinger, and Melissa A. McManus. 2011. "STEMing the Tide: Using Ingroup Experts to Inoculate Women's Self-Concept in Science, Technology, Engineering, and Mathematics (STEM)." *Journal of Personality and Social Psychology* 100(2): 255–70.

Streb, Matthew J., Barbara Burrell, Brian Frederick, and Michael A. Genovese. 2008. "Social Desirability Effects and Support for a Female American President." *Public Opinion Quarterly* 72(1): 76–89.

Sweet-Cushman, Jennie. 2023. *Inspired Citizens: How Our Political Role Models Shape American Politics*. Philadelphia: Temple University Press.

Swers, Michele L. 2013. *Women in the Club: Gender and Policy Making in the Senate*. Chicago: University of Chicago Press.

———. 2020. *The Difference Women Make: The Policy Impact of Women in Congress*. Chicago: University of Chicago Press.

Swim, Janet K., Kathryn J. Aikin, Wayne S. Hall, and Barbara A. Hunter. 1995. "Sexism and Racism: Old-Fashioned and Modern Prejudices." *Journal of Personality and Social Psychology* 68(2): 199–214.

Tackett, Michael. 2017. "Women Line Up to Run for Office, Harnessing Their Outrage at Trump." *The New York Times*, December 4. https://www.nytimes.com/2017/12/04/us/politics/women-candidates-office.html (accessed August 31, 2022).

Tate, Katherine. 1991. "Black Political Participation in the 1984 and 1988 Presidential Elections." *American Political Science Review* 85(4): 1159–76.

———. 2001. "The Political Representation of Blacks in Congress: Does Race Matter?" *Legislative Studies Quarterly* 26(4): 623–38.

Thomas, Deja. 2019. "In 2018, Two-Thirds of Democratic Women Hoped to See a Woman President in Their Lifetime." *Pew Research Center: Short Reads*, July 26. https://www.pewresearch.org/fact-tank/2019/07/26/in-2018-two-thirds-of-democratic-women-hoped-to-see-a-woman-president-in-their-lifetime/ (accessed February 10, 2023).

Thomsen, Danielle M. 2015. "Why So Few (Republican) Women? Explaining the Partisan Imbalance of Women in the U.S. Congress." *Legislative Studies Quarterly* 40(2): 295–323.

REFERENCES

Thomsen, Danielle M., and Bailey K. Sanders. 2020. "Gender Differences in Legislator Responsiveness." *Perspectives on Politics* 18(4): 1017–30.

Towler, Christopher C., and Christopher S. Parker. 2018. "Between Anger and Engagement: Donald Trump and Black America." *Journal of Race, Ethnicity, and Politics* 3(1): 219–53.

Tyler, Matthew, and Shanto Iyengar. 2022. "Learning to Dislike Your Opponents: Political Socialization in the Era of Polarization." *American Political Science Review* 117(1): 347–54.

Uhlaner, Carole Jean, and Becki Scola. 2016. "Collective Representation as a Mobilizer: Race/Ethnicity, Gender, and Their Intersections at the State Level." *State Politics & Policy Quarterly* 16(2): 227–63. https://doi.org/10.1177/1532440015603576.

US House. 2023a. "Hispanic Americans in Congress." https://history.house.gov/Exhibitions-and-Publications/HAIC/Hispanic-Americans-in-Congress/ (accessed May 15, 2023).

———. 2023b. "Total Members of the House & State Representation." https://history.house.gov/Institution/Total-Members/Total-Members/ (accessed May 15, 2023).

———. 2023c. "Women in Congress." https://history.house.gov/wic/ (accessed May 15, 2023).

Valentino, Nicholas A., Carly Wayne, and Marzia Oceno. 2018. "Mobilizing Sexism: The Interaction of Emotion and Gender Attitudes in the 2016 US Presidential Election." *Public Opinion Quarterly* 82(S1): 799–821. https://doi.org/10.1093/poq/nfy003.

van der Pas, Daphne, Loes Aaldering, and Angela L. Bos. 2023. "Looks like a Leader: Measuring Evolution in Gendered Politician Stereotypes." *Political Behavior*.

Vanderleeuw, James M., and Baodong Liu. 2002. "Political Empowerment, Mobilization, and Black Voter Roll-Off." *Urban Affairs Review* 37(3): 380–96.

Verba, Sidney, Kay Lehman Schlozman, and Henry E. Brady. 1995. *Voice and Equality: Civic Voluntarism in American Politics*. Cambridge, MA: Harvard University Press.

Volden, Craig, Alan E. Wiseman, and Dana E. Wittmer. 2013. "When Are Women More Effective Lawmakers Than Men?" *American Journal of Political Science* 57(2): 326–41.

Wahlström, Mattias, and Katrin Uba. 2023. "Political Icon and Role Model: Dimensions of the Perceived 'Greta Effect' Among Climate Activists as Aspects of Contemporary Social Movement Leadership." *Acta Sociologica*, October 11. https://doi.org/10.1177/00016993231204215.

Washington, Ebonya. 2006. "How Black Candidates Affect Voter Turnout." *The Quarterly Journal of Economics* 121(3): 973–98.

Waters, Elizabeth and Anastasia Posadskaya. 1995. "Democracy Without Women Is No Democracy: Women's Struggles in Postcommunist Russia." In *The Challenge of Local Feminisms: Women's Movements in Global Perspective*, edited by Amrita Basu, 351–73. Boulder, CO: Westview Press.

Weinraub, Bernard. 1984. "Running Mate Joins Ferraro for a Rally in Queens: Mondale Salutes Ferraro in Queens." *The New York Times*, August 1. https://www

REFERENCES

.nytimes.com/1984/08/01/nyregion/running-mate-joins-ferraro-for-a-rally-in-queens.html (accessed May 19, 2022).

Weissberg, Robert. 1978. "Collective vs. Dyadic Representation in Congress." *The American Political Science Review* 72(2): 535–47.

Wells, Dylan. 2024. "Haley Trails Trump but Is Winning with Young Girls." *The Washington Post*, February 24. https://www.washingtonpost.com/politics/2024/02/24/nikki-haley-young-girls-legacy/ (accessed February 27, 2024).

Wells, Dylan, and Maeve Reston. 2023. "As Haley Climbs in the Polls, She Confronts Attacks Criticized as Sexist." *The Washington Post*, December 23. https://www.washingtonpost.com/politics/2023/12/26/nikki-haley-sexism-republican-politics/?_pml=1 (accessed February 29, 2024).

White, Ariel. 2016. "When Threat Mobilizes: Immigration Enforcement and Latino Voter Turnout." *Political Behavior* 38(2): 355–82.

Wilcox, Clyde. 1994. "Why Was 1992 the 'Year of the Woman'? Explaining Women's Gains in 1992." In *The Year of the Woman: Myths and Realities*, edited by Elizabeth Adell Cook, Sue Thomas, and Clyde Wilcox, 1–24. Boulder, CO: Westview Press.

Winslow, Barbara. 2014. *Shirley Chisholm: Catalyst for Change, 1926–2005*. Boulder, CO: Westview Press.

Winter, Nicholas J. G. 2010. "Masculine Republicans and Feminine Democrats: Gender and Americans' Explicit and Implicit Images of the Political Parties." *Political Behavior* 32(4): 587–618.

Wolak, Jennifer. 2009. "Explaining Change in Party Identification in Adolescence." *Electoral Studies* 28(4): 573–83.

———. 2015. "Candidate Gender and the Political Engagement of Women and Men." *American Politics Research* 43(5): 872–96.

———. 2019. "Descriptive Representation and the Political Engagement of Women." *Politics & Gender* 16(2): 1–24.

———. 2020. "Self-Confidence and Gender Gaps in Political Interest, Attention, and Efficacy." *The Journal of Politics* 82(4): 1490–1501.

Wolak, Jennifer, and Eric Gonzalez Juenke. 2021. "Descriptive Representation and Political Knowledge." *Politics, Groups, and Identities* 9(1): 129–50.

Wolak, Jennifer, and Michael McDevitt. 2011. "The Roots of the Gender Gap in Political Knowledge in Adolescence." *Political Behavior* 33(3): 505–33.

Wolbrecht, Christina. 2000. *The Politics of Women's Rights: Parties, Positions, and Change*. Princeton, NJ: Princeton University Press.

Wolbrecht, Christina, and David E. Campbell. 2007. "Leading by Example: Female Members of Parliament as Political Role Models." *American Journal of Political Science* 51(4): 921–39.

———. 2017. "Role Models Revisited: Youth, Novelty, and the Impact of Female Candidates." *Politics, Groups, and Identities* 5(3): 418–34.

Wolbrecht, Christina, and J. Kevin Corder. 2020. *A Century of Votes for Women: American Elections Since Suffrage*. Cambridge and New York: Cambridge University Press.

Youniss, James, Jeffrey A. McLellan, and Miranda Yates. 1997. "What We Know About Engendering Civic Identity." *The American Behavioral Scientist* 40(5): 620–31.

Zaller, John. 1992. *The Nature and Origins of Mass Opinion*. Cambridge and New York: Cambridge University Press.

Zetterberg, Pär. 2009. "Do Gender Quotas Foster Women's Political Engagement? Lessons from Latin America." *Political Research Quarterly* 62(4): 715–30.

Ziegler, Sianna Alia, and Sapna Cheryan. 2017. "Role Models and Gender." In *The SAGE Encyclopedia of Psychology and Gender*, edited by Kevin L. Nadal, 1427. Thousand Oaks, CA: Sage.

Zukin, Cliff, Scott Keeter, Molly Andolina, Krista Jenkins, and Michael X. Delli Carpini. 2006. *A New Engagement? Political Participation, Civic Life, and the Changing American Citizen*. Oxford and New York: Oxford University Press.

INDEX

Note: Page numbers in italics indicate figures or tables.

abortion, 184
Access Hollywood (television show), 87
Adams, Abigail, 18
Adams, John, 18
adults: attitudes about democracy, 176–77; impressionability of, 171–81, 187–88; Republican candidates experiment's effect on, 212n15; role models' effects on, 11, 171–81, *179–80*; on women's capacity for politics, 175–76; young people's responses compared to those of, *179–80*. *See also* men and boys; parents; women and girls
African Americans: as candidates/officeholders, 41, 131–32, 136; co-racial political effects of, 41, 135, 142–46, *143*; discrimination against, 134; political representation of, 134; role model effects of, 132–33, 135, 142–46, *143*; voter mobilization among, 32–33
Aldrin, Buzz, 112
Alexander, Amy C., 27
Allen, Peter, 27
Armstrong, Neil, 112
Asian Americans, 131, 132, 147
attitudes toward democracy. *See* democratic representation/legitimacy

backlash, 32–34, 116, 122–25, 169, 184, 197
Baker, Brea, 131
Barbie (doll), 3, 6
Beaman, Lori, 27
Bice, Stephanie, 151
Biden, Joe, 9, 61–62, 132, 133, 141, 148

Bobo, Lawrence, 141
Bos, Angela, 37
boys. *See* men and boys; young people
Braun, Carol Moseley, 108
Brown, Kate, 212n11
Buice, Melissa, 27
Burns, Nancy, 208n2
Bush, George W., 183
Buttigieg, Pete, 148

Campbell, Angus, 43
candidates. *See* women candidates
CBS Evening News (television show), 110
ceiling effects, 100
Cellucci, Paul, 212n11
children. *See* young people
Chisholm, Shirley, 85, 131–32, 147, 149
Clayton, Amanda, 29
Cleopatra, Queen, 47
Clinton, Bill, 114
Clinton, Hillary, xv, 3, *4*, 9, 15, 33–34, 44, 48, 59–61, 70, 85–88, 100, 103, 109, 112, 114, 126, 160, 162, 171, 183, *195*, 199
Collaborative Multiracial Post-Election Survey (CMPS), 133, 139–40, *140*
communal vs. agentic approaches to life's activities, 7–8, 17, 25–26
Cooperative Election Study (CES), 174–75, *175*, 212n3
Crenshaw, Kimberlé, 136
Cuomo, Mario, 106
Cutts, David, 27

Davids, Sharice, 96, 132
Deckman, Melissa, 38

Declaration of Independence, 18
Delli Carpini, Michael X., 31
democratic representation/legitimacy, 85–104; adults' perceptions of, 176–77; Democratic perceptions of, 89–92, *91*, 97–104, *97, 98, 101, 102*; disillusionment with, 38, 87–88, 91–92, 99, 103, 126, 199; dyadic vs. collective, 49–50; factors in, 28; intersectional role models' effects on perceptions of, 146–47; men's perceptions of, 40, 89–92, *91*, 97–104, *97, 98, 101, 102*; mind-changing about, *102*; minority role models' effect on perceptions of, 41; political engagement linked to, 35, 96; Republican candidates experiment's effect on perceptions of, 160–62, *161*; Republican perceptions of, 89–92, *91*, 97–104, *97, 98, 101, 102*; role models' effect on perceptions of, 5–6, 9, 11, 19, 28–29, 35, 40, 49–50, 88–92, 96–104, 194, *194*; women's necessary role in, 5–6, 189, 197–200; women's perceptions of, 28–29, 40, 88–92, *91*, 97–104, *97, 98, 101, 102*; young people's perceptions of, 85–92, 96–104, 207n5
democratic theory, 5, 11, 16
Democrats/Democratic Party: attitudes about democracy, 89–92, *91*, 97–104, *97, 98, 101, 102*; and feminine traits, 67, *78*; impact of role models on members of, 11, 42–44; and masculine traits, *79*; political engagement of women members of, 113–14; race of, 138–39; sexist attitudes of, *79*; women candidates/officeholders, 9, 11, 12, 42, 60–61, 67, 80–81, 92, *93*, 94–100, *95*, *97*, 151–54, 198–99; on women's capacity for politics, 61, 63–65, *64*, 67–68, *78*, 80; women voters in, 11, 42, 67
Dolan, Kathleen, 137
Dole, Elizabeth, 85
Driscoll, Kim, 164

Eagly, Alice, 24, 33
Edelman, Marian Wright, 3

Educational Longitudinal Study (ELS), 181–87, *182*
efficacy. *See* political efficacy
Electoral College, 88
Emily's List, 94
enduring effects hypothesis, 173–74, 181–88, *186*
Escobar, Veronica, 96

Family Matters 1 survey, 89–90, *90*, 92, 96–97, 99
Family Matters 2 survey, 58, 73–74, *74*, 100, 116, 118, 132–33, 140, 174, 178, 181, 193, 198
feminine traits: ascribed to Democrats, 67; ascribed to women politicians, 26; Democrats' perceptions of, *78*; men's perceptions of, *78*; Republicans' perceptions of, *78*; women's perceptions of, *78*. *See also* gender roles/stereotypes
Ferraro, Geraldine, 44, 48, 105–6, *107*, 109, 112–14, 126, 162, 171–73, 190
Fifteenth Amendment, 134
Finkenauer, Abby, 95, 100
Fiorina, Carly, 34, 86–87
Fox News, 81
Foxx, Deja, 105

Gandhi, Indira, 47
Garcia, Sylvia, 96
gender: defining, 39; impact of role models by respondent's, 39–41, 52, *53*. *See also* gender roles/stereotypes; men and boys; women and girls
gender roles/stereotypes: of Black women, 136; challenging of, 120, 138, 146, 169; of leaders, 17, 18, 25–27, 33, 37, 57, 158; perceptions of political parties reflective of, 42–43; religion and, 65; social sanctions enforcing, 25, 30; social significance of, 16–17, 24–25, 30; updating of, 26, 30, 40, 43, 48, 52, 66, 67, 82, 115; vicious cycle of, 25–26; young people's beliefs in, 37. *See also* feminine traits; gender; masculine traits/masculinity
General Social Survey, 61

INDEX

Gillard, Julia, 15
Gilliam, Franklin, 141
girls. *See* women and girls; young people
glass ceiling, 3, 19, 86, 164, 200
governor, women as or campaigning for, 9–10, 94, 164
Greene, Marjorie Taylor, 152–53, 198

Haaland, Deb, 96, 132
Hajnal, Zoltan, 135
Haley, Nikki, 3, *5*, 9, 18, 37, 152, 164
Harris, Kamala, xiii–xv, 9, 15, 37, 48, 61, 70, 132–33, 141, 147–48, 153, *195*, 210n3
Healey, Maura, 164–65, 212n11
Herrnson, Paul S., 32
Hill, Anita, 94, 106–7
Horn, Kendra, 151
Horvath, Lindsey P., 148

identity politics, 164
immovable adults hypothesis, 171–81, 187–88
intersectionality, 136–37
intersectional role models: effects of, 41–42, 137–49; political engagement of young people after exposure to, 141–49; questions concerning, 138

Jones, Mondaire, 149

Karau, Steven J., 33
Keeter, Scott, 31
Kelly, Megyn, 87
Klobuchar, Amy, 9
Kotek, Tina, 164, 212n11

Latinos/as: as candidates/officeholders, 41, 132; co-racial political effects of, 41, 135, 143–46; discrimination against, 134–35; political representation of, 134–35; role model effects of, 135, 143–46; voter mobilization among, 32
Lay, J. Celeste, 32
leaders, stereotypes of, 17, 18, 25–27, 33, 37, 57, 158. *See also* women's capacity for politics

Levesque, Cassandra, 171
LGBTQ Americans, 148–49, 164–65, 200, 212n11
list experiments, 60, 64
location: geographic distribution of women candidates, 68–70, *69*; local exposure to role models, 115–25
longitudinal surveys, 181. *See also* panel surveys
Luce, Clare Booth, 47

MacManus, Susan A., 27, 66, 189
Mansbridge, Jane, 18, 24, 28, 65, 66, 82, 135, 148, 193, 199
Margolin, Jamie, 85
Mariani, Mack, 44, 209n18
Marshall, Bryan, 44, 209n18
masculine traits/masculinity: ascribed to men politicians, 26; ascribed to Republicans, 67; Democrats' perceptions of, *79*; men's perceptions of, 66, *79*; perceived threats to, 32–34, 40–41, 116, 122, 144, 184; Republicans' perceptions of, *79*; women's perceptions of, 66, *79*. *See also* gender roles/stereotypes
Mathews-Schultz, A. Lanethea, 44, 209n18
Matland, Richard E., 27
Mattel, 3
McDonald, Jared, 38
McLellan, Jeffrey A., 119
media coverage: novelty as focus of, 191; political engagement in response to, 110, *111*, 112; of women politicians, 95, *95*, 106, *107*, 110, *111*, 112, 191
Meir, Golda, 47
men and boys: attitudes about democracy, 89–92, *91*, 97–104, *97*, *98*, *101*, *102*, 168–69, 160–62, *161*; effect on, of women's political participation, 31; and feminine traits, *78*; gender identity threat experienced by, 32–34, 40–41, 116, 122, 144, 184; and masculine traits, *79*; sexist attitudes of, *79*; stereotypes of, 17, 25–26, 30; on women's capacity for politics, 63–67, *64*, *78*, 80, 158–60,

[241]

men and boys (*cont.*) 159. *See also* adults; gender; gender roles/stereotypes; masculine traits/ masculinity; political engagement of men and boys; white Americans: leadership capacity ascribed to male; young people
MeToo movement, 100, 184
Mink, Patsy, 131
minorities. *See* intersectional role models; race
misogyny. *See* sexism
Mondale, Walter, 106
Monitoring the Future survey, 90, 108–9, 119
Monkey Cage (website), 86
Montoya, Celeste, 137
Morgan, Jana, 27
Murray, Patty, 28, 108

Native Americans, 96, 132
NBC Evening News (television show), 110
Neal, Melissa Olivia, 32
New York Times (newspaper), 110, *111*, 112
novelty/exceptionality: importance and ironies of, 196–97; of political role models/women candidates, 11, 13, 18, 31–32, 34, 45–47, 71, 102–3, 108, 152–53, 168, 190–97; study for testing of, 192–95, *194*, *195*

Obama, Barack, 90, 112
O'Brien, Diana Z., 29
Ocasio-Cortez, Alexandria (AOC), 95–96, 100, 141, 153, 198
Omar, Ilhan, 96, 141

Pacific Islanders, 132
Palin, Sarah, 44, 48, 60, 112, 114, 171, 183
panel surveys, 51–52, 74–75, 89. *See also* longitudinal surveys
parents, research on political attitudes of, 73–74, 178. *See also* adults
partisanship: in contemporary America, 101, 103; as factor in judging women's capacity for politics, 68, 80–81; as factor in political engagement, 113–15, *113*; formative age for, 37–38, 43–44; impact of role models on, 42–44; polarization linked to, 11, 42, 44, 68, 103, 152; political engagement affected by, 122–24; race and, 138–39
Pelosi, Nancy, 44, 48, 60, 110, 112, 153, 171, *195*
Pew Research Center, 15
Phillips, Anne, 65
pinkie promises, 3, 57, *58*, 83, 124, 173
Piscopo, Jennifer M., 29
Pitkin, Hanna, 16
polarization: in contemporary America, 11, 42, 101, 103, 152; partisanship linked to, 11, 42, 44, 68, 103, 152; in political engagement, 113
political activism. *See* political engagement of men and boys; political engagement of women and girls
political efficacy, 123, *124*, 163, 165–66, *166*, 206n5
political engagement of men and boys: compared to that of women and girls, *109*, *111*, 112, 114; gender identity threat as impetus to, 32–34, 40–41, 116, 122–25, 184; intersectional role models' effects on, 144–46, *146*, 148; media coverage as influence on, *111*, 112; Republican candidates experiment's effect on, 162–67, *166*, 212n13; responses of, to women of color in politics, 144–45, *145*
political engagement of women and girls, 105–27; activities defined as, for young people, 109, 141–42; adults, 177; democratic representation/ legitimacy linked to, 35, 96; duration of, 184–86, *185*; history of, 34–35; interest, attention, and knowledge as factors in, 30–32, 46, 108, 120; intersectional role models' effects on, 141–44, *142*; media coverage as influence on, 110, *111*, 112; men's political trust influenced by, 29; minority role models' effect on, 41; obstacles to, 89; office-seeking and officeholding by women, 9–10, 25,

INDEX

47–48, 57, 67, 92, *93*, 94–96, *95*, 100, 107–8, 110; partisanship as factor in, 113–15, *113*; polarization in, 113; Republican candidates experiment's effect on, 162–67, *164*, *167*; research on, 34–35; in response to Trump, 94–95; rises and drops in, 109–12; role models' effect on, 7–8, 9, 11, 19, 29–36, 40, 48, 105–7, 117–27; types of, 117–18; underrepresentation of women, 9–10, 18, 25, 47–48, 106, 108, 112, 183, 198; young people, 108–27, *109*, *111*, *121*, 141–45, *142*, *143*. *See also* political efficacy; women candidates; women's capacity for politics

political role models: age of respondent as factor in effects of, 8, 11, 37–39, 52, 171–88; candidates vs. officeholders as, 49; characteristics of, 7; contingency of, 18; definitions of, 6–9, 15–17, 20; duration of effects of, 172–74, 181–88, *185*, *186*; effects of, 7–9, 10–11, 17, 20, *21–23*, 36–44, 83, 189–200, *191*; expectations for, 65–66; importance of, 3; local exposure to, 115–25; negative responses to, 98, *98*, 102, 103, 122–25, 144–46, *145*, 165–66, *166*, 197, 212n13 (*see also* backlash); novelty/exceptionality of, 11, 13, 18, 31–32, 34, 45–47, 102–3, 108, 152–53, 168, 190–97, *194*, *195*; perception/conscious recognition of, 46, 119–20, 126; popular conceptions of, 15, 28; presence of, 44–50, 119–20; Republican, 151–69; research on, 3–4, 6, 13, 20, *21–23*, 35–36, 38, 50–52; respondents to, 36–44; salience of, 44–50, 71, 86, 96, 110, 113–15, 125–26, 183, 208n3; STEM research relating to, 7–8; time and context for, 47–48, 82, 106–15, 183; from underrepresented groups, 17–18; visibility of, 44–45. *See also* democratic representation/ legitimacy; intersectional role models; political engagement of women and girls; women candidates; women's capacity for politics

Pressley, Ayanna, 96, 141
public opinion: about political role models (folk theory), 15, 19–20, 28, 37, 171–72, 190; receive-accept-sample model of, 19; on women's capacity for politics, 57–62, *59*, 131

race: of candidates/officeholders, 41, 96, 132, 138–39; challenging of stereotypes based on, 138; Democrats and, 138–39; partisanship and, 138–39; Republicans and, 138–39; role model effects of, 133; underrepresentation in politics associated with, 133–36, *134*. *See also* African Americans; Asian Americans; intersectional role models; Latinos/as; Native Americans

religion: as factor in judging women's capacity for politics, 62, 65; and gender roles/stereotypes, 65

Republicans/Republican Party: attitudes about democracy, 89–92, *91*, 97–104, *97*, *98*, *101*, *102*; and feminine traits, 78; impact of role models on members of, 11–13, 42–44; and masculine traits, 67, *79*, 116; political engagement of women members of, 113–14; race of, 138–39; role model effects for, 76–79, 83; sexist attitudes of, *79*; women candidates/officeholders, 12–13, 42, 60–61, 67, 80–81, *93*, 94, 98–100, *98*, 151–69, 198–99; on women's capacity for politics, 61, 63–65, *64*, 67–68, *78*, 80; women voters in, 42

Resistance, 94, 100, 114
role models. *See* political role models
roles, 16–17

Safarpour, Alauna C., 45
Sanders, Sarah Huckabee, 82, 164–65
Sapiro, Virginia, 65–66, 82
Schlozman, Kay, 208n3
September 11, 2001, terrorist attacks, 183
sexism: of adults, 176; boys' attitudes and, *79*; Democratic attitudes and, *79*; female, 34; girls' attitudes and, *79*;

sexism (cont.)
    hostile, 63–64, 116, 175–76; male, 33–34; modern, 63–64; Republican attitudes and, 79; Republican candidates experiment's effect on, 211n5; traditional, 63–64; Trump and, 86–87. *See also* gender roles/stereotypes
Shelby County v. Holder (2013), 134
social desirability bias, 59, 62, 73, 118, 119
social psychology, 5, 8, 11, 16, 24, 31
social roles, 16–17
social role theory, 24, 26, 30, 152
Squad, the, 96, 141, 148
STEM role models, 7–8
stereotypes: of Black women, 136; challenging of, 5, 6, 8, 9, 17–19, 25, 27, 32–33; genesis of, 57; of leaders, 17, 18, 25–27, 33, 37, 57; of men, 17, 25–26, 30; modification of, 26–27, 30; in STEM fields, 7; vicious cycle of, 25–26; of women, 17, 24–26, 30, 57. *See also* gender roles/stereotypes; women's capacity for politics
stereotype threat, 8
Stokes-Brown, Atiya Kai, 32, 137
survey experiments, 12–13, 153–55
Swift, Jane, 212n11
symbolic representation, 16

Thatcher, Margaret, 47
theory of political role models, 5, 15–54; and attitudes toward democracy, 28–29; building of, 16–23; factors in salience of political role models, 44–50; folk version of, 15, 19–20, 28, 37, 171–72, 190; key questions for, 16; and political engagement of women, 29–36; research approaches to, 50–52, 68–76; respondents' role in, 36–44; summary of, 52–54; and women's capacity for politics, 24–27
Thomas, Clarence, 94, 106–7, 108
threat. *See* masculine traits/masculinity: perceived threats to; stereotype threat
Thunberg, Greta, 48
Time (magazine), 95, *95*, 106, *107*

Time-Sharing Experiments in the Social Sciences (TESS), 153, *154*
Tlaib, Rashida, 96, 141
Torres, Ritchie, 149
Trump, Donald, xiv, 9, 32–34, 48, 81–82, 86–88, 91–92, 94, 99, 103, 114, 116, 137, 160, 184, 199

underrepresented groups: attitudes toward democracy of, 28; necessary role of, in representative/legitimate democracies, 199–200; perceptions of representation in political office by members of, 46; racial minorities, 133–36, *134*; role models' effects on, 17–18, 148–49; vicious cycle faced by, 25–26; women in politics as, 9–10, 18, 25, 47–48, 106, 108, 112, 183, 198
US Constitution, 18
US Department of Education, 181
US Supreme Court, 94, 106, 134

Verba, Sidney, 208n3
Victoria, Queen, 47
Vinson, Ashley, 100
voting: as form of political engagement, 117, 120, *121*, 123; persistence of, 186; racial discrimination in, 134–35
Voting Rights Act (1965), 134

Wall Street Journal (newspaper), 108
Warren, Elizabeth, 3, 9, 57, *58*, 83, 173
white Americans: domination of politics by, 25, 38, 131–33, *134*, 199; identity threat experienced by, 33, 136; leadership capacity ascribed to male, 7, 25; responses of, to African American officeholders, 41, 136, 143–44, 146
Whitmire, Kathy, 27, 189, 200
women and girls: attitudes about democracy, 28–29, 40, 88–92, *91*, 97–104, *97*, *98*, *101*, *102*, 160–62, *161*, 194, *194*; and feminine traits, 78; and masculine traits, 79; political issues especially relevant to, 31–32, 198; role of, in democracy, 5–6; sexist attitudes of, 79; stereotypes of, 17,

INDEX

24–26, 30, 57; on women's capacity for politics, 63–67, *64*, *78*, 80, 158–60. *See also* adults; feminine traits; gender; gender roles/stereotypes; political engagement of women and girls; women candidates; women's capacity for politics; young people

women candidates: backlash against, 33; barriers to minority, 137; in Democratic Party, 9, 11, 12, 42, 80–81, 92, *93*, 94–100, *95*, *97*, 151–54, 198–99; and economics, 32; as focus of study, 52–53; geographic distribution of, 68–70, *69*; gubernatorial, 9–10, 94, 164; novelty/exceptionality of, 45–46, 71, 102–3, 108, 190–97, *194*, *195*; perception/conscious recognition of, 46, 71–73, 119–20, 126; presence of, 44–50, 70–71, 82–83, 88, 96–100, 105, 119–20; for president, 9, 85–86; in Republican Party, 12–13, 42, 80–81, *93*, 94, 98–100, *98*, 151–69, 198–99; role model effects of, 49; time and context for, 47–48, 82, 106–15, 183; viability of, 45, 71, 96; visibility of, 44–45, 71; and women's issues, 31–32, 198; young people's intention to become, 118, *121*, 123, 143, *143*, 166–67, *167*, 194–95, *195*. *See also* intersectional role models; political engagement of women and girls; political role models

women of color. *See* intersectional role models; race

women's capacity for politics, 57–83; adults' perceptions of, 175–76; Democrats' perceptions of, 61, 63–65, *64*, 67–68, *78*, 80; intersectional role models' effects on perceptions of, 146; men's perceptions of, 39, 63–65, *64*, *78*, 80; mind-changing about, 65–68, 75–76, 80–82, *81*; minority role models' effect on perceptions of, 41; popular conceptions of, 57–62, *59*, 131; religion as factor in judging,

62, 65; Republican candidates experiment's effect on perceptions of, 158–60, *159*; Republicans' perceptions of, 61, 63–65, *64*, 67–68, *78*, 80; role models' effect on perceptions of, 5, 9, 11, 19, 24, 26–27, 39, 57–68, 73–83; vicious cycle concerning, 25–26, 57; Warren and, 57; women's perceptions of, 39, 63–65, *64*, *78*, 80; young people's perceptions of, 57–59, 62–67, 73–83. *See also* political engagement of women and girls

Women's March (2017), 94

World Values Survey, 99

Yates, Miranda, 119

Yeakel, Lynn, 107

Years of the Woman (1992, 2018), 8, 44, 45, 50, 92–100, 106, 109, 112, 113, 126, 162, 183, 190

young people: adults' responses compared to those of, *179–80*; attitudes about democracy, 85–92, 96–104, 146–47, 160–62, *161*, 194, *194*, 207n5; duration of role model effects on, 172–74, 181–88, *185*, *186*; gendered stereotypes held by, 37; impressionability of, 37, 171–73, 187–88; partisanship of, 37–38, 43–44; political engagement of, 108–27, *109*, *111*, *121*, 141–46, *142*, *143*, 162–67, *164*, *166*, *167*, 194; and Republican women candidates, 151–69, *169*, *159*, *161*, *164*, *166*, *167*; research on political attitudes of, 38, 73–76; role models' effects on, 8, 11, 37–39, 52, 171–73; their knowledge of candidates, 116–17; on women's capacity for politics, 57–59, 62–67, 73–83, 146, 158–60, *159*, 193. *See also* men and boys; parents; women and girls

Youniss, James, 119

Yousafzai, Malala, 48

Zaller, John, 19